D1238960

WEYERHAEUSER ENVIRONMENTAL BOOKS
WILLIAM CRONON, EDITOR

Weyerhaeuser Environmental Books explore human relationships
with natural environments in all their variety and complexity. They
seek to cast new light on the ways that natural systems affect human
communities, the ways that people affect the environments of which
they are a part, and the ways that different cultural conceptions of
nature profoundly shape our sense of the world around us. A complete
list of the books in the series appears at the end of this book.

ICELAND IMAGINED

Nature, Culture, and Storytelling in the North Atlantic

Karen Oslund

FOREWORD BY WILLIAM CRONON

UNIVERSITY OF WASHINGTON PRESS | SEATTLE & LONDON

Iceland Imagined *is published with the assistance of a grant from
the Weyerhaeuser Environmental Books Endowment, established
by the Weyerhaeuser Company Foundation, members of the
Weyerhaeuser family, and Janet and Jack Creighton.*

University of Washington Press
P.O. Box 50096, Seattle, WA 98145 U.S.A.
www.washington.edu/uwpress

Library of Congress Cataloging-in-Publication Data
Oslund, Karen.
Iceland imagined : nature, culture, and storytelling
in the North Atlantic / Karen Oslund
p. cm. — (Weyerhaeuser environmental books)
Includes bibliographical references and index.
ISBN 978-0-295-99083-5 (hardback : alk. paper)
1. Human ecology—Iceland. 2. Natural history—Iceland.
3. Ethnology—Iceland. 4. Folklore—Iceland. 5. Iceland—
Social life and customs. 6. Iceland—Description and travel.
I. Title   GF645.I25O75 2011   949.12—dc22   2010033491

Title-page spread: Þingvellir lava field; photo by William Cronon
Cover illustration: Reyðarfjördur, East Fjords; photo by Martin
Sejer Danielsen

CONTENTS

FOREWORD

Amid the Mists of Northern Waters and Words

WILLIAM CRONON

I should probably confess right at the outset that I myself am among the people described in Karen Oslund's *Iceland Imagined* who have had a life-long fascination for this remote and eerily intriguing island in the North Atlantic. When my fifth-grade class back in the mid-1960s spent a semester doing "country reports" on a chosen foreign nation, I selected Iceland. I wrote off to the tourist bureau for maps and pamphlets, did what research I could in the public library, and put together a detailed compilation of the geographical, historical, and cultural features that make the place so uniquely fascinating even for those who have never seen it. I still have that report in a box in my basement and doubt I'll ever bring myself to throw it away.

As time went on, seemingly unrelated intellectual fascinations carried me back to Iceland in unexpected ways. My youthful passion for *The Lord of the Rings* led me to the realization that J. R. R. Tolkien's scholarly expertise as a linguist of Old English and Old Norse had enabled him to draw quite extensively on the literature of medieval Iceland in weaving together and even inventing languages for his vast novel. The very name he chose for the imagined landscape in which he set his story—Middle Earth—derived in part from the Norse word *miðgarð* (by way of the Old English word *middangeard*), a realm in Norse mythology in which we humans live surrounded by a vast ocean inhabited by a world-encircling serpent named Miðgarðsormr. (By the way, that strange Icelandic character "ð" is pronounced like the "th" sound in "bathe.") Having been introduced to this mythological world by Tolkien, I read the Icelandic sagas and Eddas, spent a year learning Old Norse, and for a while even imagined that I would become a scholar of the medieval North Atlantic. At almost the same time, my college studies of geology drew me to Iceland for a very different reason: its location atop the Mid-Atlantic Ridge, whose spreading boundaries have produced the repeated volcanic eruptions and peculiar igneous landforms without which the island would not exist. There are few places on the planet where one can so easily and vividly witness the consequences of plate tectonic movements at first hand. From that perspective, it was hardly surprising to me when I learned that Jules Verne started his travelers on their *Journey to the Center of the Earth* by way of a secret tunnel in the crater of the Icelandic volcano Snæfellsjökull—and that they learned of this tunnel from a mysterious parchment in runic letters that falls into their hands from the leaves of a saga by the great Icelandic writer Snorri Sturluson.

Then, finally, in the 1990s, long after I had abandoned the Middle Ages to become a scholar of American environmental history, I had the good fortune to hire as an assistant a woman named Salvör Jónsdóttir. Salvör, a native Icelander, happened to be living in the small Wisconsin town that I was then researching. Trained as a cartographer, she had been responsible for producing a beautiful historical atlas of Reykjavík before moving to the United States, and she would eventually return to her home country to become the director of city planning for its capital city. It was through Salvör's good graces that I finally managed to visit a place that had been living in my imagination for more than four decades. Iceland was everything I expected it to be and far more, so that I now name it to my students as one of those places "not to miss seeing before you die." In making that trip at long last, I reenacted the kind of journey that Karen Oslund explores with such subtlety in this remarkable book.

Oslund's key insight in *Iceland Imagined* is that this distant northern island has existed on the margins not just of European maps but of European minds for over a millennium. Until the ninth century, it had remained one of the last large islands anywhere on earth never to have been permanently settled by human beings. (For some reason, the Inuit peoples who first occupied the northern latitudes from Alaska to Greenland never made it to Iceland.) This began to change in 874 CE, when the Norwegian chieftain Ingólfur Arnarson first settled at the place he named Reykjavík: Bay of the Smokes. Over the next sixty years, he was followed by wave after wave of migrants, so that by 930 CE the coast of Iceland—really its only inhabitable territory—was completely claimed and occupied. This "age of settlement," as Icelanders now call it, was recorded in a classic early history called *Landnámabók* (*Book of the Land-Taking*), and practically everyone now living on the island is descended from immigrants who arrived at that time. It was all part of an extraordinary wave of outmigration from the western fjords of Norway and other parts of Scandinavia that changed forever the face of northern Europe. Skilled as they were in ship construction, maritime navigation, trade, raiding, and warfare, these Vikings, as we now call them, ranged from Iceland, Greenland, and even Newfoundland in the west to England, France, Russia, and the Black Sea in the east, wreaking havoc wherever they went. In 793, they sacked the Northumbrian monastery of Lindisfarne and began the ninth-century settlement of what came to be called the Danelaw in England. A century later, they occupied the northwest coast of France, where the province of Normandy—the name itself means home of the Norsemen—would become the base from which William the Conqueror would undertake the Norman Conquest of Anglo-Saxon England in 1066. Farther to the east, comparable Viking beachheads were established in Poland and Russia.

This Scandinavian occupation of far-flung territories had more or less come to an end by the eleventh century. Places like Norman England and Kievan Russia followed their own divergent histories with little relationship to Scandinavia. In the Viking homeland, first Norway and then Denmark asserted their authority over the lands and peoples of Scandinavia, so that by the end of the fourteenth century Iceland had become a colony of the Danish Crown; it would remain so until World War II. From that point forward, Iceland—along with the Faroe Islands, which had served as Viking waystations, and the Greenland settlements, which had died out by the fifteenth century during the Little Ice Age—would recede ever further to the outer fringes of European geopolitics and cultural life.

It is there, on the far margins of Europe, that Karen Oslund begins to explore these northern regions. By the eighteenth century, the glory days of the Viking Age were half a millennium in the past, and the North Atlantic seemed very much a backwater in comparison with Enlightenment Europe. Using a boldly kaleidoscopic approach that traces changing European perceptions of Iceland and its neighbors in language, literature, geography, science, tourism, ethnography, and politics, Oslund demonstrates the unstable and often contradictory ways that Iceland could be portrayed: as an icon of wild nature; a remnant of Europe's own medieval past; a primitive exemplar of pre-modern humanity; and, in the twentieth century, a place in which all these qualities were either transformed or threatened (or both) by the rapid onset of modernity. In so doing, she demonstrates the ways that Edward Said's classic analysis of the colonial "other" can be applied with surprisingly rich effect to Iceland, a place that is indisputably so European and yet also so peripheral.

Travelers to Iceland in the eighteenth and nineteenth centuries, for instance, invariably commented on the raw wildness of its terrain. The devastating Laki volcanic eruptions of 1783—among the most violent in all of recorded world history—demonstrated the explosive nature of the island's geology, the speed with which its landscape was capable of transforming itself, and the challenges that human beings faced trying to make homes there. At the dawn of an age that was increasingly fascinated by the romantic sublime—those parts of nature that were roughest, darkest, most chaotic and dangerous—Iceland seemed as wild and sublime a place as European minds could imagine. And if romantic intellectuals were intrigued by Iceland's nature, they were no less intrigued by its medieval past, so that this same period saw the rediscovery of the Icelandic sagas, the collecting of the manuscripts on which those ancient stories survived, and their translation into modern languages. The sagas enjoyed a widespread literary revival—perhaps most famously in Wagner's operatic Ring Cycle, which combined elements of the German Nibelungenlied with the Icelandic *Völsunga saga*. (Jules Verne's choice of an Icelandic manuscript as the starting point for his *Journey to the Center to the Earth* is, of course, another example.) Suggestively, the word Viking entered modern English during the romantic age as part of this literary revival. The word derives from Old Norse *víkingr* by way of the root word *vík*, meaning bay or inlet—as in Reykjavík—so that a Viking is one who frequents or comes out of bays or inlets like the fjords of Norway. The word did not exist in English until scholars and writers popularized it in the early nineteenth century.

The great contribution of *Iceland Imagined* is to help us understand the mental geographies that over the past quarter millennium have come to define the North Atlantic—and that teach us more than we might think about the rest of the world. When travelers made their way to Iceland (or to Greenland or the Faroe Islands) right up until the mid-twentieth century, they saw themselves traversing several different imaginary paths. They traveled geographically outward from their European homelands to what they saw as the far periphery of European civilization. This was the traditional path from empire to colony, which was all the more striking in the north because it for the most part lacked the racial overlay so apparent elsewhere. Visitors also saw themselves moving back in time into the mythic space of the Eddic poems and the seemingly more historical landscapes of the sagas. Another path to the north led from the pastoral to the wild. The sublimity of its landscapes meant that Iceland could serve as the purest European example of nonhuman wilderness, standing in stark contrast to the domesticated countrysides that travelers had left behind. And, not least, the farming, sheepherding, and fishing families of coastal Iceland became icons of a peasant past for European intellectuals who felt a decided ambivalence about their own industrializing nations and the working-class proletarians whose deracinated journeys from farm to factory seemed among the most troubling symptoms of modernity. Here the traveler's symbolic path led toward seemingly simpler, more organic communities that were still firmly rooted in their native soils. Even after World War II, when Iceland joined the rest of Scandinavia in embracing the modernism and postmodernism of the second half of the twentieth century, it continued to straddle these imperial/colonial, modern/premodern, inorganic/organic, unnatural/natural oppositions in ways that displayed the country's ambiguities and contradictions as powerfully as anywhere in the world.

For all these reasons, Oslund argues, Iceland and the North Atlantic have served for the past two centuries as a landscape and region for meditating on a peripheral "other" that has stood as a defining counterpoint to everything that Europe and the rest of the modern world were ceasing to be. Partly because they were becoming modern at the same moment that other Europeans were beginning to question the price of modern progress,

Icelanders in particular came to pride themselves for achieving a more balanced integration of nature and culture on the strange and challenging island that was their home. By the start of the twenty-first century, they had long been using the geothermal energy of their volcanic landscape to produce hot water so inexpensively that there was no need to charge for it, and they could argue with some truth that they had adopted low-carbon, environmentally friendly alternative energies more fully than had any other nation. Having made themselves one of the most literate and highly educated human populations on the planet, Icelanders were at the cutting edge of the digital revolution, making their country a destination for high-tech start-up firms willing to pay dearly for such a talented workforce. And, of course, their growing ties to the global economy helped produce the banking crisis and attendant currency collapse of the Icelandic *króna* starting in 2008—clear evidence of how much the North Atlantic had become fully a part of the modern world. One can make a similar claim about the worldwide chaos caused by the Eyjafjallajökull eruption in 2010, when volcanic ash from Iceland disrupted air traffic worldwide and stranded travelers all over Europe for days. Both the *króna* collapse and the Eyjafjallajökull eruption offer compelling evidence for Karen Oslund's core insight: to understand the deepest paradoxes of modernity, whether they lie in the realm of nature or culture, whether they have to do with economic globalization or the future implications of climate change, there are few better places to go looking for answers than Iceland and its neighbors, which are not nearly so far away as they may seem.

ACKNOWLEDGMENTS

In Christina Sunley's novel *The Tricking of Freya*, the Icelandic "bad boy" Sæmundur—a stand-in for the trickster god Loki—explains to the heroine why the terrain at Þingvellir is so rocky and hard for her to balance on: "Think of the earth as an egg with its shell cracked. We are standing on one of those cracks . . . underneath, lava rises up and pushes the two plates apart. . . . California is on the opposite side of the North American plate. Iceland is pushing California into the ocean!"

Finally, finally, I have an explanation for why I had to come to Iceland from California: I was pushed. So, here, I have to thank those who pushed, pulled, gritted their teeth, and otherwise helped bring this book into existence (with apologies to anyone I might have overlooked).

In California, Jim Massengale, Ted Porter, Peter Redfield, Chris Stevens, Tim Tangherlini, Mary Terrall, and Sharon Traweek encouraged me and read many, many drafts. The UCLA History Department supported me with fellowships during my doctoral studies, while Robert and Heidi Rudd provided some necessary distractions and Eric Stepans supplied me with books that were not about Iceland. My parents, Carol and Kenneth Oslund, were the first to show me Iceland and Greenland from above on a trans-Atlantic flight.

When I was in Denmark, Katrine Andersen, Pelle Ove Christiansen, Marianne Sjøholm, and Thomas Söderqvist welcomed me; Thomas Højrup and the Institute for Archaeology and Ethnology, University of Copenhagen, and the Danish-American Fulbright Commission gave me a place to study and to think about Danish-Icelandic connections. Christina Folke Ax enlightened me with many exciting discussions about Icelandic farmers, and she also performed the arduous task of reading the entire book in proof. For seeing me through a Danish Christmas, I thank Andrea Handsteiner and Meike Wulfers. Martin Sejer Danielsen kindly allowed me to use his photograph for the cover of *Iceland Imagined*. Across the Ørsund in Lund, Harald Gustafsson invited me to the first year of Icelandic seminars at the university.

In Iceland, by hosting me, Steinn Eiríksdóttir, Sumarliði Ísleifsson, Kristján Róbertsson, Angela Walk, Ian Watson, and Þóra Sigurðardóttir made it possible for me to study one of the most expensive regions of the world. In addition, Sumarliði made my work much easier by writing such excellent books so much more quickly than I do. Hrefna Róbertsdóttir provided me with many sources and much encouragement, and greatly enhanced my understanding of eighteenth-century Icelandic history. Ingibjörg Eiríksdóttir and Sharpheðinn Þórisson generously allowed me to use their photographs in the book and Sigmund Jóhannsson was kind enough to let me reproduce his Keikó cartoon. Jakob Guðmundur Rúnarsson diligently looked up sources and pictures of reindeer at Landsbókasafn Íslands, which also deserves my thanks for allowing me to reproduce the Ortelius map without charge.

In Great Britain, Stuart Hartley hosted me while I worked at the National Library in Edinburgh. In London, Neil Chambers (National History Museum, London) helped me with the Joseph Banks material, and in between Ashley Holdsworth and Ken Jukes made sure I didn't spend all my time in libraries. In Munich, Helmuth Trischler and the Deutsches

Museum gave me a place to write. Whether in Germany, Iceland, or any other place, Skúli Sigurðsson's energy and resourcefulness in finding books and contacts for me were inexhaustible.

In Atlanta, Georgia, Gregory Nobles at the Georgia Institute of Technology arranged interlibrary loan privileges for me, which greatly helped with the climate adjustment from north to south. I returned to the north again when the Science and Technology Studies Program and the Society for the Humanities at Cornell University hosted me for a year, supported by the Andrew W. Mellon Foundation. During that time, Kenneth Baitsholts and Patrick J. Stevens assisted me with the Fiske Icelandic Collection at Cornell. I also thank John Carson and Gabrielle Hecht for their thoughtfulness during a Michigan winter in Ann Arbor.

When I finally landed in the capital region, former colleagues in the History Department at the University of Maryland, College Park, especially Robert Friedel, Andrea Goldman, and David Sicilia, offered helpful critiques of portions of these chapters. Some of the material in *Iceland Imagined* appeared previously in the *British Journal for the History of Science*, in *Environment and History*, and in my co-edited volume with David L. Hoyt, *The Study of Language and the Politics of Community in Global Context, 1740-1940* (Rowman and Littlefield, 2006). The American Council of Learned Societies and a Mellon Fellowship allowed me to spend a year at the John Kluge Center with the collections at the Library of Congress. The German Historical Institute (GHI), Washington, D.C., and especially its former director, Christof Mauch, deserve my thanks for understanding why the Institute should hire someone writing about a place that was neither Germany nor America, but somewhere in between. My colleagues at the GHI, especially Richard Wetzell, also gave me constructive criticism on some of this material during my time there. My colleagues in the Towson University History Department have consistently and warmly offered me a stimulating atmosphere in which to think about the North Atlantic and the world. I also thank its chair, Robert Rook, for securing financial support for the picture reproductions in *Iceland Imagined*.

At the University of Washington Press, the advice of Marianne Keddington-Lang, William Cronon, and four anonymous reviewers greatly improved the book. Copyeditor Julie van Pelt had a superb eye for detail, designer Pamela Canell made the pictures complement the text beautifully, and managing editor Marilyn Trueblood expertly steered the book through the entire process.

Then there are the people who were everywhere, all the time: my husband, Thomas Zeller, who came in late one morning in Berlin, but never leaves before the end, even if that means having to read two hundred pages about places north of the Alps. Our children, Tobias and Sebastian, deserve my thanks for being good travelers and for not letting their parents write long books. I hope they will also be pushed and pulled by forces of their own making to one edge of the world and another.

K.O.

ICELAND IMAGINED

For Europe is absent. This is an island and therefore Unreal.
—*W. H. Auden (1937)*

Few outside the Scandinavian world know much about Iceland. . . .
To write about early Iceland and intend to be understood is to supply
background that would be inappropriate if supplied by the historian
whose turf had the (mis)fortune to become populous, powerful, and
central to the story western nations like to tell about themselves.
—*William Ian Miller (1990)*

INTRODUCTION

Imagining Iceland, Narrating the North

On my first visit to Iceland, an Icelandic acquaintance took me for a driving tour around the Reykjanes peninsula. On this south-western corner of the island, the capital of Reykjavík is surrounded by a cluster of outlying suburbs and neighboring communities where almost two-thirds of Iceland's approximately 317,000 inhabitants live. As we passed over traffic bridges between Reykjavík and the old port town of Hafnarfjörður, I thought about the visual contradictions of the Icelandic landscape. Signs of modernity mark the city; for a European capital, Reykjavík appears strikingly new. Öskjuhlíð, the silver-grey geothermal water towers topped by a gourmet restaurant, Perlan (The Pearl), is sometimes jokingly compared to a UFO because of the sleek, high-tech appearance of its dome. The architecture of the University of Iceland (Háskóli Íslands), founded in 1911, is modernistic and functional. The Nordic House (Norræna Húsið) on the university campus was designed by the Finnish architect Alvar Aalto in his distinctive Scandinavian modern style, and the National Library of Iceland (Landsbókasafn Íslands), with its courtyard fountain and café, might strike the visitor as the entrance to a shopping mall rather than a research institution. Kringlan, one of the actual Reykjavík shopping malls located at the other end of one of the major thoroughfares from the university, uses high ceilings, windows, and natural light in a way that I found more appropriate to the sunnier climes of Los Angeles than to cloudy, drizzly Iceland that summer.

When I left Los Angeles for Iceland, I had imagined that I was going to "Europe" and thought of the features of European built landscapes that Americans are trained to be impressed by: cathedrals, castles, and monuments, structures that derive their historical authority through their age and their memory of the past. In Iceland, a historical memory invoked by the built landscape seemed to be missing at first glance.

If the Icelandic cityscape seems modern, so too does the Icelandic soundscape. Since the early 1990s, Iceland has been marketed by the tourist industry as a site of breaking pop culture and electronic music. The notoriously frantic Reykjavík weekend "pub crawl" (*rúntur*) is noted in the guidebooks as an attraction equal to Hallgrímur's Church (Hallgrímskirkja) and the National Museum (Þjóðminjasafn Íslands) for the foreign understanding of Icelandic culture. In the mid-1980s, the Icelandic art collective Bad Taste (Smekkleysa) launched itself with the manifesto of rejecting the established conventions of the Icelandic art world. The most famous artists to emerge from the collective on to the international scene have been Björk and the Sugarcubes, although many other Icelandic bands, including Sigur Rós, Gus Gus, and Mum, have also become internationally well-established. The tension between this Icelandic modernity and notions of its history and traditional beliefs has even provoked a cynical commentary from Björk herself, who remarked that "when record company executives come to Iceland they ask the bands if they believe in elves, and whoever says yes gets signed up."[1]

Iceland does have a long written history, but, as I was beginning to understand that summer, its history was not the kind that left its mark on the landscape. The architecture and sounds of Reykjavík might be modern, but Icelandic history, as it is told in that country and elsewhere, is almost exclusively concerned with the remote past. As I had learned during the prior month, in Iceland a foreign student is always assumed to have come in order to study the medieval sagas—the stories that were written about the earliest days of Icelandic settlement from Norway, the Viking-age period of Icelandic independence from about 871 to about 1262. Icelandic tourist brochures promote the country as the "land of the sagas" where one can still experience aspects of the "age of the Vikings." Since the beginning of saga study in Europe in the seventeenth century, this period in Icelandic history has been considered the golden age (*gullöld*) of Icelandic literature and culture, when the events of many of the Old Norse sagas took place and Eddic poems were composed. Tales about the heroic Leifur Eiríksson and his discovery of North America, of Viking warriors like Ragnar loðbrók (Ragnar the Hairy Pants) and Egill Skallagrímsson—who, when captured by his arch-enemy the Norwegian king Eiríkur blóðöx (Erik of the Bloody Ax) saved his own life by composing a poem so magnificent that it moved the king to mercy—continue to dominate the historical narrative of the country.[2] For centuries, the saga literature has been a major source of foreign interest in Iceland, and it was natural that Icelanders would casually assume that a foreign student was there to study it.

When foreign travelers came to Iceland, as they did in increasing numbers beginning in the eighteenth century, obsessed by catching a glimpse of the "sites of the sagas," they traveled for long distances, often in difficult conditions, and they were frequently rather disappointed by what they saw. If you visit Bergþórshvoll in southern Iceland, which tourist brochures typically describe as the "site of *Njáls Saga*, the most famous of the Icelandic sagas," you may well see nothing in particular that stands out.[3] A modern farmhouse on a low mound is all that represents the farmstead of the tenth-century farmer Njáll Þorgeirsson and his last stand with his sons against the men who burned his home with his family inside. If one looks to the landscape for history, as the tourist eye is instructed to do, the landscape reveals very little, and certainly nothing so obvious as a medieval castle with reconstructed walls and a museum and a gift shop next door. The medieval history, the period of Icelandic greatness, has left but little impression on the landscape.[4]

For a traveler better educated in Icelandic history, all of this might have been less striking. Even a few moments of reflection on the poverty of the Icelandic past and the inhabitants' inability to build lasting structures of the type to satisfy the naïve expectations of later travelers would have helped to resolve this contradiction in my mind. Indeed, my Icelandic acquaintance seemed unimpressed by my musings. "Well," she said, "you have to remember that, except for the technology, we're a third world country." Although one risks cliché here, I came to think of this as a "typically Icelandic" remark: laconic, ambiguous, perhaps critical of Iceland and its inhabitants, or perhaps of foreign expectations of the country. If it was meant to be the latter, she surely had grounds for this: while I was naïve about Iceland on my first visit, at least I wasn't the only one. Since the eighteenth century, European and American writers have been thinking, describing, classifying, imagining, and writing about Iceland and the North Atlantic region with surprise and wonder about its "contradictions," "paradoxes," and "extremes." Their stories, the reactions of the natives to their stories, and the consequences of these narratives and counternarratives for the region, are the topic of this book.

At that moment in Iceland that first summer, however, the idea of Iceland as part of the third world only intensified my surprise, curiosity, and lack of understanding. What does it mean, to be a "third world country except for the technology"? Since the term "third world" was invented after World War II, it has been used primarily to signify impoverished regions of technological underdevelopment.[5] Those areas of the globe designated the third world and thus coded deficient, in need of modernization, Westernization, and industrialization were most often the former colonies of Western powers in Africa, Southeast Asia, or Central and South America, regions considered to be well outside the main trajectories of European history. According to the schema outlined by this classification, these were places acted upon by Westerners and rendered passive, static, and outside of historical time.[6] In a series of historical moments, eighteenth-century Enlightenment thinkers, colonial administrations of the nineteenth century, and post–World War II aid programs modeled on the Marshall Plan delineated the deficiencies of the regions and people outside the areas where they themselves lived. Although the Enlightenment, colonialism, and the Marshall Plan are considerably different from each other, they share a tendency toward dualism, dividing the world between the modern self and the nonmodern, primitive, others.

So where and what is Iceland? Is it part of "Europe" or a technologically advanced and prosperous part of the "third world?"[7] Or is it something in between? Categorizing Iceland, or any other country, as part of "Europe" or as part of the "third world" helps to reveal what these terms mean, as their meaning is continually being explained and defined through use. According to which standards of measurement can we call this small island in the North Atlantic European? If we find it different in some way, in some way not European, as European travelers to Iceland from the eighteenth to the mid-twentieth century often did, how are these differences then used to define European norms? The anthropologist Fredrik Barth has pointed out that identities are constructed at borders, at the points where differences can be seen most clearly.[8] By looking at the edges of Europe in the North Atlantic, we can understand what it means to be European by identifying which aspects of life on these borders traveling Europeans found to be exotic, strange, and disconcerting.

Iceland Imagined examines how Iceland and the rest of the North Atlantic region, which includes Greenland, northern Norway, and the Faroe Islands (see map 1), have been envisioned by travelers and observers from the eighteenth century to the time of the Second World War. (The epilogue discusses certain developments in late-twentieth- and twentieth-first-century Iceland that parallel the themes of the earlier period.)

This book is also a cultural history of the North Atlantic as a European periphery. The North Atlantic, which was in the eighteenth century a marginalized region of the Danish-Norwegian kingdom, was gradually transformed—culturally, environmentally, and technologically—into modernity. Considered an exotic and unfamiliar wilderness by travelers from western Europe when the story begins, the North Atlantic was, by roughly the end of World War II, generally understood as belonging to the developed areas of the world. The image of a wild and untamed North Atlantic frontier, filled with dangerous nature and unpredictable inhabitants, was gradually transformed into a place of beautiful, well-regulated, and manageable nature, inhabited by simple but virtuous people. *Iceland Imagined* analyzes the process of this change by looking at the people who participated in it—both in the North Atlantic and those looking at the region from outside—and their reasons for considering the North Atlantic a "wilderness" or a "homeland." When they looked at the nature, the landscape, the language, or the material conditions of the North Atlantic, they read into these observations a position for the North Atlantic on the globe.

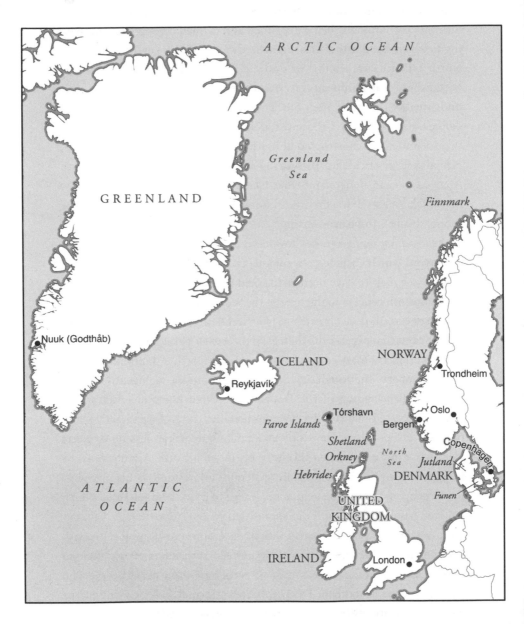

MAP 1. THE NORTH ATLANTIC

This change did not take place only in the centers of European power like Copenhagen and London. European images of the North Atlantic often interacted with how the natives of the North Atlantic saw themselves and the place in which they lived. The dynamic exchange between the different visions of the North Atlantic assumed meaning in larger political, economic, and cultural contexts. Images were created, used, contested, and replaced to serve political motivations or to promote economic and cultural interests.

"OTHER" OTHERS IN EUROPEAN VISIONS

The North Atlantic, of course, is hardly unique for having been treated as a figment of the European imaginary. European travelers invented imaginary geographies for many areas of the globe, and these geographies have been investigated by scholars in great detail under rubrics such as "Orientalism" and "alterity." Since the publication of Edward Said's *Orientalism* in 1979, European thinking about the other large regions of the globe, like Asia and the Americas, has often been used as a lens to investigate the European intellect itself. Additionally, studies in the history of travel, of science, and of artistic representations have also analyzed how eighteenth- and nineteenth-century Europeans thought about very distant regions, such as the South Pacific islands, for example, as ways of understanding cultural and intellectual transformations within Europe. Although the ways in which European travelers saw the North Atlantic were in part shaped by the same factors that influenced how they saw the Orient and the Pacific, there is something also fundamentally different about the European gaze toward the North. European thinking about very large and very distant territories, like the Orient, did not call their categories into question. Europeans were not generally confused about the position and status of China or of Hawaii; their impressions of these places were so utterly foreign, so absolutely other, that their experiences only served to confirm and solidify the basic integrity of their conceptual apparatus. Indeed, their experiences of these parts of the world helped to shape these categories from the beginning: eighteenth-century Europe was "European" in a large part because it was not like China or a Pacific island.[9] But in the North Atlantic, a region considered both "close" and "small" in the European imagination, the categories of "self" and "other," "home" and "away" became less distinct. The result was a sense of confusion about where the North Atlantic was with respect to the "civilized world" and by what measures this civilized world could be recognized. This ambiguity was the starting point for the creation of different narratives about the North Atlantic.

In the North Atlantic, the categories of race and religion by which traveling Europeans generally demarcated the world were largely, although not entirely, absent. Yet their absence did not make Europeans less aware of difference, both of the people and of the country, when they traveled in this region. For them, the North Atlantic was a place that became less recognizable by degrees and according to certain categories and standards of measurement. Through an analysis of travel books and other primary sources, we can see the categories according to which the North Atlantic appeared to be outside of European norms: its landscape and nature, its technology and material culture, and its language and literary heritage. These were not only categories used by traveling Europeans but also ways in which natives of the North Atlantic perceived themselves as distinct from Europeans. Naturally, both parties attached different meanings to this difference, but they tended to hold this set of categories as fixed markers of either being inside or outside of Europe.

This perceived divide between Europe and the North Atlantic did not remain constant over time. Between the mid-eighteenth and mid-twentieth centuries, the North Atlantic, as seen from both sides of the ocean, gradually drew closer to Europe. In the decades following World War II, the technology and material culture of the North Atlantic no longer seemed as foreign to visitors as it had before. Likewise, sometime around the end of the nineteenth century, although the transition is a little harder to pinpoint, the landscape of the North Atlantic ceased to be understood as a visible departure from European landscapes into a "New World." Taken together, these changes meant that the North Atlantic region transitioned into modernity during this period and ceased to be a strange place outside Europe. It instead became part of Europe and thereby underwent a historical process that never, despite the colonial *mission civilisatrice* or even globalization processes, took place in Africa or other regions considered exotic in Enlightenment Europe. With a few exceptions—some of which are discussed in the epilogue—the North Atlantic became, as seen by European eyes, regulated and normalized, losing the exotic qualities that had set it as a place apart prior to this period. *Iceland Imagined* tells the story of how this process evolved, identifies the actors in the process, and explains their interests in the transformation of the North Atlantic.

GEOGRAPHICAL AND HISTORICAL OUTLINE OF THE NORTH ATLANTIC

From the early Middle Ages on, the North Atlantic can be best understood as the Viking-age settlers themselves probably saw it: as a series of landfalls, as a chain of islands bridging the Atlantic from the European continent to North America, although of course the earliest settlers had no idea that North America was a continent. They left Norway in the ninth century—according to their own founding myth to escape the tyranny of a Norwegian king—and settled in the Shetlands, Orkneys, Faroes, and Iceland. From Iceland, after a pause of about a century, they went on to settle in Greenland and explore briefly in North America, which they called Vínland (Wine Land). According to their own sailing directions from the twelfth-century *Book of Settlements* (*Landnámabók*), it took them about seven days to sail from Stad (north of Bergen) in Norway to eastern Iceland. From western Iceland, it was four more days sail to Greenland. This means they might cover about 130 kilometers per day in the best conditions; the coast of Norway is about 965 kilometers from east Iceland, and Greenland is almost 300 kilometers from the west coast of Iceland. The Faroe Islands, where some of the settlers remained, lies roughly at the midpoint between Norway and Iceland.

When the Norse settlers came, the North Atlantic islands were sparsely inhabited, if at all, and population density remained low in the centuries after Norse settlement. The explanation for this is mostly environmental. Iceland's coast is warmed by Gulf Stream waters, but the interior is an uninhabitable sub-Arctic desert. The Norse, probably after expelling a few Irish monks who were living in Iceland sometime around 870, settled in isolated farmsteads around the coast. Most of their food came from farming wheat (and corn in the medieval period), raising cattle and sheep, and was supplemented with fish, seals, whale, and birds' eggs. The Viking-age settlement of Greenland and the discovery of North America were a continuance of this westward movement. According to the saga sources, the Norse discovery of Greenland was prompted by Eiríkur Þorvaldsson's ("the

Red") expulsion from Iceland around 985 for murder—a common way of making people "outlaws" in medieval Iceland was to expel them from the country. About fifteen years later, his son Leifur Eiríksson ("the Lucky") sailed from Greenland and became the first European to establish a camp in the Americas, on the site of L'Anse aux Meadows in Newfoundland. One of the reasons for the abandonment of the North American settlement was the hostile encounter between the Norse and native peoples there, ending with the death of Leifur's brother, Þorvaldr, according to the story from the sagas. The Norse called these Indians *skrælingar* (wretches), the same word that they used to describe the Inuit people of Greenland, whom their descendants met later, perhaps in the fourteen or fifteenth centuries.

During the early Middle Ages, the natives of the North Atlantic traveled seemingly frequently, and without great comment in the sources, between Norway, the Orkneys, the Shetlands, the Faroes, and Iceland. This period of unrestricted North Atlantic expansion and settlement did not last beyond this early medieval period, however. Because of a period of internal unrest in Iceland and the political weakness of local leaders in the Faroes, the Norwegian kings dominated the North Atlantic after 1262. Intermarriages among the Scandinavian monarchies in the fourteenth century, formally recognized by the Kalmar Union in 1397, united Norway with Denmark and Sweden. As Iceland, Greenland, and the Faroe, Orkney, and Shetland islands were politically part of Norway at this time, they too became legal parts of the combined Danish-Norwegian kingdom. When the Kalmar Union ended in 1536, Denmark declared that the North Atlantic provinces came directly under rule of the Danish Crown. Until the seventeenth century, however, when Danish kings began to pursue a more active centralizing policy toward the various parts of the state under absolute monarchy, the North Atlantic territories were in practice allowed a large measure of local control.

The English and Scottish states began to extend their power over the North Atlantic in the fifteenth and sixteenth centuries. The British historian Harold B. Carter refers to the "triangular relationship" between the North Atlantic, the British Isles, and Denmark, in the sense that both European powers exercised considerable cultural influence, even where formal legal ties were missing.[10] In 1472, the Shetlands and Orkneys were annexed by Scotland as part of the unpaid royal dowry from Christian I of Denmark to James III of Scotland upon his marriage to Christian's daugh-

ter Margaret. In some respects, however, these islands remained culturally Norse. Norse laws of landholding, the so-called *odal* laws, continued
in force until the imprisonment of Patrick Stewart, the earl of Orkney, in
1611. The Norn language, which is etymologically related to Old Norse,
was spoken on the Shetlands until the nineteenth century, although it was
gradually replaced by English and Scottish dialects as the languages of the
fishing trade. With the Act of Union between Scotland and England in
1707, these islands passed with little attention under British control, where
they remain to this day.

Over the centuries, however, Denmark gradually loosened its hold
in the North Atlantic, along with shedding the other dominions of its
global colonial empire. Even though the Danish state might have at one
time profited from its holdings in India and Africa, the North Atlantic was mostly an economic loss for the country. After its defeat in the
Napoleonic wars in 1814, the Danish state gradually contracted over the
course of the nineteenth century from the height of its expansion in the
seventeenth. It sold its African territories on the Gold Coast, in present-
day Ghana and Upper Volta, and its Indian possessions, in Tranquebar
and Bengal, to Great Britain in the 1840s, while the islands of St. Croix,
St. John, and St. Thomas in the West Indies went to the United States in
1917. Norway was ceded to Sweden by the Treaty of Kiel in 1814. The con-
vention between Sweden and Norway gave Norway its own parliament
under the Swedish monarch, but Norway achieved full independence
in 1905.[11] Iceland was granted home rule in 1903–4, and a 1918 Danish-
Icelandic treaty stipulated a twenty-five-year period of transition to full
independence, which expired in 1944 during the World War II German
occupation of Denmark. Today, only the Faroe Islands and Greenland
remain parts of the Danish kingdom, although home rule was granted
in 1948 and in 1979, respectively. Independence for these islands continues to be a topic of discussion between these countries and Denmark. In
June 2009, after a referendum on greater autonomy passed, Greenland
assumed responsibility for self-government in judicial affairs, policing,
and natural resources, while Denmark maintains control of finances,
foreign affairs, and defense. This has been interpreted as a step toward
full independence from Danish rule.[12] Significantly, Greenlandic, rather
than Danish, became the official language of Greenland at the historic
ceremony.[13]

A NORTHERN BORDERLANDS

With this history in mind, the map of the North Atlantic, as regarded from Europe, appears as a series of outposts charting the progressive landfalls of Scandinavian settlers from the mid-ninth century to the year 1000, a date that marks both the introduction of Christianity into Iceland and the Norse discovery of North America. The territories of the North Atlantic were "outposts" in several different senses. Environmentally, they were outposts, as the climate and the margin of subsistence became increasingly more severe and slimmer the farther the settlers ventured into the North Atlantic. In his book, *Collapse: How Societies Choose to Fail or Succeed*, Jared M. Diamond explains the demise of the Norse Greenlandic colony by understanding the North Atlantic as a series of settlements in which the settlers attempted to import European methods of agriculture and subsistence, such as cattle farming, into an increasingly fragile environment that could not sustain it.[14] Diamond claims that it was the failure of the medieval Norse to recognize these changes and adapt—by abandoning European agriculture and adopting Inuit hunting methods of survival—that doomed the colony. He argues that the Norse placed such a high cultural value on farming and cattle raising as essential elements of European Christian culture that they were unable to switch to more viable forms of sustenance as the climate began to change. The medieval Norse settlers were probably less culturally rigid than Diamond has portrayed them, however. Up to 80 percent of all bones found in some Norse archeological sites in Greenland are seal bones, and fish were also a substantial part of the diet.[15]

Thus, although Diamond's claim about the medieval Norse diet is not well substantiated, his argument points to a second sense in which the North Atlantic has been seen historically as a series of outposts, that is, as cultural as well as environmental outposts. Civilization, which was most often equated with Christianity during the medieval period, was feared to be in danger of deteriorating as one ventured farther into the North Atlantic, especially on the shores of Greenland or the North American coasts, where the European encounter with the heathen native posed a spiritual as well as physical threat. Many of the travelers in the North Atlantic related the theme of civilization to the environment, noting how difficult it was to sustain spiritual and moral life under the conditions of privation they found. One of the nineteenth-century Danish governors of the Faroe Islands, Christian Pløyen, for example, blamed the Faroese tendencies toward stealing and begging on their poverty and the difficult farming conditions on the islands.[16]

In one or both of these senses, that is, with respect to nature or with respect to civilization, the idea that the North Atlantic was a series of stepping stones on a journey to another world is implicit in the writings of many European travelers. The birdlife of the Faroes, one nineteenth-century German visitor, Carl Julian Graba, imagined as he set out from Kiel, would be "even stranger" than that of the Orkneys, Shetlands, and Hebrides, where he had already visited.[17] A better-known traveler, the great Victorian explorer Richard Burton, declared that "Iceland . . . is an exaggeration of Scotland, whilst Greenland exaggerates Iceland," although he had never been any farther than Iceland himself, which he detested.[18] Why, then, did he make this claim in his "Zoological Notes" section in his two volumes about his trip to Iceland? His remark illustrates a belief in a European imaginary geography of the North Atlantic that was well-established by the late nineteenth century: the farther north one traveled from the European continent, the less recognizable the world became. It became less recognizable by degrees and was measured in set categories. The North Atlantic was a zone of change, a territory encompassing a range of variation on a certain type of difference from the traveler's home. There was no firm dividing line separating the known from the unknown, Europe from the Orient; rather, one got lost gradually, and, what was worse, unexpectedly. Places that one might expect to be ordinary were in fact strange, and what was made exotic in the imagination turned out on the journey to be disappointingly normal. The aspects of North Atlantic journeys that confused travelers, and left them wondering whether they were still within familiar territory, were landscape and nature, religion, technology and material culture, and literature and language. They serve as indications of the perceived distance between European places and those on the peripheries of the North Atlantic. These categories were used by both visitors and natives to measure and determine the extent of difference and change on the journey.

Burton's notion of the North Atlantic as a zone or range of difference from European norms was expressed in another way by the Danish exhibition Northern Dwellers in the Colonial Pavilion at the 1900 World's Fair in Paris. Across from the Eiffel Tower, the visitor could see polar bear furs displayed with Icelandic manuscripts and maps, while Greenlandic kayaks and hunting gear were arranged with a bridal dress worn in a Lutheran wedding. Margit Mogensen, who has written about Denmark's self-presentation in exhibitions, poses this question about the display: "One might wonder why Iceland and the Faroe Islands should be included, when the exhibition was placed in the colonial section, and when in other respects the fragments of Greenlandic culture were the point of departure for the exhibition."[19] Since the Faroes and Iceland had been granted political representation within the Danish kingdom by 1900, the placement of these islands together with Greenland, which was still a colony, might have appeared to be a slight to the Icelanders and Faroese on the part of the Danish organizers.[20] Daniel Bruun, the chief curator of the exhibition, actually had great respect for the North Atlantic culture and was well-known there from several trips he had made to Norway, Iceland, the Faroes, and Greenland. His intention was almost certainly not to insult the Icelanders or the Faroese by the arrangement of this exhibit. Mogensen analyzes the rationale behind the arrangement of the exhibition with reference to the aesthetics of museum exhibitions, rather than politics:

> [Danish arrangers] had placed "dependencies" of all sorts together without precise explanations in exhibitions abroad before, and when Bruun wrote his proposal to the National Museum, it was the 900-year anniversary of the Christianization of Iceland, which was in itself a good opportunity to display the Christian culture . . . from the beginning it was an important point for Bruun that Iceland and the Faroes should be included because he thought that the traces of the Northern culture in Greenland could be better understood if the visitor could compare them in the same exhibit with the better-preserved houses and other material artifacts from Iceland and the Faroes. The idea of *visualizing* cultural connections over the ocean was quite advanced for exhibitions, and nothing similar had been attempted earlier in the Danish exhibitions at the World's Fairs.[21]

Here, Mogensen makes explicit a Danish conception of the North Atlantic that had been implicitly understood from at least the mid-eighteenth century on: that all the North Atlantic islands shared a particular type of nature and culture, one different from European norms, different by degrees and in recognizable and measurable ways. The idea of spectators "visualizing cultural connections across an ocean" might have been advanced for the organization of museum exhibitions, but the idea of these connections in the North Atlantic was actually quite well-established by 1900. Furthermore, this was not solely a Danish understanding but an image that was transmitted by Denmark—on occasions like the World's Fair exhibition— to other European countries. It was also an idea that many other Europeans arrived at independently, without the intervention of Danish cultural brokers. At the World's Fair, these images were displayed as evidence of the Danish paternalistic role as a helpful bringer of civilization to less-advantaged peoples, as Mogensen goes on to interpret the presentation in Paris: "To the rational gaze, the hierarchy of civilization was drawn very clearly: first came the old, cultivated Iceland with the church and altar, and one could understand the sad story of how these northern-dwelling Christians had disappeared from Greenland, and therefore how we must strive to bring them to civilization from this wilderness."[22]

The construction of this "hierarchy of civilization" and the tools used to construct it is the point of the inquiry in *Iceland Imagined*. Mogensen points out one of the yardsticks: the division between heathen and Christian. This was one of the most obvious European measures of a culture and also one of the most rigid—in the early eighteenth century a line could simply be drawn with Norway, Iceland, the Faroes, the Shetlands, and Orkneys on one side and Greenland on the other. Furthermore, religion is a binary marker: the closer dependencies, such as Iceland, Norway, and the Faroes, are Christian Europeans, and the Inuit of Greenland are heathens in need of European civilization. This was one, but only one, of several ways of ordering the North Atlantic. Placing regions at the right places on the map was not as simple as that, and travelers and natives used a number of factors to orient themselves there.

The North Atlantic situation was all the more complex because, unlike travel in Africa or North America, the nature and people that Europeans encountered in the North Atlantic were not perceived as utterly foreign and exotic in all their aspects. Rather, they were in some respects familiar and in some respects different. At times travelers invented exotic stories about Icelanders and Icelandic nature, while others tried to deemphasize or discredit such stories. These descriptions of nature are in some ways accurate but cannot be taken entirely at face value. Rather, they are indicative of political, cultural, and economic relationships between the visitors and the natives. Identifying the various measures of civilization and familiarity in the following chapters, sorting out the order of the North Atlantic as measured from Europe, and the distance to Europe as measured from the North Atlantic, helps to provide a view of the relationship between knowledge and power that is both nuanced, in terms of showing various types and degrees of viewing, and also broad, showing the commonalities throughout the large zone.

OTHER EUROPEAN PERIPHERIES: EAST, WEST, AND SOUTH

At first glance, the moment of European-native encounter in the North Atlantic appears relatively reciprocal and evenhanded, as least as compared with this encounter in other parts of the globe. Because of relative proximity to the European continent, a long shared history, and well-developed channels of administrative communication, the inhabitants of the North Atlantic were also able to travel and develop familiarity with the areas of the world from which visitors came. Icelanders, Faroe Islanders, Norwegians, and Greenlanders came to Europe in many different roles—as representatives of the administrative bureaucracy, as scholars, as soldiers, as prisoners, even as human exhibitions and spectacles, for example, the Inuit captives who were brought to the court of Denmark's King Christian IV in the early seventeenth century.[23] North Atlantic peoples were also in a position to evaluate the relationship between their homelands and the distant territory, and they did so in the form of poetry, administrative reports, folktales, and travel books, just as travelers from the European continent did. All of these voices did not reach the same audiences, but they were not unimportant or negated either. Often, native expertise was crucial to the establishment of knowledge of the North Atlantic territories in ways that have not always been adequately recognized. Unlike the invented native from China or Africa of the "Persian letters" genre, the native of the North Atlantic was often not just a European mouthpiece but an actual voice.[24] In measuring these distances, it was not only the Europeans who had the privilege of observing the natives but the natives who looked back at Europe and also at the distance between their homelands and those of the travelers they encountered. Still, the sense of reciprocity in the North Atlantic encounter is incomplete. Within the region there is a hierarchy of privileged voices, heard through the filter of central power structures. Despite the apparent fluency of the cultural exchanges in the North Atlantic, the bargain struck remained uneven. These places could be almost European—but not quite, and not always, and in different ways, and to different degrees. In the North Atlantic, making these measurements, which has been identified by some scholars as a characteristically European practice, blurred those very categories at the moment of their construction.

This imagining of the North Atlantic took place within a context of relationships with the larger European powers. Whatever travelers saw in the North Atlantic, they saw in comparison with what existed in a European homeland, a home that was most frequently Denmark or Great Britain, although also often the German-speaking countries, Sweden, or France. Travel writers from these regions used the journey into foreign lands to reflect on conditions at home. Their use of non-Western regions as mirrors of themselves is a dominant motif of this literature. European writers, prominently Denis Diderot and Jean-Jacques Rousseau, as well as many others, who looked at the non-West frequently saw these places as exemplars in a catalogue of binary oppositions between the familiar and the foreign: civilized versus savage, enslaved versus free, enlightened and progressive versus primitive and stagnated. This eye for dualism was especially directed toward the Pacific after Captain James Cook's voyages in the 1760s but was present even before the scientific voyages of the later eighteenth century provided evidence in support of this view. As much of the literature on the Western constructs of the non-West has demonstrated, it has made very little difference whether the Western home came out on the positive (Cook's) or negative (Rousseau's) side of the balance sheet in these reckonings: the notion of binary opposition remains fundamental to the evaluation of other cultures. This dualism has been identified as a rhetorically powerful element of the discourses of colonialism and imperialism as, during the nineteenth and twentieth centuries, the West came to dominate the non-West economically and politically as well as intellectually and culturally.[25]

Many of the oppositions by which the West classified the non-West applied equally well to regions nearer to home. European peasants, as well as Tahitians, could also be described as impoverished, dirty, and uncivilized in contrast to the sophistication of metropolitan centers. Similarly, marginalized peoples also could be seen as retaining a pure, uncorrupted culture that Europeans, who were corrupted by the decay of civilization, sought to rediscover. Some previous attempts to theorize the relationship between European metropoles and peripheries have been proposed under rubrics such as internal colonialism and demi-Orientalization. Although both focus on European perception and treatment of regions that, like the North Atlantic, are relatively small and close compared to those examined by other studies of colonialism and Orientalism, neither concept precisely fits the European relationship with the North Atlantic.

The concept of internal colonialism has been used to describe colonial practices that take place within the borders of a state, in which the actors and those who are the subjects of these practices often share a common ethnicity, language, or religion, although not necessarily all three. The former Soviet Union's relationship toward its indigenous peoples and the English relationship with Scotland and Wales are frequently cited as examples of internal colonialism.[26] Like much of the work on overseas or external colonialism, internal colonialism largely depends on a single core-periphery model, in which the practices of the metropolis—the monopolization of commerce, discrimination on the basis of language or ethnic identity, and the maintenance of a lower standard of living in the colonized areas—are imposed on the internal colony unilaterally, with irreconcilable differences between the center and the periphery. This was not the case in the relationship between the North Atlantic periphery and Danish and British centers of power. The North Atlantic region was rather a zone of progressive degrees of subjugation and imposition of power, and of degrees of perception of difference and similarity. Furthermore, internal colonies are often described as those areas in the "hinterlands" or "within the natural frontiers" of the state.[27] From the point of view of Copenhagen or London, the North Atlantic was not "within a natural frontier" but was rather an extension of that frontier across the natural barrier of the ocean.[28] The area was a series of outposts that extended the reach of European civilization and the European state at the same time that the stability and levels of this civilization were questioned and being reassessed and recalculated. Despite some difficulties with the concept of internal colonialism, it remains a useful idea for expressing that European colonialism was not contingent on factors such as race, physical appearance, language, or geographical location but was a deeply embedded practice.[29]

In his book on the western European "invention" of eastern Europe, Larry Wolff argues that the world order of the Enlightenment classified eastern Europe as an ambiguous borderland between Europe and the Orient: it was "within Europe, but not fully European."[30] Following Said's work, Wolff calls this perception of eastern Europe on the part of the

West a "demi-Orientalization" and situates eastern Europe as a space of mediation between the "ordinariness/rationality" of eastern Europe and the "strangeness/irrationality" of the Orient. The reports of travelers from western Europe to eastern Europe that he cites seem, however, to place the most weight on the strangeness and exoticism of the travel experience, and a sense of familiarity with the Western home does not emerge so readily from the primary sources. Furthermore, this exoticism is understood primarily, if not entirely, in a negative sense: eastern Europe was a place in the Western mind that needed to be disciplined and ordered. The travelers complain about the Polish peasants' "incomprehensible" language and filthiness and find little in their culture worthy of praise, in distinction to the Western travelers' experience with the actual Orient. This sets the western European experience of the North Atlantic quite apart from its experience of eastern Europe as Wolff describes it.

At least in part, this problem arises from the selection and availability of sources. Travelers, whose books Wolff primarily relies upon, tend to write about what is different and noteworthy in a foreign place rather than about what is the same as it is at home. In the North Atlantic, as in every other region visited frequently by outsiders, it was easy for common ideas about landscape and cultural differences to be repeated into clichés. Despite travelers' tendency to exaggerate, fabricate, or retell stories from other books uncritically, their perception of difference should be taken seriously. But an important question for the historian reading these travel accounts is to consider what the author expects to find on the journey. What is considered natural in this territory? What is the point of departure, and where do things become different? Travelers often see what they expect to see, and any surprises they encounter along the way are reconstructed into the discourse set up by their outlook and goals for the journey, at least by the time they come to write the narrative. If they think themselves still within the boundaries of their home territory, they manage to rationalize the strangeness they encounter. Away from home, they are eager to perceive slight variations as wildly exotic. In the North Atlantic, travelers did both, and quite purposefully so, for example in their efforts to win trading privileges and grants from the Danish Crown, to make collections of folktales, or to investigate nature in the North Atlantic.

Unlike some of the other "Orients" of Europe, however, the North Atlantic region was legally part of two European states. In addition to travel books, administrative reports were written about the conditions there.[31] The concerns and style of those who wrote these reports are certainly different from what is found in the travel books and can provide a useful balance to the exotic descriptions the latter sometimes contain. A census was taken in Iceland in 1702–12, a major land commission visited in 1770, and a second commission was appointed following the environmental crises of 1783–84. Officials in eighteenth-century Norway, the Faroes, and Greenland also produced a plethora of reports, and in the Shetland and Orkney islands the local lords began in the early eighteenth century to introduce projects for improvements along the same lines as in the Danish-managed North Atlantic.[32] There was often a great deal of congruence between the projects proposed by the Danish and British officials. State administrators in the North Atlantic tended to be confused and fascinated by the same characteristics as other travelers: nature, technology and material circumstances, and language. These issues are often reformulated as problems in these texts, especially the problem of management of technology and the environment. The tone is often one of earnest encouragement in the face of difficulties rather than amazement, but the discussions and the points of confusion are similar. Looking at the range of sources about the North Atlantic, one can see these islands both rationalized as part of Europe, as utterly normal provinces of the Danish and British kingdoms, and also exoticized as completely strange and bewildering places outside the borders of home. *Iceland Imagined* takes as its point of departure the sense of confusion and difficulty that travelers had in locating, measuring, and understanding this territory.

While internal colonialism and demi-Orientalization are thought-provoking if not entirely accurate terms when applied to the North Atlantic, the types of power arrangements between the North Atlantic provinces and the European states might be best categorized by Jürgen Osterhammel's designations of "informal empire," or "colonialism without colonies."[33] In these relationships, the power of the larger state (the "big brother") is generally maintained through such means as favorable trade agreements and largely without recourse to the force of arms, or the threat thereof. Osterhammel concludes that informal empire offers the big brother state many of the same advantages over the little brother as formal empire or imperialism does, but without the attendant military costs. By examining the European treatment of the North Atlantic as a zone of outposts of civilization, *Iceland Imagined* takes up the cultural aspects of this informal empire or big brother–little brother relationship. The story shows how both the big and little brothers were active, if not equal, partners in shaping this relationship. In the North Atlantic, it was complex, difficult, and confusing for Europeans to evaluate the levels of civilization there. In other European encounters with the rest of the world this judgment was often made simple by European *mission civilisatrice* theories or by racist assumptions. Such techniques did not prove applicable to the North Atlantic, where racial difference could only be perceived in Greenland, and the natives were already Christian and literate. In the absence of these broad, overarching ways of demonstrating European superiority, European travelers in the North Atlantic were forced to delineate their measures of civilization more precisely, in terms of nature, language, and technology. Placing the North Atlantic on European maps was an ongoing process that did not reach a conclusion in a simple way. Untangling how the discussions over these categories progressed demonstrates how Europeans viewed the borders of civilization and how they sought to extend these borders.

In the North Atlantic, and especially in Iceland, the earlier traveler was, as I was myself, alternately impressed and disappointed by the horizons and landscapes presented to him. As outlined in many eighteenth- and nineteenth-century travelogues on expeditions to the North Atlantic, the object of the journey was the majesty of vistas shaped by volcanoes and glaciers, by fire and ice, as Iceland has so often appeared in travel literature. The traveler expects strangeness, difference from the landscapes to which he is accustomed, and is disappointed by settings that appear mundane and familiar. In these accounts, Reykjavík, which effectively represented Iceland's connection to the European mainland, often depresses the visitor with its poverty and banality, and the traveler is more satisfied when he reaches the sites of the sagas on horseback. The discussion about landscapes in the North Atlantic centers on the meanings of this perceived difference from European landscapes, even if the so-called remarkable features of Iceland—such as glaciers and volcanoes—were not in fact completely unknown to individuals who had often undertaken a European grand tour that included Italy and Switzerland.

Icelandic landscapes took on symbolic meanings for travelers; they came to represent different historical narratives, contested among travelers from different countries and the Icelanders themselves. Other sources also contributed to informing visitors about nature in the North Atlantic, for example, the European natural histories characteristic of the eighteenth century. Using descriptions of flora and fauna in the North Atlantic, Icelanders entered into European scientific discourse during the eighteenth century to establish themselves as authorities about nature in their own country.

When turning an eye from distant horizons to local conditions, however, the traveler expected certain familiar material comforts in Reykjavík, the administrative center of a province of a European state, and was often shocked to realize that conditions of poverty and material underdevelopment could exist in part of the Danish kingdom. Another sense of confusion was created by the encounter with technology and material conditions in the North Atlantic and the reaction to these conditions. A number of eighteenth-century proposals for improvements and modernization in Iceland and the Faroes, which urged the natives to learn to use the land better and adapt themselves to the climate, emerged in response to the perceived problems of material deficiencies in the provinces. The writers, usually officials in the state administration, often express distress that people who are otherwise on such high cultural levels could be living in conditions of such depravity, and they look toward the regions of the North Atlantic zone closer to civilization, such as the Scottish islands, for models for improvement. In Greenland, however, Arctic explorers began to confront, to their disadvantage, the deficiencies of their own technology. By the end of the nineteenth century, European travelers in Greenland had discovered that, despite their allegedly primitive cultural state, Inuit tools were much better suited to this environment than their own were, and they had to rely upon native expertise to survive in a climate so different from European norms. Thus, they were forced to reevaluate that equivalence of technology and civilization fundamental to the European self-image at the end of the nineteenth century, which had not been called into question, but only solidified, by their previous experiences in the North Atlantic.[34]

When Europeans began to pay attention to Greenlandic tools and technology, they also began to learn about the people who used them. Beginning in the eighteenth century, they did this largely through Christian missions. Christianization, which had taken hold already in Norway, Iceland, the Faroes, Shetlands, and Orkneys in the Middle Ages, was introduced to the Greenlandic Inuit via European missionaries in the early eighteenth century. Religious conversion can be understood as a parallel process to the study of the Greenlandic language, which began with these missionaries in Greenland in the eighteenth century and was taken up by professional linguists during the nineteenth. In the same way that the missionaries attempted to shape Greenlandic religious and spiritual life in accordance with the norms of European civilization, linguists tried to codify and relate the Greenlandic language to the Indo-European languages, which were an important locus of European identity in the nineteenth century.

Although this story shows how language was an important aspect of the North Atlantic encounter, it was also a frequent source of confusion for the traveler. The linguistic situation in the North Atlantic was multilayered. Danish was the administrative language in Norway, Iceland, Greenland, and the Faroes, but it was only spoken by officials and people of higher status, who had often received some of their education in Copenhagen. By the time Norway left the Danish kingdom in 1814, the standard form of Norwegian was essentially Danish, although with a considerable number of dialects with differences in pronunciation and vocabulary. During the Norwegian nationalist movement in the nineteenth century, two separate forms of Norwegian were standardized, one that remained close to Danish conventions and one that was based on the dialects of western Norway, far removed from the urban center and thus allegedly retaining pure Norwegian forms.[35] Icelandic and Faroese (which did not exist as a standardized written language until the invention of an orthography in the nineteenth century) were spoken on these islands, and these were often the only languages spoken by people in rural areas whom travelers met. The Inuit languages spoken in Greenland were substantially unknown in Europe until the arrival of explorers to the island in the seventeenth and early eighteenth centuries. Although the folk culture was collected and the languages were systemically studied, the Greenlandic languages and Faroese never achieved the status of Icelandic, with its written medieval literature, in European cultural estimations.

The highest administrative officials in the North Atlantic, the first people to whom the traveler usually paid an official visit, often spoke English, German, or French. As late as the end of the nineteenth century, travelers report resorting to Latin as a lingua franca in Iceland. An exchange conducted in Latin, a symbol of European cultural achievement, with people who appeared otherwise primitive in their living conditions, was a surprise to travelers and generated much comment on the linguistic abilities of Icelanders, as well as occasionally sheepishly self-critical assessments of the traveler's own proficiency. Visitors also regarded Icelandic as a highly sophisticated European language and as the origin, or at least the oldest living example, of the Germanic languages, with a status comparable to Latin. Encouraged by the reencounter with medieval literature and by the grammatical codification of the language, late-nineteenth-century visitors such as William Morris—who was differently disposed toward the island than his contemporary Richard Burton—adopted learning Icelandic as something of a hobby. Thus, instead of the usual situation in the colonized or marginalized peripheries of a single administrative language of higher status and a native language, or an assortment of languages and dialects, of lower status, the linguistic situation in the North Atlantic was inverted and jumbled. European travelers sought to reconcile the high literary and cultural levels that they found in the North Atlantic—represented above all by the Icelandic sagas—with their experience of technology and material culture there, which they often took as evidence of the primitive state of the North Atlantic provinces.

Does this history of foreign and native imaginations in the North Atlantic have any lasting legacy? Can any European or American think of the North Atlantic as exotic anymore when several direct flights depart every day from the East Coast of the United States to Iceland during the summer months, and when Icelandair markets the country as a stopover destination between Europe and the United States? How, in fact, are Iceland and the North Atlantic perceived today? Iceland, along with the other North Atlantic countries, modernized rapidly following World War II. It was a beneficiary of cold war politics, as its geographical location was considered strategically ideal by the Americans, who financed the construction of the country's transportation infrastructure, including its roads and international airport.[36] The airport where one arrives via direct flight from New York or Boston is a legacy of the U.S./NATO base at Keflavík, about fifty kilometers outside the capital. This base, of course, was also the entry point for other kinds of modernity, about which the Icelanders were much more ambivalent: American television and rock music.[37] With Iceland's high standard of living and new technological modernity, it would appear that the discussion outlined in *Iceland Imagined* is now closed and that the country—independent of Denmark since 1944—has become indisputably part of Europe (although not of the European Union). The anthropologist E. Paul Durrenberger declares decisively that: "Iceland is not exotic. It has electricity and central heating and cars and buses. It has telephones that work and supermarkets and electric milking machines and tractors. People live in high-rise apartment buildings or modern single-family houses. Icelanders have credit cards, money machines, color TV. Except for a couple of letters the alphabet is the same as we use for English. Iceland is a thoroughly modern country."[38]

In most respects this is true. In the terms that Durrenberger understands modernity in this passage, which are mostly technological, the country today is a modern place. While Iceland is still routinely spoken of as "Europe's last wilderness," this language is mostly used in tourist literature, where such exoticism is a marketable commodity. A few contemporary episodes show, however, how the definition of North Atlantic nature is still, or again, a contentious issue. One of these is the whaling controversy, which came to international attention following the International Whaling Commission's (IWC) introduction of new regulations and a zero-catch quota for commercial whaling in 1986. In this dispute some North Atlantic inhabitants, including many Norwegians, Icelanders, Greenlanders, and Faroe Islanders, argue for a certain relationship to nature—the right to hunt and eat whales—that most European countries, including Great Britain, France, Germany, and also the United States, have rejected. Today, all four of these North Atlantic countries kill and eat whales, although these hunts are classified and treated in different ways under IWC guidelines. Thus, the choices made in the North Atlantic about the human relationship to nature conflict with values that an international community wishes to establish as normative. This conflict has its roots in the lengthy discussion about North Atlantic nature conducted by natives and foreigners over the preceding centuries. How does the post–World War II status of the North Atlantic region change the power relationship between these natives and foreigners and the perception of the North Atlantic?

THE POSTCOLONIAL NORTH

Having experienced the contradictions of the peripheries during a summer in Iceland, I went farther east to the centers, to London and to Copenhagen. Traveling backward in this fashion, reversing the journey that many of the subjects of this book took, once again calls attention to the question of distance between the North Atlantic and Europe. Two events took place in Copenhagen in the final years of the twentieth century, and both of these represented an aspect of the postcolonial relationship between Denmark and the North Atlantic.

The first, which in fact drew very little public attention, was the final stage of the return of the saga manuscripts to Iceland from the Royal Library in Copenhagen (Det Kongelige Bibliotek) and the University of Copenhagen (Københavns Universitet), where they had been since the seventeenth and eighteenth centuries. The Danish parliament had decided in 1965 to return the manuscripts to Iceland on the grounds that they were part of the Icelandic cultural heritage and not Danish. This decision had been celebrated by Icelanders as a crucial step in their cultural independence and protested in Denmark by student marches and flags flown at half-mast. In 1997, more than thirty years later, however, the actual repatriation was hardly noticed by the general public. Danish newspapers interpreted the lack of controversy over the final stage of this process as part of the maturing relationship between Denmark and its former colony. The transfer of these documents was taken for granted as a standard part of the postindependence process between the new state and its former motherland.

A second issue, the topic of much more extensive discussion in newspapers and in public life in Denmark, was the ongoing revelations about the role of the Danish government in the forcible relocation of Inuit away from the American air base at Thule in Greenland in 1953.[39] Although the Danish government represented itself as merely following American wishes in moving about a hundred Inuit away from their lands, and claimed that the Inuit had agreed to this move, the Danish High Court found instead that the group had been forced to move on very short notice and under unfavorable conditions. A group of Inuit filed suit against the Danish government in 1996 and received compensation, although considerably less than they had requested, and an official apology from the government in 1999. This discussion, together with the portrayal of Greenlanders in Bille August's dramatization of Peter Høeg's novel *Frøken Smillas fornemmelse for sne* in 1997 (*Smilla's Sense of Snow*), awakened much interest in Danish-Greenlandic history and relations. Unlike the case of the Icelandic cultural heritage of written material, the Greenlandic claim to the cultural heritage of the land and the traditions it embodied was not regarded as a routine matter or a closed issue as seen from Copenhagen at the end of the twentieth century. It appeared that, in the Danish public eye, the reconciliation of Icelandic-Danish history, and the integration of Iceland into the cultural norms of European states had already taken place, while the Danish-Greenlandic relationship and the status of Greenland were still in question.

Imagining Iceland examines this process of integration from the eighteenth century, taking account of how the North Atlantic was marked as a territory outside Europe and how these lines of demarcation on the map gradually moved. How was the landscape, nature, technology, material culture, religion, and language of the North Atlantic understood as part of a new world in eighteenth-century Europe, and how did these same features become part of the modern Europeans' own world? What was the process of this transformation? Who participated in it and for what reasons? What actually changed about the environment, culture, and technology of the North Atlantic, and what changed about the perceptions of the travelers? A remarkable number of historical actors—some who lived in the countries of the North Atlantic and knew them intimately and others who never visited—expressed opinions on these issues. *Iceland Imagined* examines writings by travelers from European states, including Great Britain, Denmark, Germany, Sweden, and France, who in the process of pursuing their own economic and cultural interests in the North Atlantic helped to shape competing visions of the regions as "European" or as "exotic." Furthermore, the present volume shows how natives of the North Atlantic—the Icelanders, Norwegians, Faroe Islanders, and Greenlandic Inuit—also participated in this process by resisting, contesting, or allying themselves with the stories and agendas of foreigners. The story concludes by pointing out the unevenness of the different strands of this transformative process, and the contested nature of it. In some respects the North Atlantic still functions and is conceived as a wilderness and frontier—as the tourist agencies selling dogsled tours in Greenland want us to believe, reaping profits themselves from this narrative of the North Atlantic.

Early in the morning of our second day of driving we came to a junction in the main dirt road. A primitive jeep trail split off, marked by a sign that pointed across a vast, barren volcanic plain: "Kverkfjöll—105 km." Civilization ends here; we had crossed Iceland's green, inhabited circumference. . . . We bounced onto the jeep trail and the clock whirred backward. . . . It seemed we had entered a time before life began—before cars, houses, animals, bushes, or birds. . . . Along with related cataclysms and natural disasters, [volcanic] eruptions have shaped Iceland's history in somewhat the same manner that the histories of other European nations have been shaped by war. —*Peter Stark (1994)*

1 | ICELANDIC LANDSCAPES

Natural Histories and National Histories

Icelandic nature, particularly in its extreme manifestations of volcanoes and glaciers and their potential to create natural disasters, has long fascinated travelers. The striking idea of a land shaped by fire and ice grips the memories of visitors, even as the tourist industry has rendered the image cliché. There is a basis for the "fire and ice" cliché; nature in Iceland does exert a powerful force on the landscape. Iceland sits on a mid-Atlantic tectonic plate boundary that is slowly being forced apart as new rock is pushed to the earth's surface, forcing the two plates farther away from each other. This geological circumstance makes many parts of Iceland seem to be continuously under construction—barren, rough, and bearing the imprints of recent cataclysms (fig. 1). While lush green meadows, fields of flowers, and even trees—despite a history of soil erosion and deforestation—are also a part of the Icelandic landscape, these are far less frequently pictured and remembered than the more dramatic mountains, lava fields, and icebergs, all of which usually contrast sharply with travelers' home terrain. Visitors came to Iceland with the desire to see natural phenomena not found at home; they often overlooked the more mundane features of the Icelandic natural world, instead heading straight for the geysers and glaciers.

Eighteenth- and nineteenth-century European travelers to the island frequently used dramatic language in describing Icelandic nature as remarkable, unique, and completely different from the landscapes, flora, and fauna they knew at home. A participant on Joseph Banks's 1772 expe-

FIG. 1 An Icelandic landscape on the Sprengisandur road (the northern part between Kiðagil and Bárðardalur). Sprengisandur crosses the interior of Iceland, which was the legendary home of outlaws and trolls. The tower of rocks in the foreground is a typical path marker in Iceland. Photo courtesy of Ingibjörg Eiríksdóttir.

dition to Iceland, Uno von Troil, a Swedish student of Linnaeus who later became the bishop of Uppsala, wrote on the very first page of his *Letters on Iceland*, "I was happy to come to a country where many traces of our ancient language still existed, and where I was certain to catch a glimpse of the most unusual aspects of nature."[1] Three-quarters of a century later, Ida Pfeiffer, the wife of an Austrian civil servant, echoed von Troil's expression when she spoke of her hope of finding in Iceland "nature in a garb such as she wears nowhere else."[2]

The idea of traveling in order to find natural extremes and wonders was, of course, not uncommon in eighteenth and nineteenth century Europe, and Iceland and the other North Atlantic countries were far from the only exotic regions spoken of in these terms. At this time, European journeys both northward and southward were expected to bring the traveler face-to-face with the unusual. In the genre of northern voyages, probably the most well-known and striking example of this trope occurs on the opening pages of Mary Shelley's 1818 novel *Frankenstein*, when the narrator Robert Walton is onboard a ship, headed north from St. Petersburg toward Archangel, where he will meet Victor Frankenstein and hear his sad tale. Walton writes to his sister that even though the North Pole is often pictured as the "seat of frost and desolation," it "presents itself to my imagination as the region of beauty and delight," and he imagines it as a country "ruled by different laws and in which numerous circumstances enforce a belief that the aspect of nature differs essentially from anything of which we have any experience." He further explains that, even though the ship was encountering ice floes, at the pole "snow and frost are banished" and they would "sail over a calm sea." For the rather counterintuitive notion that natural conditions would abruptly reverse themselves at the pole, Walton cites the authority of "preceding navigators."[3] Shelley's formulation of northern nature, written in the epitome of the Romantic style, is so extreme that not just natural phenomenon but the very laws of nature were imagined to be different in the North.[4] The North was a wild place, uncontrolled by the physical laws and standards familiar to the traveler.

This construction of the North as a wilderness where all the laws of nature are turned on their heads is fundamentally one-sided, however. It takes for granted the Western notion of the difference between *homeland* and *wilderness*, ignoring the fact that people who live in so-called wildernesses do not consider them in these terms.[5] Mark Nutall, an anthropologist who studies land use in Greenland and the Arctic, writes that the

Western-Inuit conflicts over land and resource use are often the result of profound misunderstandings of the categories of the other; what is for Westerners a wilderness is the landscape that the Inuit would describe as home—a place not to be "protected" from humans but to be inhabited and used by them.[6] Historically, many European travelers to the North Atlantic ignored the natives' perspective of their own landscapes and instead dealt with the possibility of differing notions of nature by projecting their own senses of uncertainty or ill ease onto all interactions with the territory. They imagined that natives of this territory possessed the same sense of distance and nature that they did. Henry Holland, a British medical student who accompanied George Steuart Mackenzie on his expedition to Iceland in 1810, described after his return home his impressions of the reaction of an Icelandic student to the landscape of Scotland:

> A young man by the name of Thorgrimson . . . is going to study medicine at the university of Copenhagen. When he landed but two days ago, he had never seen a tree, or a house built of stone; carts, carriages, roads, and a thousand other things, were all new to his eyes and understanding. Conceive then his astonishment in passing through the richly wooded country between Leith and Edinburgh, and still more the feelings with which he beheld every thing around him in this metropolis, which perhaps more than any other place in the world is fitted to afford an entire contrast to the scenes he had left behind him in the desert place of his nativity. The Latin language (in which alone I can converse with him) is not favourable perhaps to the expression of strong emotion; but I could see his wonder in his countenance, and the eager gazing of his eyes. The feeling to me is a singular one of seeing these people here, after meeting them before in scenes and situations so very different.[7]

In this passage, Holland's home and the student's appear as utterly alien places to each other, and both travelers could experience a similar sense of wonder in gazing at the strange landscapes they found. Holland, however, is in the position to define the terms of the encounter: Iceland, the place of the student's nativity, is characterized as a "desert place," while Edinburgh is a "metropolis" that provides an "entire contrast" to the other. The landscape of the "desert" is defined by the features that this environment lacks— trees, roads, stone houses—and the other elements of European nature and culture. It is only the student's ability to converse directly with Holland, albeit inadequately, that distinguishes the encounter from the purely alterian. And even language is not here treated as a civilized gesture; it is rather through the student's "gaze" that Holland claims to understand the other's feelings.

Some of the natural wonders that traveling Europeans found in Iceland, as well as in other parts of the world, were curiosities to be collected and placed in cabinets, museums, and gardens.[8] But others—like the most characteristic features of the Icelandic landscape, the volcanoes, glaciers, and hot springs—had to be seen in situ in order to invoke wonder. While flasks of mineral water from the hot springs and rocks from the volcanic eruptions could be taken back home to be analyzed, for the literary traveler the landscape of the North Atlantic had to be experienced in its entirety, not in scientifically dissected pieces. Scientific and literary motives for visiting Iceland were not in fact generally separated from each other by travelers, just as von Troil linked his interests in Iceland's "ancient language" and "unusual nature" in the same sentence. The same was true of Sir Joseph Banks, the leader of the expedition that von Troil participated in and a later president of the British Royal Society. Banks was not initially particularly interested in northern travel, and the Iceland excursion was for him only a hastily arranged substitute for a second Pacific journey after his 1768–71 *Endeavor* voyage. The trip left him with an unexpected taste for things Icelandic, and he became a lifelong collector of saga manuscripts and volcanic rocks, as well as a friend of Icelanders and Iceland enthusiasts.[9]

Clearly, the environment and landscape of Iceland made the strongest impression on those Europeans who actually visited the island. However, Iceland's unusual nature did also sometimes impact the environment of people who remained at home. The Laki volcanic eruptions of 1783, which are ranked as one of the ten largest in recorded world history, not only devastated the country, but the volcanic smoke also affected the climate and agriculture of England, Germany, southern Europe, and even North America.[10] The cultural memory and meaning of this disaster and its transformation of the Icelandic landscape has been a subject of central importance in Icelandic history for some time, but its implications for the linkages between landscape and cultural and political meanings extend beyond the small island's shores, just as the smoke from the volcanic eruptions itself did. The Laki catastrophe focused attention on Iceland, the Icelandic landscape, and the problems of living with Icelandic nature. At the end of the eighteenth century, these problems were the business of many different kinds of people. Following the Laki eruptions, natural historians, Danish officials, visiting tourists, and Icelandic political leaders all offered interpretations of the event, of the landscapes created by the lava flows, and of the late eighteenth century in Iceland. In these discussions, native Icelanders as well as Danish and other foreign visitors used the barren landscapes of volcanic rock and the consequences of the eruptions to reflect upon Icelandic history and the role of human agency in that history. These writings reveal how very different stories and meanings can be found in the same landscape and natural events. Who offered interpretations, and why? What interests did they have in defining Icelandic nature in these ways? The various reactions to the Laki eruptions—which can be roughly categorized as scientific, religious, and political/historical—show how Icelandic nature had different meanings for people with different interests. Some thought of Iceland as a wilderness of potential that needed better management to bring it under control; others believed that Iceland was beyond human control but was rather a place where humans could observe nature's basic forces at work.

The Laki eruptions occurred at a moment when Iceland was becoming a destination for scientific and literary European tourism, while at the same time the Danish state was pursuing a centralizing administrative policy, begun under the leadership of the kings Christian IV (1588–1648) and his son Frederick III (1648–70), to bring the various colonies and dependencies more directly under Copenhagen's control. Because of these historical circumstances, a plethora of historical records exist for examining the Laki eruptions, written from the viewpoints of inhabitants who experienced the crisis, of visitors to the island, and of officials concerned with the management of agriculture. A central question for all these writers, although taken up in different ways, was the description of Icelandic nature—not only what had occurred during the disaster, but what was characteristic of Icelandic nature in general. What kind of place was Iceland, these writers wondered? Was it a place that nature had rendered uninhabitable through the collision of extreme forces? Or was it an island where nature could be tamed through proper management? And, if the latter was the case, in whose hands should this management rest?[11]

THE LAKI DISASTER AND ITS AFTERMATH

The Laki disaster, which is known in Icelandic as the Móðuharðindi (famine of the mist) or the Skaftáreldar (fires of the Skaftá river) began on June 1, 1783, when a series of earthquakes shook the Skaftafell district in southern Iceland (map 2).[12] On June 8, after seven days of earthquakes and aftershocks, smoke carried by a northeast wind covered the district with a layer of ash, sand, and finely ground minerals. The following day the lava streams from fissures adjacent to Laki, a glacier-covered volcano in the Skaftá mountain range, burst forth, while the earthquakes, smoke, and rains of ash continued. The mountain itself did not actually erupt in 1783; the lava poured rather from these fissures. Over the next days, the river Skaftá dried up. Lava began to pour from the canyon of the river and continued to flow, in stops and starts, until early December. Fish, birds, and sheep were the first animals to die, followed by the cattle and horses. The lava was slow moving enough that most of the efforts to evacuate the farms in the district were successful, and few people died directly from the lava flows; but the health of vulnerable members of the population was severely compromised by the smoke and ash, and many died of famine in the following years.

The Móðuharðindi resulted in the death of 70 percent of the island's sheep and the destruction of the island's offshore and inland fisheries for the next three years, both from fluorine poisoning and the thick layers of ash that covered the grazing land. Furthermore, the Móðuharðindi had been preceded by years of cold winters, famine, a smallpox epidemic, and a plague among the sheep in midcentury. More than 10,000 inhabitants perished in the famine in the years after the eruptions, reducing the population to about 38,000—about the number of people estimated to have inhabited the island after its settlement in the ninth century. Because of a smallpox epidemic and continuing famines in 1785–87, the population did not regain its predisaster size until the mid-nineteenth century.

This catastrophe, coupled with other troubles of the eighteenth century in Iceland, was remembered long after the island had begun to recover. When the chief justice of Iceland, Magnús Stephensen, looked back at the history of the eighteenth century in 1808, what first came to his mind were all the problems that his country had faced for the last hundred years. In his book, he counted up a long list of all the "bad years" (Uaar) and listed the causes to which he attributed these problems—cold winters, sea ice, famine, disease, and so on. Magnús's contemporary, the Icelandic bishop Hannes Finnsson, commented that the eighteenth century only saw the worsening of all the problems of the seventeenth, a period that had been characterized by raids from Algerian pirates and the introduction of the

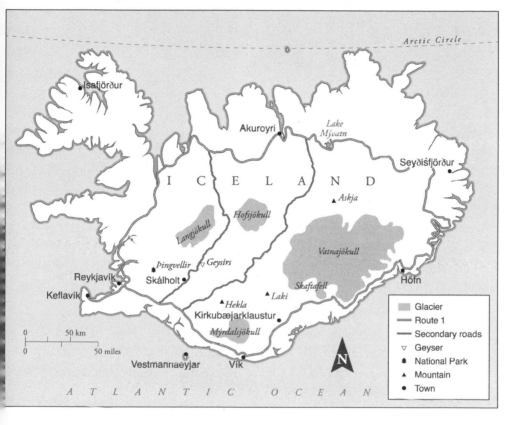

MAP 2. ICELAND

Danish-owned monopoly trade, which Hannes regarded as highly disadvantageous to Icelanders.[13] According to these Icelandic authorities, the late eighteenth century was a period of great natural and social crisis in their country. During the nineteenth century, one group of Icelanders looked back at this period of crisis and argued that the blame for it should be laid at the feet of one entity: the Danish government, and in particular the Danish-monopoly trading company.

Throughout the eighteenth century, the Danish government had been confronting environmental problems in various parts of the kingdom, including sandstorms and soil erosion in the Jutland peninsula and deforestation on the island of Zealand.[14] Furthermore, the impoverished conditions in Iceland had already been the subject of a land commission investigation in 1770–71. The official response to the news of the Laki eruptions was both long- and short-term: aid was sent from Copenhagen and an investigative body was appointed to recommend a course of action. The central recommendation of the land commission of 1785, the last of the eighteenth-century commissions on Iceland, was that the monopoly trade, which had been instituted in 1602, be lifted and trading opened to all the subjects of the Danish kingdom, including the Icelanders.[15] This company had been put into place primarily to break the hold of the Hamburg merchants—members of the strong Hanseatic trading league centered around the northern German cities of Hamburg, Bremen, and Lübeck—on Icelandic trade. Denmark had also prohibited the export of Icelandic products to Hamburg in 1620. During the period of the Danish monopoly, from 1602 to 1787, only between twenty-two and twenty-five merchants were licensed to trade in Iceland, each with a fixed trading post served by one or two boats.

Both Danish and Icelandic officials had criticized this trading system for its inflexibility and inefficiency even before the Laki eruptions. Many of the criticisms appeared to be justified after the catastrophe, since the monopoly company's boats sailed to Iceland in the summer of 1784 without carrying any additional food supplies but still exporting the regular quota of fish from the island.[16] Although news of the crisis had reached Copenhagen in September 1783, the system was so slow that the decision to send extra food to the Icelanders was not made until late July of the following year, and a collection in the churches in the other parts of the kingdom for the relief of the Icelanders was not begun until 1785.[17] The land commission's recommendation thus fell upon receptive ears, and the decision was made to abolish the monopoly company in 1786.

But another outcome of the Móðuharðindi, one much less direct and less noticed by historians of this period than the economic and political results, was its contribution to the discovery of Iceland as a site of scientific investigation. Volcanic upheavals were of immediate interest to European geologists investigating the origins of the earth. Ironically, the very changes in the landscape that caused the Icelanders so much distress came to be considered the most attractive to European explorers. After 1783, travel books about Iceland devoted considerable space to describing the new landscapes and speculating about the composition of rock formations caused by these lava flows. Some travelers found these sights ugly, barren, and desolate, although scientifically intriguing. Beginning in the nineteenth century, however, these barren landscapes began to be reevaluated in the more positive terms of Romanticism as majestic and awesome. Furthermore, panoramas created by fire and ice were considered to be the most characteristically and uniquely Icelandic vistas; these visions were the very objects of the travelers' quests. Far from seeking to restore Iceland to the condition it might have been in before these upheavals, the upheavals themselves became the defining essence of Iceland and its so-called unique nature. Elsewhere in the Danish kingdom, as in other European countries, eighteenth-century agricultural improvers tried to alter barren landscapes in accordance with their standards of beauty by using stone walls, clover, and beech trees to create garden environments.[18] In the North Atlantic, where such efforts had little effect, there was a gradual redefinition of what a "beautiful" landscape was.[19]

Many of the early reports of the Laki crisis reified an image of "Iceland as hell," as the island had been portrayed in fifteenth- and sixteenth-century travel accounts, with descriptions of an isolated place remote from the centers of civilization, covered with ice and fire, shrouded in clouds of poisonous smoke, the inhabitants like doomed souls, begging for relief. Mount Hekla, perhaps the most well-known Icelandic volcano (which is situated about eighty kilometers west of Laki but did not in fact erupt in 1783), had long figured in medieval legend as the mouth of hell and was pictured as perpetually vomiting flames on Abraham Ortelius's 1570 map of Iceland (fig. 2). Ortelius's map, like other European maps of exotic places from this period, also shows the Icelandic waters inhabited by monsters. This map, together with Olaus Magnus's 1555 map with similar features, was much reproduced and spread the image in Europe of Iceland as an exotic, extreme, and remote land inhabited by strange creatures and strange men.

But unlike many earlier Icelandic eruptions, the Laki eruptions were not merely the stuff of legend but were the topic of firsthand reports, both from observers on the scene and those noticing the more widespread environmental effects. Journeying on his European grand tour in 1783, the naturalist and later member of the British parliament John Thomas Stanley was denied the vision of sublime beauty of the Alps that he anticipated: "this splendid and beautiful scenery was concealed from us for a considerable time after our arrival by a fog which had spread itself over a great part of Europe. it was of a peculiar kind, having no apparent moisture. An Eruption was taking place at the time in Iceland and there can be no doubt of the volcanik smoke having affected the Atmosphere of the Countries where the Fog prevailed. The Mountains of Skaftafell vomited its columns

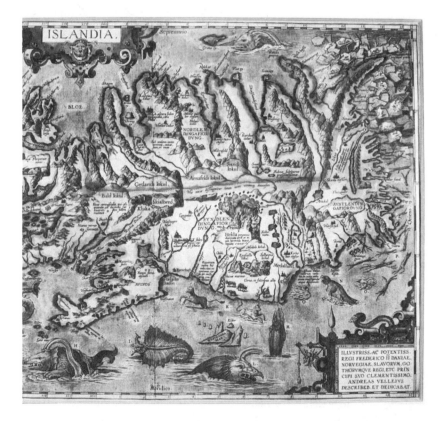

FIG. 2 Mount Hekla erupting on Abraham Ortelius's 1570 map of Iceland. Ortelius's map showed Hekla continually spewing fire. Glaciers border the mountain on the south, and the Icelandic waters are inhabited by monsters. Photo courtesy of Landsbóksafn Íslands.

of fire precisely during the period the fog lasted. The wind blew chiefly from the North West. I traced the fall of ashes from the Orkneys through the Faroe Islands to Iceland & some fire dust was noticed to have fallen in Germany."[20]

Six years later, when Stanley launched his expedition to Iceland, he was too late to witness the volcanic activities that had ruined his appreciation of alpine vistas. Not being fortunate enough to see the spectacle himself, he imagined it in a landscape painting of a fiery nocturnal view of a mountain, probably Hekla, erupting.[21] In his watercolor, the erupting volcano dominates the landscape as two tiny human figures in the foreground assume a reverential posture of powerlessness toward the mountain in the face of nature's might (fig. 3). The diabolic black and red colors of the painting are particularly evocative of Hekla's status in legend.

This watercolor was the only painting that Stanley himself completed (although he made many sketches in his unpublished journals). The other paintings from the Stanley expedition are the work of the professional

FIG. 3 John Thomas Stanley's *Eruption of Hekla* painting (9 × 13 cm, watercolor, 1794). This diabolic portrayal seems to have been inspired more by Stanley's reading about Iceland than by his experiences on his trip. Photo by Helgi Bragason, courtesy of Landsbókasafn Íslands.

artist Edward Dayes, who was not on the trip but who based his work on Stanley's sketches and descriptions. These paintings are quite different in character from Stanley's; the hardships and deprivations of Icelandic life six years after the Laki eruptions mentioned in the written accounts of the expedition do not appear in Dayes's pictures, which show unthreatening, parklike images.[22] In one encounter between the explorers and the natives, Stanley and his party dominate the picture's center. Although the painting, called *Icelandic Farmstead*, suggests a chance meeting with ordinary folk, Stanley is directing attention toward clean and well-dressed people who are seated before a house of wood rather than turf, the usual Icelandic building material.[23] The encounter, set against a background of farmers haying before Hekla in the distance, portrays a serenely pastoral and rather unlikely scene.

Not only were the images of volcanic eruptions fascinating, but the landscapes resulting from the 1783 eruptions also drew interested visitors. Following Stanley's trip, the island was visited again in 1810 by the Scottish mineralogist George Steuart Mackenzie, accompanied by Henry Holland, a medical student who later rose to prominence in London society, counting Queen Victoria among his patients. Mackenzie, an enthusiastic geologist and member of the Edinburgh Royal Society, was, at the time of his Icelandic expedition, participating in the massive ongoing scientific conflict in Britain over the geological origins of the earth. At the turn of the century, debate was polarized between two theories of rock formation: one by Abraham Gottlob Werner, a professor at Freiberg in Saxony, which proposed that the surface features of the earth were formed primarily by water erosion during a single, catastrophic flood; and the other by James Hutton in Edinburgh, which postulated that rocks were continuously being formed by great heat and pressure below the ocean floor and forced up to the earth's surface. Mackenzie was an ardent supporter of Hutton and realized that an expedition to Iceland could find evidence to advance Hutton's theory.[24] Holland's journal from their visit to the lava fields northeast of Hekla describes

a landscape more extraordinary in all of its features than any other which had before occurred to our notice in Iceland. The extreme wildness and desolation of the scenery was its most prominent feature—a desolation derived not only from the absence of every trace of human existence but still more from the many marks of convulsion & disorder in the operations of nature, which present themselves on every side. . . . Further to the East, there appears another assemblage of mountains, still more wild & desolate in their character. This is the *Skaptaar-Fiall Jokull* the tract of country from which proceeded the great volcanic eruption of 1783, one of the most extensive & dreadful of which there has been any record preserved. This vast tract of country, forming the interior of Iceland, & wholly unknown even to the natives themselves, is currently reported to be inhabited by a race of men, differing much from the Icelanders. This story is credited even by some men of accuracy and good-sense, though attended in itself with circumstances of great improbability.[25]

In the scientific account of the expedition, *Travels in the Island of Iceland, 1810*, the North Atlantic island appears as an ideal site for studying the natural history of the earth for the Huttonian geologist.[26] Here, the explorer could find the earth constantly in a state of upheaval and renewal, as Hutton's theory outlined. Hutton's emphasis on gradual processes over time and on regular and repeated mechanisms of change became accepted geological doctrine after the Huttonian-Wernerian controversy was laid to rest in the 1820s, although all the details of Hutton's theory did not survive. In the classic text of nineteenth-century British geology, Charles Lyell's *Principles of Geology*, first published in 1830 and running through many editions, the Laki eruptions are presented as evidence of the regular operation of mechanisms of heat and pressure in the formation of the earth's surface.[27]

Because Holland was interested in the lava fields primarily as a record of the natural history of the earth, he ignored the human aspects of the crisis and characterized the region as "wholly unknown even to the natives." In fact, it was only through the reports of native observers that the scientific record of the eruptions came to be written in Europe. Already in 1785 the chief justice of Iceland, Magnús Stephensen, had published a report in Danish on the eruptions and their results. In 1794, an Icelandic doctor and naturalist, Sveinn Pálsson, visited the lava fields to describe and measure the volcanic rocks. His manuscript was unpublished, but a handwritten copy was given to the Scottish missionary Ebenezer Henderson when he lived in Iceland in 1814–15, and it is Henderson's travel account that Lyell cites in *Principles*.[28] Two other accounts by Icelanders also exist: one by Sæmund Holm, a secondhand report based on the letters of inhabitants who fled the lava; and one by Jón Steingrímsson, the priest of the district who witnessed the eruptions but who did not write down his recollections until the end of his life.[29]

The eighteenth-century Icelandic accounts of the Móðuharðindi differ greatly in character and in focus. Magnús Stephensen wrote seemingly in his official capacity, accounting for the numbers of people, animals, and homes affected. Naturalists and other observers, however, were inclined to make much more general interpretations of the crisis. As the literature on European reactions to the Lisbon earthquake of 1755 has shown, natural catastrophes in eighteenth-century Europe were the subject of religious, philosophical, and scientific speculation.[30] The Laki eruptions, like the Lisbon earthquake, provoked a crisis that demanded not only a practical but also a philosophical response (although the Lisbon disaster was the subject of much more widespread and intense attention in Europe than Laki was). Jón Steingrímsson, who became known as the "fire priest" because of the miracle that occurred when the lava approaching the church where he was celebrating mass halted its onslaught and saved the church and parishioners, came to the rather typical conclusion for the time that the eruptions were punishment from God for the sins of the Icelanders. Yet God showed his mercy by allowing the slow-moving lava flows to serve as a warning of his wrath, so that many of the wicked were spared. On the other hand, Sveinn Pálsson, like the British naturalists, was only interested in the scientific causes of volcanic eruptions and the descriptions of the lava flow and volcanic rocks; he declined to speculate about sin and the will of God in natural disasters. In this, he may have been following something of an Icelandic tradition: a story from the time of conversion to Christianity in Iceland around the year 1000 tells of an argument between pagans and Christians during which the pagans claimed the volcanic eruption going on at the time showed the anger of the old Norse gods at the Icelanders' treachery in considering another faith. The leader of the Christians, however, raised his hand to point at the old lava cliffs at Þingvellir and asked whom the gods were angry with when this lava flowed.

For Holland and other British geologists, the scientific importance of Iceland was paramount. The 1783 eruptions were seen as part of a pattern of history in Iceland and the entire world. The event and the resulting landscape showed that the earth's history was constantly renewing and repeating itself, that, rather than a single catastrophic event such as the Flood, there were many cycles of collapse and renewal. The new lava fields and the transformed Icelandic landscape stood for the history of the entire earth. Iceland was a site where one could observe processes of change that were hidden elsewhere, exceptional for the clarity of these phenomena but not unique in these processes. Rather, the small island was important for not being unique, for instead illustrating the cyclical history of the globe.

No observer seems to have reacted to the Laki eruptions with the philosophical equivalent of Voltaire's abandonment of optimism after the Lisbon earthquake. However, over the next decades a third interpretation of the Móðuharðindi emerged alongside the scientific and the religious: a political/historical explanation.[31] There was another history that could be read out of the landscape besides the natural history—a human history. During the nineteenth century, the story of the Móðuharðindi and the lava fields created by the Laki eruptions became part of an Icelandic history of foreign oppression, material and spiritual decline, and the struggle against these forces. The Icelandic nationalist movement, which began in the 1830s, was primarily led by Icelandic students educated in Copenhagen who learned of Johann Gottfried Herder's ideas of "national spirit" during their studies there.[32] The barren lava fields left behind by the Laki eruptions could be seen as evidence of nature's forces at work, but they also represented the failures of the Danish state and its administration of the island. While volcanic eruptions were natural occurrences, the responsibility for controlling them and their effects lay with people. This point of view had already been suggested by the arguments advanced for the loosening of the trade monopoly immediately after the eruptions. During the nineteenth century, Jón Sigurðsson and other nationalist leaders blamed Danish rule, not for the eruptions themselves, but for the series of catastrophes of the Icelandic eighteenth century, which could have been prevented or at least mitigated with better—that is, by local—management. The categories of natural and social events were conflated in this reading, and Danish rule was substituted for the evil forces of fire and ice. According to this interpretation, the 1783 eruptions should not be seen as an isolated event but as the culmination of a series of troubles—harsh winters, a smallpox epidemic, trade deficits—that marked the eighteenth century in Iceland, placing the island in sharp contrast with the picture of its rich, imaginary medieval past that was built up by nationalists' reading of the Icelandic sagas. Although modern scholars have argued persuasively that Iceland was probably neither economically worse off under Danish rule than it would have been otherwise, nor was it treated worse than other regions of the Danish kingdom,[33] a link between the natural and social events of the miserable Icelandic eighteenth century was drawn broadly in nineteenth-century Icelandic writing. Commenting on the Móðuharðindi one hundred years afterward, in a treatise mostly devoted to a day-by-day account of the 1783 eruptions and their effects, Þorvaldur Thoroddsen wrote:

> Iceland was never visited by so many and such great catastrophes as in the eighteenth century, when bad years, plague, volcanic eruptions, and earthquakes unleashed themselves. According to Magnus Stephensen, that century had no fewer than 43 bad years, some because of harsh winters, coastal ice, and the decline of fisheries, and some from volcanic eruptions, earthquakes, and plague. In 1707, 18,000 people died of smallpox, in 1757–9, 9,744 people died of accidents, hunger, and so on. The list could be added to almost endlessly, and in truth it is strange that this tiny population with their poverty and unhappy circumstances of their trade, which oppressed them more than all the rest put together, was strong enough to withstand all of these troubles.[34]

Here, the natural disasters of earthquakes and disease are linked with the social disaster of the monopoly trade, which is judged to be the worst of all. For many of the nineteenth-century Icelandic patriots, the appearance of the country was to be understood as a direct reflection of its history: in Iceland, history had gone wrong with the arrival of the Danes upon the scene.

The idea that the physical appearance of a landscape displays the land's and people's history was not confined to nationalist rhetoric by politically interested parties but spread broadly in the nineteenth century. Even those with no particular axe to grind in struggles over political representation were taken with the simple and appealing notion of directly equating the features of a landscape and the character of its people. For example, nineteenth-century nature-protection organizations in Germany, according to Thomas Lekan, saw the preserving of meadows and forests as an important step toward protecting cultural heritage in the same way that "restoring peasant cottages, researching rural customs, and publishing poetry and stories in regional dialects" was. Emblematic landscapes such as the Rhine River and the Siebengebirge (Seven Mountains) hill country in the Rhineland represented the enduring character of the local people through the flux of historical and political change.[35] Increasingly, when travelers in Iceland looked at the landscape, they read a narrative of a people and used the visit as an opportunity to think about Icelandic history and culture. The motifs of Icelandic nature were commonly viewed as literal signifiers of a folk history and a national history. Volcanoes and glaciers became suggestive of the Icelandic spirit of independence and stoicism, preserved through centuries of Danish oppression. Lava fields deemed "barren," as they were in Lord Dufferin's 1857 *Letters from the High Latitudes*, represented the "dullness and aridness" of Icelandic history under Danish rule, when the "glory of the old days is departed."[36] These rock formations represented a story that had sadly come to an end.

This trope was frequent with British visitors, who compared the differences in cultural and material conditions in their North Atlantic islands, the Shetlands and Orkneys, with Iceland and the Faroes, thus placing themselves in the role of benevolent managers against the Danish exploiters. And the Icelanders themselves were fully willing to exploit this constructed alliance in their arguments against Danish rule. In a paper delivered before the Philosophical Society of Great Britain, Jón Stefánsson opened by declaring, "Geographically and geologically Iceland is part of—a continuation of—the British Isles." After running through a brief geological, political, and social history of the island, Jón summarized the seventeenth and eighteenth centuries in Iceland as follows: "The Hanseatic trade was succeeded by a Danish monopoly of trade, which completed the economic ruin of Iceland. Algerine pirates appeared off the coast and carried off hundreds of people into slavery in 1627. Smallpox caused the death of one-third of the population in 1707, a famine raged in 1759, and the volcanic eruptions of 1765 and 1783 laid waste large tracts of the island. Nature seemed in league with man to render Iceland uninhabitable."[37]

Ending the paper by calling Iceland "a living Pompeii where the northern races can read their past," Jón both reemphasized the link between landscape and people and included his audience as part of the "northern races" who might find their history in Iceland. The lecture was rhetorically and strategically powerful. By claiming that Iceland was naturally—geographically and geologically—part of Britain, Jón made it clear that Danish rule in Iceland was an interference with the natural order that had resulted in disaster. If Iceland were restored to its rightful political place, then Icelandic nature would surely prove as benign as it had been in the years of medieval settlement, the years from around 870 to 930. It was lucky for Jón's argument that he did not have to explain climatologists' later discovery of the Little Ice Age, which coincided roughly with Danish rule in Iceland, following a warmer period in the Middle Ages.[38]

For both British naturalists and Icelandic political writers, therefore, looking at Icelandic landscapes was a way of reading history. However, they did not find exactly the same story there. Interpretation of the sites vis-àvis humans was different from a natural-history interpretation: the former stressed linear movements of progress and decline over cyclical patterns. In the views of nationalists, and those influenced by such accounts, lava fields tended to represent stasis, an end of development, rather than dynamic processes of change (which they did for Mackenzie and Holland). When the link was made between the present "decline," the "glory of the old days" when Iceland was free and the saga manuscripts were written, and an imagined future of independence and prosperity, however, the cyclical pattern of human history in Iceland emerged clearly. Themes of renewal in nature's history corresponded with the theme of restoration in human history—Iceland could rise again to the great days of its medieval independence. Comfortingly, human and natural histories composed a unified story. Furthermore, it was, in both views, an accessible story, readable on the surface of things, like the features of the landscape.[39]

AFTER LAKI: PORTRAYALS OF ICELANDIC NATURE IN THE LATE NINETEENTH CENTURY

The social history of the island, of course, was under the direction of humans. For nineteenth-century politicians, both Icelandic and Danish, the central questions were which humans should be in control, and how should Icelandic nature best be understood and managed? Iceland's next major volcanic eruption—Hekla's in 1845—brought another scientific expedition to Iceland, this one assembled and supported by the Danish Crown. This party, which also reached Iceland only after the volcanic fires had cooled, included naturalists, chemists, mineralogists, zoologists, and one of the Danish Golden Age painters, Emmanuel Larsen, who was then only twenty-two years old.[40] Once again, if a volcanic eruption could not be witnessed, it could certainly be imagined, as Larsen did in his etching, which first appeared in the picture book *Danmark*, in 1856.[41] His conception is strikingly different from John Thomas Stanley's and typical of the serene style of the Danish Golden Age artists (fig. 4). The explorers do not cower in fear in front of the mountain but stand safely on a hilltop in the foreground, observing the flames. The volcanic fire is not overwhelming but is a distant spectacle, and the lava fields around it, formed in the recent eruption, are not jagged and barren but are smooth and gentle hills. If they were green instead of gray-black, they could be called pastoral. The waters of the river run calmly through the hills, untroubled by any violent shakings of the earth. Nature in this image is controlled, unthreatening. Only the darker colors of the sky and landscape distinguish Iceland from the Danish farmlands, gentle hills, and woodlands pictured in the rest of the book. Sumarliði R. Ísleifsson, in his study of foreign pictorial representations of Iceland, calls Larsen's vision "enjoyable and pleasant . . . totally unlike the catastrophic representations of Icelandic eruptions which had long been customary."[42]

The volume in which this picture of Hekla appeared, *Danmark*, contained seventy-seven pictures of various parts of the Danish kingdom, including Greenland, and was one of the first popular portrayals of nature

FIG. 4 Emmanuel Larsen's drawing of Mount Hekla's 1845 eruption, published in the picture book *Danmark* in 1856. This depiction of Icelandic volcanism contrasts sharply with previous images like Stanley's but is composed in the same serene style in which *Danmark* portrayed other regions of the Danish kingdom, including landscapes in Norway, Greenland, and the Faroes. Photo courtesy of the Division of Rare and Manuscript Collections, Carl A. Kroch Library, Cornell University.

aimed toward the growing Danish middle class. By presenting Icelandic eruptions within the context of the entire Danish kingdom, *Danmark* portrayed a tamed version of wild Iceland. Larsen's painting shows nature being observed under the scientifically detached gaze of the explorers, not as a nature that would overpower them, as Stanley had seen Hekla. This later portrayal corresponded to some degree with the realities of the Icelandic experience. Hekla's 1845 eruption was not the disaster that the Móðuharðindi had been. Although the smoke and volcanic ash remained for two years, much of the grazing land was once again destroyed, and the livestock died, the long-term population decline and the perception of grave catastrophe of the previous century were avoided. The recommendations of free-trade advocates and the action of the 1785 land commission appeared to have been implemented to good effect. All restrictions on North Atlantic trade were lifted in 1854, not specifically in response to any events in Iceland, but as part of a series of liberalizing movements in the Danish kingdom in general. These included granting representation to Iceland and to the German-speaking provinces in southern Jutland at the national parliament in 1834 and the revocation of absolute monarchy in 1848, as elsewhere in Europe. In this political context, Larsen's painting might be interpreted as an expression of confidence that the disasters of the previous century would not be repeated.[43] Conditions in this remote corner of the Danish kingdom had been brought under control through a series of actions on the part of the central government. In fact, this attitude was generally the response of Copenhagen officials to Icelandic nationalists: the Danes were quite willing, even eager, to make reforms that were in keeping with their own liberal principles but insisted that these reforms be directed from the center. The future of Iceland lay in continued union with Denmark. Icelandic independence was economically unfeasible and disadvantageous for both parties, the Danish government maintained. The most radical proposals for Icelandic economic independence, such as Jón Sigurðsson's calculation of the amount of reparation Denmark owed to Iceland from taxes and income from the trade monopoly over the centuries, never received serious consideration by the Copenhagen government.[44]

Societies for the study of history and literature in Denmark did not directly contest Icelandic claims of the unity between Iceland and other European nations, such as the British Isles, that Jón Stefánsson advanced. Instead, they promoted a vision of Iceland that pointed out the many commonalities between the island and mainland Scandinavia; they advocated a spiritual and literary pan-Scandinavianism that would replace diminished political realities. Orla Lehmann, the future leader of the Danish National-Liberals, wrote about the Icelandic landscape and culture in the pages of *Maanedsskrift for Litteratur* (Literary Monthly), asserting that

> in these bare mountains [of Iceland] we see our own past, a gigantic monument raised in a distant time, which stands in stark loneliness in a world where everything is new and altered. In the old days, some Scandinavians emigrated there [to Iceland] and introduced the life and customs of the old North. Since that time, a life of great changes and transitions has transformed the surface of the earth and its inhabitants among us; the mighty hand of civilization has ploughed under every trace of ancient life and everything that accompanied it. But, as though frozen among these distant icy mountains, where the storms of time never reached, it is preserved in Iceland in an almost unaltered purity, so we can see there a living past, a rich picture of past life. Therefore the Icelandic people must be beloved by every Scandinavian, and we will find in the present-day Icelandic character, lifestyle, and customs, the trace of our past physiognomy, for which we would look in vain in our own moldering ruins and lifeless annals.[45]

It is interesting to see in this passage how Lehmann considered the preservative qualities of ice, rather than the transformative qualities of fire, to be the most characteristic of the Icelandic landscape. Rather than discussing geology and geography, Danish scholars gave weight to the common cultural ties of language, literary culture, and religion that made Iceland part of Scandinavia, and not a lost province of Great Britain. For them, the facts that many of the Icelandic sagas were set in Sweden or Norway and that the original settlers of Iceland had emigrated from Norway were more relevant for political management than the scientific classification of rock types.[46] The picture of Iceland in nineteenth-century Denmark was primarily as the birthplace and inspiration of the sagas, the manuscripts that were then kept in Copenhagen.

Icelanders had two kinds of responses to this Danish vision of Icelandic nature and the Pan-Scandinavian future: political and artistic. They continued negotiation and agitation for representation and independence. Their path was a nonviolent and legalistically oriented struggle culminating in a new constitution in 1874, home rule in 1903–4, and independence in 1944, following a 1918 treaty between Denmark and Iceland stipulating a twenty-five-year transition period to full independence. Nineteenth-century Denmark was a country that had gradually come to recognize its own political decline, and it turned culturally toward an outlook that sought to make a virtue of its status as a minor power in Europe. Only the memory of the Danish empire of the seventeenth and eighteenth centuries remained, when the state had included Norway, Iceland, the Faroes, Greenland, Schleswig and Holstein (the German-speaking provinces in southern Jutland), the Virgin Islands, and possessions on the west coast of Africa and in India. Denmark had fought several wars with its major rival, Sweden, for regional dominance and had once taken possession of the southern part of Sweden. But after Denmark's disastrous alliance with France in the Napoleonic Wars, the bankrupt state gradually sold off its southern possessions in Africa and India to Great Britain and later the Virgin Islands to the United States. Norway was given to Sweden in the Treaty of Kiel in 1814, and Schleswig and Holstein were lost in wars with the German Confederation in 1864 (although part of Holstein was returned following Germany's defeat in World War I). From a purely economic point of view, it would have been a good idea for the state to rid itself of Iceland as well, but the arguments for the prestige of Iceland as the source of a common Scandinavian heritage remained compelling. The struggle to establish claims to identity in the nineteenth-century North Atlantic was firmly grounded in literary and cultural discussions.[47]

Alongside these political developments, an Icelandic artistic vision of their own nature also emerged in the first decades of the twentieth century. It is more difficult to trace than the political developments because, as Sumarliði R. Ísleifsson has noted, there was little Icelandic tradition of landscape or nature painting until the later decades of the nineteenth century.[48] In the 1920s and 1930s, however, one group of Icelandic painters, including Guðmundur Einarsson of Miðdal and Finnur Jónsson, rebelled against a Danish tradition of painting Icelandic landscapes that they found to be too soft and European. Instead, this group of Icelanders sought out landscapes that had been previously thought unattractive as the subjects of paintings, claiming that these most represented the character of Icelanders.[49] In 1940—just four years before the island's independence—Finnur chose the Laki landscape for his painting *Lakagígar* (Laki Craters).[50] In his portrayal, no observer, native or foreign, stands in the picture to comment upon it. The craters are stark and jagged, yet the landscape does not seem desolate; the horizon in the background of the painting beyond the craters is bright. In 1983, which was the two-hundredth anniversary of the Laki eruptions, Finnur's painting was reproduced on a fifteen-kronur stamp by the Icelandic Postal Service (figs. 5 and 6). Although from one perspective it might seem odd to commemorate as a national symbol the disaster that killed more than 20 percent of the population, two centuries after the crisis the Laki craters had come to stand for the memory of the Icelandic national

FIG. 5 The Laki craters as they appear today, as seen from Mount Laki, looking to the southwest. Photo courtesy of Ingibjörg Eiríksdóttir.

spirit against times of hardship and oppression. Iceland is indeed a wilderness, the stamp seems to assert, but it is our wilderness. It may appear uninhabitable, and yet we are the ones who live there, and this landscape is representative of the Icelandic character.

Natural phenomena, including volcanoes, flora, and fauna, have been frequently depicted on Icelandic stamps after independence. For example, a series was issued to commemorate the 1947 eruption of Hekla, for the submarine volcano that erupted to create the island of Surtsey in 1963, and for the 1973 eruption in the Westman Islands. In all of these portrayals, the perspective on the erupting volcano is that of a distant observer. In the three stamps showing Hekla erupting in 1947, a single plume of smoke rises from the mountain. The eruption is a spectacle that threatens no one.[51] In 1970, a stamp showing the Laki craters was issued as part of the Náttúruvernd (Nature Conservation) series. Here, the craters are distinct in the foreground but fade away into blue mountains and a bright horizon in the distance. The depiction suggests that volcanic craters are part of Iceland's unique nature, worthy of protection, and not a symbol of destruction, hopelessness, or foreign oppression.[52] The Icelandic landscape appears in these pictures—in contrast to both the Stanley and Larsen paintings—neither threatening nor pastoral. Icelandic nature is extreme, unpredictable, and even wild, but people live within this wilderness, and their character has been formed by the struggle with this nature.

MEN AND THE MOUNTAINS: ICELANDIC NATURE AND THE ICELANDERS WITHIN IT

Although these Icelandic pictures of volcanoes and the Laki craters did not include people, some foreign portrayals of Iceland during the nineteenth century did suggest a link between the people and the land, integrating the natives into the landscape in a way not seen in the eighteenth century. This change follows some of the general movements toward realism and emphasis on portrayals of ordinary people and peasant life characteristic of European painting in the nineteenth century. Rather than using the countryside simply as a backdrop against which to pose explorers, as in pictures by Edward Dayes, the Icelandic people seem to become part of the natural landscapes over the next hundred years of foreign gazing. One drawing, in a German book from the later half of the nineteenth century, shows Icelandic women with children at their sides using the island's "unique" natural forces in a very practical way: washing clothes at the hot springs. The figures dressed in everyday clothes stand and sit amid the hills and escaping steam vents, working, relaxing, or chatting. In this group activity, no one particular individual is set apart from the others; they all blend into their surroundings. If William Jackson Hooker noted during his visit in 1809 that the Icelanders did not seem interested in the land's "natural wonders" and were accustomed to look at the geysers and hot springs "with the utmost indifference," this picture might suggest one reason why.[53] To the natives of the place, the European "unique" was everyday, and the hot springs were about as remarkable and interesting as a laundromat might be to us.

In another well-known and much-reproduced image of Iceland, the Icelandic people are even more thoroughly integrated into the landscape. In 1897 the British author, painter, and saga translator W. G. Collingwood visited Iceland together with Jón Stefánsson. Their book, *A Pilgrimage to the Saga-Steads of Iceland*, was published two years later. The book is meant, as they explain, "to illustrate the sagas of Iceland. It is intended to supply the background of scenery which the ancient dramatic style takes for granted. . . . The intense tenderness and the intense passion of the sagas could only be developed among scenery which, whether the actors felt it or not, reacted upon their sentiment. It was in this belief that we undertook our pilgrimage. We went to see the very places where events so familiar in books occurred in reality; and we found that the belief was true."[54]

As he was mainly attracted to Iceland by the medieval literature, Collingwood's picture imagines medieval Icelanders gathering at the site of their national assembly, Þingvellir, as they did during the settlement of the island in the ninth and tenth centuries (fig. 7). This setting, a landscape of plains, cliffs, and a valley with a river running through it, was formed by a much older volcanic eruption unrecorded by the historical sources. Only a short journey from Reykjavík, by the end of the nineteenth century Þingvellir had become imbued with enormous cultural and historical significance. The assembly (Alþingi) had continued to meet there during periods of Norwegian and Danish domination, but it gradually lost parliamentary power, becoming first a judicial court and then being disbanded in 1800. The reconvening of the Alþingi was a major project of the Icelandic nationalists, and some even argued that they should continue to meet at its original site rather than in Reykjavík. In 1843 the Alþingi was restored, but in the modern capital. In 1874, however, when King Christian IX presented a new constitution to Iceland, the ceremony, which also commemorated the thousand-year anniversary of the island's settlement, was held at Þingvellir. Collingwood's painting shows men conversing in small groups on and between the rock cliffs. The figures are tiny and quite indistinct; the view is from a long distance and the groups of people simply appear as part of the landscape. The tents in the bottom center of the picture that have been erected for people to live in for the duration of the assembly have the same coloring as the rocks, which are part of old lava flows. In his painting, the Icelandic people are part of the nature of Iceland.

The notion of the fundamentally wild quality of Icelandic nature emerged in more banal, everyday matters as well as in the wake of major catastrophes. One of these routine affairs was a matter of local governance of agriculture in the late eighteenth century, a time when the problems of agricultural improvement were a major concern of the Danish state, as in other European countries. In most regions of the Danish kingdom, central administrative efforts to alter and improve the landscape, such as the enclosure laws of the eighteenth century, were generally considered to be successful. In Jutland, which was, like the North Atlantic, a marginalized region from the point of view of Copenhagen, the environment also created problems of management—sandstorms and soil erosion. According to Danish authorities, such environments should be combated, not romanti-

FIG. 7 W. G. Collingwood's *The Icelandic Thing* (90 by 69.5 cm, watercolor, ca. 1897). Collingwood imagined medieval Icelanders gathering at the site of their national assembly, Þingvellir, after having visited it on his 1897 "pilgrimage to the saga-steads." Photo by James Rossiter, courtesy of the Trustees of the British Museum, London.

cized by foreign artists, and one of the strategies of combat was fence building.[55] The Danish environmental historian Thorkild Kjærgaard shows how increasingly strict legislation, combined with the influence of discussions in agricultural societies of the benefits of fencing, led to the erection of more than 7,500 kilometers of fences in Denmark before 1790.[56] After this project was successfully implanted, according to Kjærgaard,

> where in the past there had been barren, cropped, greyish, scentless, silent out-lying areas and poor pastures of self-sown couch grass, the countryside now became full of life, colors, scents, and sounds. . . . The Danish landscape became

tamed and idyllized. . . . In combination with the abundance of animals, the new colors, sounds, and scents imbued the landscape with an increasing wealth and variety, balanced in other respects by a new atmosphere of order and stability. This was primarily due to the fences. Whereas the old landscape had been characterized by borders winding in various directions and by soft transitions between fields, outlying areas, and open forests, the new fences now extended through the landscape in regular, military lines, dividing not merely forest from field, but also field from field.[57]

A painting by Jens Juel, one of the most renowned Danish portrait painters of the eighteenth century, of the landscape of the island of Funen illustrates what Kjærgaard describes. In this painting, upper-class people in fine clothes are riding horses through a gate in the fence held open for them by a peasant woman. The gate separates the well-ordered estate from the barren moor, and the riders appear to be enjoying the garden qualities of their property, since they see that nature in their land is pleasant and not frightful—just as all the pictures of Danish nature shown in the 1856 *Danmark* demonstrate. Even places as distant and wild as Iceland and Greenland were tamed in the pages of this text and made to look like Danish farms.

But in Iceland, the process of taming the landscape was different from that in Jutland. As in the rest of the kingdom, enclosure laws were in effect there, including one in 1776 that demanded that Icelanders construct fences, promising rewards for compliance and threatening recalcitrant farmers with fines.[58] However, this ordinance had little success, and both local Danish officials and travelers repeatedly commented on the wild quality of the Icelandic landscape in contrast to Denmark, as well as the stubbornness of Icelanders who refused to do as they were advised by scientific agriculturalists.[59] The precise reasons for this failure in contrast to Jutland are unclear. Since fences enclosing farms were built from stone during the Middle Ages in Iceland, Iceland's lack of forestation during the eighteenth century would not have played a significant role. But the results of this unregulated landscape, compared to the other provinces of the Danish kingdom, gave the impression, repeated by many foreign visitors, that in Iceland nature slipped from the grasp of human control.

What changed in Iceland from the late eighteenth century on was not so much the landscape itself, as it did in Jutland, but the way in which the landscape was viewed and understood. Convincing narratives with long traditions maintained that nature in the North Atlantic was supposed to be "wild" and "untamed." These stories, which were already invented in the first European travel accounts about the island in the fifteenth and sixteenth centuries, were expanded by visitors and natives in the aftermath of the Laki eruptions. Foreign geologists saw the Laki craters as representative of the earth's entire history, while Icelandic nationalists gave the event a specifically local interpretation: it was one of the symbols of their country's decline under foreign rule and the need to return the island to the independent rule of the early Middle Ages. Some Danish observers sought to create images of an unthreatening and pacified Icelandic landscape consistent with their belief in the island as an integral part of the Danish kingdom and Danish nature, while Icelandic painters at the time of independence rejected this idea and sought out "wild Iceland." Creating such stories can be seen as another way of taming a landscape, not by altering it, but by turning it into an entity for cultural consumption. While the Móðuharðindi certainly did not by itself cause this transformation, it did provide—in the most literal sense—the ground upon which to build it. The Laki eruptions drew the attention of Icelanders, of the Danish administration, and of other European explorers. The catastrophe became an opportunity for Icelanders to reflect upon their own history and the role of human agency in that history and also a chance for outsiders to write a natural and social history of the landscape.

In the decades following the disaster of 1783, several different ways of imagining Icelandic nature emerged. These visions served different purposes. John Thomas Stanley's painting clearly follows in the long European tradition of imagining a wild, unpredictable North Atlantic. This representation of the environment promoted a certain ideal of the explorer himself: an individual with a taste for extreme environments; with a desire to seek out the unusual; with a hardy, implicitly masculine tolerance for rough conditions; and characterized by a willingness to sacrifice oneself for the larger causes of advancement of scientific knowledge. In the Emmanuel Larsen painting, on the other hand, the explorers are not in any danger, since nature in all parts of the Danish kingdom has been tamed and regulated, as the reader is told through all the pictures in the book.[60] If there is little difference between traveling to Iceland and staying at home on a Jutland farm, then both regions have the same qualities and rightfully belong to the same state. As a consequence, the explorers can no longer be heroic in the same sense; indeed, the names of the individuals who visited Iceland (as well as

Greenland and the Faroes) are not even mentioned in the text of *Danmark*.

When Icelanders turned their attention to the same landscape, however, they read a different history than either the British geologists or the Danish visitors. Rather than seeing a history that connected Iceland to other parts of the world (or, for the British scientists, to the entire earth), during the nineteenth century the Laki eruptions in Icelandic texts were made to stand for the specific injustices and hardships that the people had suffered during the eighteenth century, especially through the Danish trade monopoly. When Icelanders did turn to their own landscape as an artistic subject, which only occurred after about 1870, the Laki craters, as well as representations of Hekla and other mountains, often appeared rough and misshapen, but volcanic eruptions did not explicitly threaten people in these portrayals. In Jón Stefánsson's painting of the landscape of Hekla, *Hraunteigur við Heklu* (Stones of Hekla), the rock has a slightly abstract appearance that lends the picture a serene quality.[61] Hardships and fear caused by Icelandic nature seemed to be, if not forgotten, at least one step removed. While some aspects of these different representations can be attributed to changing artistic styles, the selection of Finnur Jónsson's painting *Lakagígar* for an Icelandic stamp and the inclusion of the Laki landscape in the Nature Conservation stamp series is significant. Icelandic views of the Laki eruptions had certainly changed over the intervening two hundred years. In an independent Iceland, uncontrolled nature was no longer a cause of distress or an indication that management had gone awry but was a sign of the country's unique qualities and character—just as the nationalists had argued in the nineteenth century. If Iceland was wild, it was meant to be so.

In Iceland no single elite or foreign power controlled and manipulated representations of the environment entirely.[62] Rather, this process was negotiated, with different groups exercising different kinds of power and advancing their visions of Icelandic nature. Outsiders did not simply impose their views upon the natives and the land. Instead, Icelanders participated in shaping foreign visions and also created their own. Rather than a simple, top-down model of power, science, and representation, the Icelandic example demonstrates the multifaceted character of these interactions. Chapter 2 turns to investigate more local and practical debates about nature in the North Atlantic—debates that, to a larger degree than those just traced, succeeded in actually shaping and altering the region's landscapes and nature.

Iceland can not be entirely separated from the Scandinavian countries. From the point of view of the historian or linguist, it is the place of the origins of the Scandinavian people, their traditions, language, and poetry; from the point of view of the physicist, of the naturalist, Iceland is, in a similar way, the source of Scandinavian climate and regular and irregular phenomena.—*Paul Gaimard and Xavier Marmier (1842)*

2 | NORDIC BY NATURE

Classifying and Controlling Flora and Fauna in Iceland

On his outward voyage from Copenhagen to the Faroe Islands in 1828, the German bird enthusiast Carl Julian Graba noted his sighting of "the first Northern birds" *(die ersten Vögel des Nordens)* of the voyage off the coasts of the Shetland Islands. Although he had previously spotted this bird—the Atlantic gannet *(sula alba)*—off the Danish coasts at the beginning of his journey, he did not regard Denmark as the genuine native territory *(Heimat)* of the bird. Even though he had already traveled north from Kiel to Copenhagen in order to begin the seagoing leg of his journey, he apparently did not consider Denmark to be part of the "North"; the edges of the North only began with the North Atlantic islands.[1]

Wherever the boundaries were drawn, Graba's reference to a "Northern bird" reflects a European nineteenth-century taxonomy of living beings, which held that different types of plants and animals developed and thrived in different climatic zones, and that these climatic zones could be mapped through identifying the natural ranges of individual flora and fauna. Brian W. Ogilvie traces the roots of this idea back to the Renaissance, arguing that during the sixteenth century "wide travel, combined with careful attention to the small distinctions between different kinds of plants, led to a view of Europe as a patchwork of different floras, with a clear line separating northern from Mediterranean floras and subtle differences within them."[2] During the seventeenth and eighteenth centuries, European knowledge about different kinds of local floras and faunas increased, as sets of handbooks and atlases, each confining themselves to a particular region, appeared, with the goal of exactly and completely tabulating all the plants and animals existing in a circumscribed area.[3]

During the eighteenth century, as James L. Larson discusses, both of the two major competing theories of natural history—the Linnaean and Buffonian—used these handbooks and atlases as the data to support their claims. Each theory, however, offered a different explanation for development of the different types of local nature or climatic variation.[4] According to the Swedish scientist Carl von Linné, known as Linnaeus, each animal and plant found the physical environment for which it was most suited. As the waters of the biblical Flood had receded, the land mass steadily increased, and through migration and dissemination from the single point of Noah's landing, animals and plants found their proper places on the globe. Regions of similar physical conditions, such as mountains or lowland areas, were therefore inhabited by similar types of flora and fauna. Linnaeus's French colleague Comte de Buffon, who opposed him on many points, countered him in this respect as well, especially stressing the differences between animals in Europe and in the Americas. Similar environmental conditions did not necessarily indicate similar types of plants and animals. Rather, different types were produced at distinct moments in the earth's history, in a long global cooling process during which larger and more vigorous animals developed before the smaller ones, when the earth was warmer and more productive, according to Buffon. As the earth cooled, the larger animals then migrated to the warmer areas of the earth, the equatorial regions, while the smaller ones who did not require so much heat remained near the poles. Thus, as in other aspects of their work, on the question of local or climatic natures, Buffon took a position marked by its emphasis on changes over time, while Linnaeus's system focused on a taxonomic classification of the existing state of nature.

Common to both theories, however, and to eighteenth-century life science in general, was the idea that each species had its proper place on the globe, a *Heimat* where it belonged and had been designed by the Creator to be. One of the goals of eighteenth-century travel was a mapping of this design in order to gain a complete knowledge of the world as God had made it. Toward this goal, Linnaeus sent his students to the South Pacific, to the Near and Far East, to Iceland, and traveled himself in the Swedish provinces, especially Lapland, to bring back specimens. In England, Joseph Banks, as president of the British Royal Society, played a similar role, traveling himself to the South Pacific from 1768 though 1771 and to Iceland in 1772, and encouraging and funding the trips of others.

The Danish Royal Scientific Society (Det Kongelige Danske Videnskabernes Selskab), founded in 1742, also propounded such encyclopedic aims for traveling natural historians. The society was involved in publishing the results of expeditions to Egypt, Iceland, and Norway.[5] The report of the 1752–57 Iceland expedition, Eggert Ólafsson's and Bjarni Pálsson's *Reise igiennen Island* (*Travels in Iceland*),[6] was an exemplar of this encyclopedic spirit, as it divided the country into regions, allotted one section of the book to each of the four regions, and repeated all the information about Icelandic plant and animal life in each section, so that the reader was informed several times about the island's most common flora and fauna.[7]

This book, which was translated into German, French, and English— even eventually Icelandic—was but one of a number of mid-eighteenth-century natural histories on Iceland and other parts of the North Atlantic. Beginning in the 1740s and 1750s, the flora and fauna of the North Atlantic were the subject of investigation and interest in new ways, by new parties, and for new purposes. This chapter examines two overlapping groups that had an interest in North Atlantic nature in the eighteenth century: natural historians, on the one hand, and reform-minded state bureaucrats, on the other. In the mid-eighteenth century, discussion of nature in the North Atlantic was not only a subject in natural histories but also in treatises on improvements and applications for entrepreneurial ventures by Danish officials. Although these two types of writing belong to different genres, and were intended for different audiences, they handled the same subject broadly understood and had congruent interests. Natural histories aimed at complete descriptions of Icelandic, and other North Atlantic, flora and fauna. Treatises on improvements dealt with specific problems, usually understood as "deficiencies," of natural circumstances and conditions in the North Atlantic. Both types of authors therefore understood, for example, the mid-eighteenth-century plague among Icelandic sheep as falling under their field of interest. The intersection between these texts was not only in their subject matter, however. Both genres assumed that there was a general type of nature, common to the North Atlantic region and relatively homogeneous throughout it, so that it was reasonable to speak of a concept such as Carl Julian Graba's "Northern bird" rather than a "bird of Iceland, Norway, or Denmark." Through both the language of natural histories and of improvement projects, an Enlightenment elite within the Danish state sought to redefine Icelandic and North Atlantic nature, reclaim a territory that had been historically viewed as a wilderness, and remodel it into a well-regulated and homogeneous part of the state. This vision of nature in the North Atlantic was a radical break with previous traditions of describing nature there and also one of the first times that Icelanders sought to establish themselves as authorities on conditions in their country.[8] They often did so with the explicit intention of resisting and contesting certain types of foreign concepts about North Atlantic nature.

Some of the prominent officials who contributed to the project of describing Icelandic nature in the eighteenth century included Magnús Stephensen, the chief justice of Iceland who also wrote about the Laki catastrophe; Hans Christian Bech, one of the directors of Iceland's Danish-owned monopoly trading company; Niels Horrebow, a natural historian sent by the Danish king to write a natural history of the island; and Skúli Magnússon, one of the most active of the eighteenth-century Icelandic reforming officials and the first Icelander to assume the post of *landfógeti* (bailiff) within the Danish state bureaucracy of Iceland. These men, members of the elite Icelandic-Danish milieu traveling between Reykjavík (which only received a charter as market town from the Danish government in 1786 and had a population of less than two hundred at the time) and Copenhagen, were investigating models for the "improvement" of Iceland, and they were concentrating on the aspects of Icelandic nature that contributed to the economic condition of the island. They wanted to know not only what Icelandic nature was like but also what Icelandic nature could become.[9]

"What are Icelandic products, and what could they be?"—this was the chief question of Hans Christian Bech's 1781 treatise on Icelandic trade. Bech believed that conditions in Iceland needed improvement and that the best method of achieving this would be for Icelanders to visit other countries and find out how things were done there, or if people from other regions could be persuaded to come to Iceland. The regions that he had in mind—where people understood how to salt meat and fish for preservation, how to spin hemp for fishing lines, and how to cultivate potatoes—were Norway, the Jutland peninsula, the Shetland Islands, and the Netherlands. Most of the places to which Bech referred in his essay were other provinces of the eighteenth-century Danish kingdom, as well as the Shetlands, which had been part of the Danish state before 1472. Thus, Bech suggested looking within the historical Danish kingdom itself for models of economic well-being for the Icelanders to emulate. This was a clever and politically sage move on his part. It placed the focus of concern for Iceland's condition on the island itself, its inhabitants and its nature, and not with Danish management. Furthermore, it also pointed to solutions already existing, put into place elsewhere within the Danish state and not requiring new innovations or foreign importations.[10]

Other officials also saw the potential appeal and advantages of such an approach. For example, the idea of transforming Iceland into a "second Norway" was quite powerful and appealing to the Danish administration. This metaphor was used successfully by Skúli Magnússon when he applied for funds in 1752 to establish the Nye Indretninger—a joint-stock entrepreneurial company that founded the first textiles factory in Iceland. With his eye turned toward tactically advantageous political rhetoric, Skúli claimed in his application to the Danish crown that

> although the country is poorer and less productive than other countries . . . this [application] is an accurate description of the condition of the country, wherein it can be seen, that the country does not lack the products and requirements to make its inhabitants happy, or its monarch the lord of a great country, which could become another Norway . . . the prevailing poverty could be improved by procuring the means so that the country's potential could be used better than it has been, by establishing manufacturing, in order to increase the country's natural products, and finally by giving the country the profit of its produce and wares, as the other provinces and territories of the monarchy enjoy, with free and voluntary trade.[11]

The prospect of transforming Iceland in this way must have appealed to the Danish king and council; Skúli received more money for his project than he had requested, and the company was launched the following year with the investment and participation of most of the leading men of eighteenth-century Iceland, including the most wealthy landholders and church officials. Clearly, the *landfógeti* had shaped his rhetoric well for his audience.

Bech, Skúli, and Magnús Stephensen aimed their treatises, applications, and histories toward the class of Danish administrative officials, the responsible parties who could bring the condition of Iceland up to the standards enjoyed in other parts of the kingdom. According to the model of enlightened cameralism, the dominant political-economic system of central and northern Europe in the eighteenth century, education should be directed from the center of the kingdom to the provinces and from the top down. The Danish state had a responsibility to provide education and resources; the Icelanders themselves had a responsibility to utilize them—and much frustration was expressed by officials about the difficulties and stubbornness of the natives in this respect. Although the plans of Bech, Skúli, and Magnús did not involve large numbers of people, and the men worked in marginalized and scantly populated regions of Europe, the implications of their projects for the state were far-reaching. By assuming that there was a single, relatively homogenous "northern nature," of which Iceland was simply a part, civil authorities sought to render all of the northern dependencies of the Danish state manageable. The eighteenth-century reforming projects had at best mixed results, but the idea behind them—to regulate and manage Icelandic nature and to transform a marginalized, wild frontier into a normal and ordinary province of the state—became the dominant mode of writing about Iceland, and the other provinces of the kingdom, by the end of the eighteenth century.

These improvement projects were supported by a new theme in Icelandic natural histories that emerged in the eighteenth century. At the same time that treatises on agricultural and other reforms of the island's economy were being written, natural histories of Iceland took on a new perspective toward Icelandic nature. Taken together, this constituted a break with previous traditions of writing about Iceland and the other northernmost provinces of the Danish state. Starting in the mid-eighteenth century, natural historians began to argue that Iceland's nature was unlike previous accounts had claimed. Rather than being an ungovernable wilderness of fire and ice, inhabited by monsters and savages, as medieval and Renaissance sailors' stories had claimed, the island was not in fact very different from the neighboring provinces of the kingdom—Norway, Greenland, or the Faroe Islands. This new conception of North Atlantic nature in natural histories can be traced to the same milieu and intellectual influences that spurred the reforming officials. Both groups of writers—who frequently belonged to the same families, social circles, and literary clubs—had a common image of the North Atlantic and a desire to establish their image as a definitive break with the past.[12]

State knowledge and state power were linked together: the new image of the North Atlantic, the solidification of state power there, and the state's active role in shaping the natural landscapes came together in the eighteenth century. Artists' representations of the landscape could, when placed in the correct context, promote a certain political reading of the land and of its nature. But the modern European states' aims and ambitions did not end there. The Danish state, as other European states, sought also to alter not just the perception of the landscape but its actual appearance. Danish officials were concerned with making the land more profitable and with managing it more efficiently. In the case of Iceland, we can discover how this management was attempted during the eighteenth and nineteenth centuries, to what degree it was achieved, and what allies and opponents the state had in this process.[13]

MANAGING THE STATE AND NATURE IN EIGHTEENTH- AND NINETEENTH-CENTURY EUROPE

The projects and ideas of the Danish state emerged from a shared European scientific consensus and community. In analyzing another eighteenth-century cameralist Scandinavian state, Lisbet Koerner has argued that Linnaeus's concerns with political economy and Sweden's negative trade balance underlay his scientific program. Ordering the natural world was but a first step toward managing it for the benefit of the country. For Linnaeus, knowledge of natural history "guarded the nation against both foreign dominance and indigenous barbarism."[14] If Swedish scientists could apply their botanical knowledge to useful projects, such as the elaborate plans for cultivating tea in Sweden designed by Linnaeus, then not only would the state of botanical knowledge improve but so would the economy of a nation that would be no longer dependant on foreign imports.[15] In his experiments, Linnaeus proposed that plants could be transferred between the tropical and temperate zones and that it would be possible to grow tropical plants in Sweden by acclimatizing them in gradual moves and by using greenhouses. As his efforts involving tea plants failed repeatedly throughout the 1740s and 1750s, he lost faith in this belief, finally concluding that plants are native to specific climates and cannot be transplanted outside them.

But the failure of Linnaeus's experiments did not mean that the scientific community abandoned the principle of acclimatization. Michael A. Osborne has argued that the acclimatization of plants and animals was an important element of the ideology of French colonialism in the nineteenth century. The projects of the Société Zoologique d'Acclimatation to raise alpacas, silkworms, and llamas in France were conceived both as evidence of the expanse of power of the French empire and as solutions to economic needs of the country for new resources and products. The directors of the society, Isidore Geoffroy Saint-Hilaire and Étienne Geoffroy Saint-Hilaire, drew upon the theories of the Comte de Buffon and Jean-Baptiste Lamarck about the adaptation of living forms according to the demands of the environment. According to Lamarck, species could change in response to newly established conditions, which gave rise to new needs. These needs in turn stimulated the creation of new behaviors and structures, which turned the animal away from its original path toward perfection of its form. The directors of the French acclimatization society (who were father and son) modified Lamarck's ideas of a drive toward perfection and deviation from that path. Instead, Isidore Saint-Hilaire believed that an idealized type of a species acted as a common center around which variation of the species "played." This became known as the "limited variability of type" theory: species could be "pushed" to adapt to local climates just enough in one direction or another to allow for silk to be spun in Paris as well as in China.[16]

By comparison to Linnaeus's plans and the French visions of empire, Danish projects in their North Atlantic provinces can be described as modest, driven by practical considerations in response to specific environmental and economic circumstances rather than theories about biological form and developments. Eighteenth-century Danish scientists and administrators did not invent elaborate schemes such as trying to grow sugarcane or raise yaks in Copenhagen. Clearly, however, the activities of natural historians and administrators in the Danish kingdom and the projects they did undertake demonstrate that they too shared a belief in climatic zones and the importance of climate in determining the characteristics of plants and animals. As in other regions, these ideas had economic as well as scientific implications. For example, reindeer were moved from northern Norway, from the northernmost province of Finnmark, to Iceland in the eighteenth century in response to famine conditions on the island. Sheep were also brought from the British Isles after a plague decimated the Icelandic flocks in the mid-eighteenth century—sheep that were unfortunately as susceptible to illness as the Icelandic variety and that brought further disease to the Icelandic flocks. There was no actual "acclimatization" practice behind these projects, merely a theory of climate. Their promoters seem to have assumed that these animals already belonged in the same climatic zone, and therefore it should be possible to relocate them without any sort of acclimatization whatsoever, since they were already acclimated to the North. By having such a broad conception of the extents of this northern climatic zone, however, the projects tended to elide substantial differences in environment and climate within this zone—failing to recognize, for example, that the marshlands of Jutland might support different crops than the volcanic, acid soil of Iceland.

European theories of the centrality of climate in determining biological form and function even extended as far as humans, as nineteenth-century discussions about the ability of white colonial officials to survive in the tropical colonies indicates.[17] For example, during Danish settlement in Greenland in the early eighteenth century, the 1729 land commission proposed that Icelanders would make the best settlers since they were already accustomed to the climate and the way of life there. Although there had been the two medieval Icelandic settlements in Greenland that perished several centuries after arriving, the notion of moving eighteenth-century Icelanders to Greenland glossed over the differences between the settled agricultural practices of the Icelanders and the nomadic hunting lifestyle of the Inuit of Greenland. From the point of view of the Danish administration, however, both Icelanders and Greenlanders were people who lived in the coldest, wildest, and most remote parts of the kingdom and were therefore assumed to be similar in character. The author of this suggestion was most likely Hans Egede, a Lutheran minister who labored for many years toward the Danish recolonization of Greenland and the conversion of the Inuit. Probably the administrators on the 1729 commission also assumed that the Icelanders could provide a link between the Danes and Inuit by

teaching European agricultural practices to the Inuit. A list of 166 Icelanders willing to immigrate to Greenland was drawn up, and preparations
were made to supply them with building materials at Nepisene. Before the
arrival of the new colonialists, however, Dutch traders who wanted to prevent further Danish footholds in Greenland destroyed the buildings, and
the attempt was given up. Ultimately, the Danish colonies in Greenland
proved to be more stable after the establishment of the royal monopoly of
Greenlandic trade in 1774 (Den Kongelige Grønlandske Handel) improved
their economic position.[18]

There were other eighteenth-century population relocation projects
within the Danish state: following the Laki volcanic eruptions in Iceland,
some officials considered moving Icelanders from their island—which had
clearly proved to be uninhabitable from the Copenhagen perspective—to
Jutland, another marginal region of the Danish kingdom. This move would
also have alleviated the problem of the eighteenth-century depopulation
of the Jutland peninsula, where the landscape was also being dramatically
altered by sandstorms and soil erosion.[19] Only eight hundred people made
plans to move, but the 1785 land commission on Iceland rejected the proposal as being unlikely to recoup the cost of resettlement, and this project,
like the proposed move to Greenland, was never realized.[20]

Another much smaller population relocation project actually was undertaken, this one with the sponsorship of Skúli Magnússon's joint-stock company: the transportation of ten farming families from Norway and Jutland
to Iceland in 1752 seems to have been based on the idea that crops grown
in Norway and Jutland would thrive with the same techniques in Iceland;
the only necessary step was to bring teachers to instruct the natives, in the
way that Hans Christian Bech would later recommend. The project ended
only ten years later, with the return of the "foreign" families home and its
instigators judging it to be failure. There is not enough evidence to pinpoint
why the scheme did not expand more broadly and involve larger numbers
of people. The report of the sheriff, Bjarni Halldórsson, who hosted two
of the Jutland families, gives a mixed and not completely conclusive picture. Bjarni claimed that one of the newly arrived families was ambitious,
but the other required instruction and supervision. According to him, the
newcomers maintained that their duties should be limited to working in
the fields and that they had the right to the same food and drink to which
they were accustomed in Denmark. There seem to have been at least as
many cultural, and possibly linguistic, differences and problems as agricul-

tural ones. After ten years, the last of the foreign farmers returned home, at company expense, in 1762.[21]

REINDEER IN ICELAND: A FOREIGN IMPORT OR NATURAL IMPLANT?

None of this experimentation with moving people and animals around the North Atlantic could have been described as fully successful even by the optimistic promoters, but at least one project did have a lasting impact on the landscape of Iceland that continues to this day: the importation of reindeer to the island from Finnmark in Norway. In some respects, this scheme could even be described as too much of a good thing. Taking a closer look at the history of reindeer in Iceland helps to sort out what the intentions and the consequences were for the Enlightenment visions of the improvement of the island.[22] The first proposal to buy six reindeer in Norway and transport them to Iceland was in 1751.[23] This idea, like so many others at the time, did not come immediately to fruition, however, and the first animals did not actually arrive in Iceland until 1771. The years in between 1751 and 1771 were particularly hard ones for the island: there was a famine from 1751 to 1758, and in 1761 an outbreak of scabies and lung disease among the English sheep that had come to Iceland began and lasted until 1770. The resumption of the plans to transport reindeer in 1771 after the twenty-year hiatus can probably be attributed to worsening environmental and agricultural conditions and the perceived need for a particularly hardy animal to replace the sheep population, which had declined by 60 percent in the previous nine years. In general the requests and inquiries to Norway for shipments of reindeer were written with reference to the specific hardships of the Icelandic eighteenth century. For example, another shipment of animals was sent by an Icelandic priest living in Norway when he heard the news of the 1783 volcanic eruptions in Iceland.[24]

In 1771 a group of thirteen reindeer arrived in the country in response to a request by the Danish governor of Iceland, L. A. Thodal, and were sent to the Westman Islands off the southern coast. This first attempt did not augur well for the future of reindeer in Iceland; of this group, about half or more died the following winter of unknown causes. Another group of seven animals was released in southern Iceland, but they disappeared as well. This was followed by larger shipments of thirty to thirty-five animals in 1777, 1784, and 1787, which were settled both on the Reykjanes peninsula and in northeast Iceland, around Lake Mývatn and north of Vatnajökull (see map 2, page 37). Their mortality rate during the shipboard journey from Norway was high; in these transports almost one-third of the animals were lost before their arrival to the island. Once they reached their destination, however, the later arrivals seem to have generally thrived. In 1781, farmers reported seeing a herd of at least seventy reindeer in an area where a small group of animals had been released.[25] Another report from local informants claimed that there were herds of several hundred reindeer in Iceland by the 1790s.[26]

This lack of precise accounting for the increases in reindeer populations, and apparent lack of knowledge about the health of Icelandic reindeer in general, however, reveals something peculiar about transplant project from the outset. Reindeer are, and were, domesticated animals in northern Norway, raised by the Saami people living in northern Norway, Sweden, and Finland. When the animals came to Iceland, there was apparently little interest in keeping them as domestic animals, and the groups were simply released into the wild. This practice is puzzling: contemporaneous sources suggest that the officials wanted the reindeer to become herding animals and replace the sheep that had died during the plague. In 1786, the new governor, H. C. D. V. von Levetzow, suggested that some Saami families should be brought to Iceland to teach the Icelanders how to keep reindeer.[27] This was never done, although it would have been consistent with Hans Christian Bech's recommendations and with other reform projects. However,

FIG. 8 Icelandic reindeer. Photo courtesy of Skarphéðinn G. Þórisson.

the idea of bringing Saami families to Iceland was dropped because the governor of Finnmark reported that the Saami nomadic lifestyle required wild meadows with large amounts of lichens and brushes in which they could find food for their animals and erect tents. Since these were clearly not part of the landscape of Iceland, the government became convinced that it would have been unsuitable to bring these people to Iceland along with their animals.[28]

Whatever the reasons for the lack of a consistent effort to establish reindeer husbandry in Iceland, the results of the policy were clear and are a familiar story in environmental history. Left to themselves, the reindeers ate lichens, which the Icelanders also used as food, and competed with the remaining sheep for pastureland.[29] The farmers began to complain and as soon as 1790 requested permission to hunt the reindeer.[30] At this time, there were an estimated 300–400 reindeer in one of the northern districts. The request was granted but was limited for three years and to one district, also with restrictions on the number, age, and sex of the animals. The quota set seemed inadequate to control the population, however, because a further demand in 1794 to hunt reindeer resulted in the extension of the permission to three districts. In 1798, farmers were allowed to hunt reindeer anywhere in Iceland.[31] In 1810, a local sheriff in northeast Iceland reported that, because the reindeer were still ruining the sheep pastures there, the animals had been more of a plague than a benefit, and he recommended not only that permission to hunt them should be extended indefinitely but that the government should distribute free bullets to the farmers for this purpose.[32] By 1849, the farmers had achieved their goal of being able to hunt reindeer anywhere in Iceland and without age or sex restrictions. It appears that they had convinced the government that reindeer were a pest and not a benefit to Iceland. Efforts to bring the reindeer population under control proceeded slowly during the nineteenth century, but by 1882 they had disappeared from many places where they had been introduced. In 1940, research to study the reindeer populations began, with the intent of protecting the stocks from further declines.[33] Today, Icelandic reindeer are hunted under a quota system, with fines levied for violation of the quotas. Culturally, a certain perception of these animals as "foreign" to Iceland, despite their now two-hundred-year-long history there, persists to some degree, and the idea of eliminating the animals continues to be raised now and then, although it is not considered seriously by the Icelandic government, which manages the reindeer population and issues hunting licenses.[34]

SCIENCE IN SERVICE TO THE STATE

The reindeer experiment in Iceland suggests that while officials may have found it theoretically unproblematic to transform and transplant the flora and fauna of the North, these ideas did not play out so simply, nor did local farmers necessarily agree with Danish administrators' concepts about the homogeneity of "northern nature." But the idea that certain types of animals, plants, and people possessed qualities particular to the North Atlantic region of the kingdom—and that this region was a relatively homogeneous one—was, despite these experiences, very persistent.[35] Although the Danish projects conceived along these lines were often interpreted as having failed by their instigators, this does not mean that these plans were in principle ill-conceived or useless. The idea of looking to neighboring regions as models and appropriating animals, plants, or people arose from the Enlightenment bureaucratic principle of seeking thorough knowledge of a governed territory. Thorough, accurate, and scientific knowledge of a place was after all the basis upon which its transformation could be envisioned. This approach combined the Enlightenment interest in science, collection, and encyclopedic knowledge with the ideal of state service, as Linnaeus advocated. The practice of royal scientific societies commissioning natural histories for regions within the boundaries of the state—as well as from more exotic realms like the Americas, the Near East, and the South Pacific—was common throughout western Europe in the eighteenth century. Niels Horrebow's *Tilforladelige Efterretninger om Island* (*Natural History of Iceland*), Eggert Ólafsson's and Bjarni Pálsson's *Reise igiennem Island* (*Travels in Iceland*), Erik Pontoppidan's *Det förste Forsög paa Norges naturlige Historie* (The First Natural History of Norway), and Olaus Olavius's *Oeconomisk Reyse igiennem de nordvestlige, nordlige, og nordostlige Kanter af Island* (Journey through the North, Northwest, and Northeast Regions of Iceland) were examples of such large, state-funded natural histories written in the encyclopedic style in the Scandinavian countries.[36]

Complete and accurate natural histories of Iceland were understood as the basis upon which agricultural reformers could build. One of the main themes in these mid-eighteenth-century natural histories of Iceland is the predictability and regularity of nature on the island. These texts point out that previous travel accounts had exaggerated stories about Icelandic nature, claiming that nature on the island was exotic and unlike anything known in Europe. For example, medieval and Renaissance books told stories about fabulous monsters living in Iceland, claimed that the Icelandic climate was perpetually cold, and the volcanoes were constantly erupting.[37] It was these stories to which Arngrímur Jónsson, the Icelandic saga scholar and church official, objected when he complained in 1592 of the "strangers" whom "it hath pleased by false rumors to deface, and by manifold reproches to injurie my sayd countrey, making it a by-word, and a laughing-stocke to all other nations."[38] Contrary to what readers had been told by others, Arngrímur informed them that Mount Hekla was not the mouth of hell, Iceland was not perpetually surrounded by ice, and Icelanders did not hold their wives in common. In addition, he added, there were neither horses that could run twenty leagues at one stretch, nor whales as large as mountains.

In the mid-eighteenth century, at about the same time as the improvement projects of the reforming officials were getting underway, Horrebow, Eggert Ólafsson, Bjarni Pálsson, and Olavius also took up the idea of writing natural histories with the intention of correcting existing false stories about Iceland. Horrebow's book pointed out that his natural history was founded on "what he himself" had "seen and experienced" during the two years he spent on the island.[39] Thus, his book portended to be a more valid source of knowledge than the 1746 *Nachrichten von Island, Grönland, und der Strasse Davis* (Reports from Iceland, Greenland, and the Davis Strait) of Johann Anderson, the mayor of Hamburg, who had based his account only on sailors' reports.[40] Among many other points, Horrebow disputed Anderson's claim that there were pools of burning water surrounding Mount Hekla that ignited spontaneously for fourteen days every year. There was no reason, argued the Danish naturalist, to think that water and fire in Iceland behaved differently than in other countries—"two opposite elements will not unite in this country any more than in any other."[41] Such pools had never existed in Iceland, since it was contrary to any experience to imagine that water can burn. If Anderson had visited Iceland and not relied on far-fetched tales spread by casual visitors, Horrebow implied, he would have realized the mistake. Horrebow then went on to explain Anderson's many other errors: that foxes in Iceland were also red, as in Norway and Denmark, and not black, and that domesticated horses also existed on the island, not just the wild varieties.

After spending two years in Iceland, Horrebow was recalled to Denmark.[42] Two Icelanders—the poet and legal scholar Eggert Ólafsson, and

Bjarni Pálsson, a physician—were sent by the Danish Royal Scientific Society to take his place and write a natural history of the entire country.[43] Their trip around Iceland in 1752–57 produced two large volumes of *Reise igiennem Island* (*Travels in Iceland*) that were translated into the major European languages. In their account, Eggert and Bjarni explicitly attempted to discredit many of the old tales about Icelandic nature. In the section on the eastern districts of Iceland, they mentioned the reports of monstrous snakes or worms living in lakes and rivers there. Since their readers were certainly too learned to believe such tales, the authors tried to pose some explanation for the existence of these stories. There were no other animals large enough in Iceland to have been confused for monsters of this size, therefore the large waves and disturbances of the water attributed to monsters must have been caused by winds and storms that are characteristic of the eastern part of the island, and the bodies of monsters must have been shadows or reflections. Eggert and Bjarni's explanation—while unlikely to persuade anyone who did believe in the existence of Icelandic sea monsters— was modeled on the methodical approach to establishing truth and authority about the natural world common during the Enlightenment, confronting "false stories" and attempting to replace them with reliable explanations based on regular laws and principles of nature.[44]

Olavius's *Oeconomisk Reyse igiennem de nordvestlige, nordlige, og nordostlige Kanter af Island* (Journey through the North, Northwest, and Northeast Regions of Iceland) was written to supplement the report of the 1770 land commission, which had not visited these areas in their investigation. Olavius did not counter the "false stories" point by point in the way that Eggert and Bjarni did. However, he complained about many authors, including Anderson, who had previously written about Iceland but who "have not even the most basic knowledge of the circumstances of the country."[45] The correction of such deficiencies in knowledge through accurate natural histories was, according to Olavius, an important step in the project of improvement in Iceland, since it was exactly this lack of knowledge and falsehoods that had caused many people to believe that the condition of the island was especially impoverished and hopeless. While Olavius recognized the many natural resources that Iceland lacked, he concluded, with the typical Enlightenment optimism that the reforming officials generally shared, that "other countries have just as many deficiencies in resources as Iceland does."[46]

In this text, the connection between the interests of natural historians employed by the Danish state and its reforming officials can be seen directly. The introduction to *Oeconomisk Reyse* was written by Jón Eiríksson, a highly placed official in the Danish Treasury, and an important advocate for Skúli Magnússon's company and its reform projects. In his introduction, Jón devoted many pages to discussing these projects, tying together the aims of the accurate and complete description of Icelandic nature that followed in the book with the goal of improving human use of this nature through useful projects. A similar congruence of interest and personal connection existed between Skúli Magnússon and Niels Horrebow. While Horrebow was writing the natural history of Iceland that King Frederick V commissioned during the winter of 1750–51, he stayed at Skúli's home at Bessastaðir in southwestern Iceland. At the same time that Skúli sent his appeal for funds to establish the Nye Indretninger to Copenhagen in the fall of 1751, Horrebow returned to the capital and presented his findings to the king. In addition to this encyclopedic, state-funded project, during his stay in Iceland Horrebow also wrote a shorter treatise, more directly addressing himself to the problems of the Icelandic economy. This fifty-one-page treatise begins with a general description of Iceland before proceeding to a discussion of particular problems, in which Horrebow discusses the industries of Iceland: namely, fishing, agriculture, forestry, tanning skins, wool spinning, and making rope. He recommends that the government invest in factories and manufacturing as the best way of improving the local economy—ideas that almost certainly were influenced by his relationship with Skúli.[47]

Icelandic and Danish naturalists during the Enlightenment attempted to use their position of authority and privileged knowledge about Iceland, as natives or as long-term visitors, to counter the romantic and wild claims of more distant writers. In the natural histories written during the early period of European exploration of the globe, the trope of a place's "exotic nature" seems to have been often linked with the idea of the inhabitants' "savage primitivism," and these were notions that the Enlightenment authorities wanted to dismiss. In Arngrímur's opinion, for example, the "strangers" who believed that the Icelandic waters were inhabited by monsters were also likely to believe that Icelanders held their wives in common, and this reasoning had led to the poor reputation of the islanders in other countries. His is an early example of the belief that was widespread in the eighteenth century, namely that the moral character of people was determined by their natural surroundings. This concern was not completely unfounded: Anderson, who repeated stories about strange Icelandic creatures, also had a very low opinion of the inhabitants of the island, considering them to be little better than animals themselves.[48] The Icelandic and Danish elite had an interest in discounting this exoticism, which separated the island from the civilized world, and argued instead in their natural histories that Iceland was just like any place that the reader might live himself. Since the mid-eighteenth-century natural histories of Iceland were translated into the major European languages, their wide readership would then gain a correct and reassuring—although perhaps less exciting—picture of the island.

THE MANAGED NORTH

Armed with the knowledge from natural histories that nature in Iceland was fundamentally similar to nature in other places, writers who were interested in improving Iceland's natural resources and economy could therefore be filled with optimism and ambition. If Iceland were a very strange place, where monsters lived and where the laws of physics operated differently than elsewhere, then the prospect of trying to transform or improve such a territory would have been daunting, if not impossible. But the latest and most authoritative scientific investigations, appearing at the same time that new agricultural and animal husbandry projects were being launched in Iceland, showed that Icelandic nature was unexceptional; the natives' economic use of their natural resources was simply less developed than in other regions of the North Atlantic, such as the Shetland Islands. For reforming officials, the path to the Icelandic future was therefore clear: Iceland could be a "second Norway" or just like the Shetlands. Improvement projects assumed that the basic circumstances and raw materials of nature were homogeneous throughout the North Atlantic. Sending Icelanders to the Shetlands to learn how to cure fish, bringing farming families to Iceland from Norway and Jutland to promote good agricultural practices, sending reindeer from Norway, and even transporting Icelanders to Greenland to start farms, were therefore thoroughly rational and scientific projects that would help to shape a more homogenous and more productive North Atlantic. If nature was everywhere the same throughout the North Atlantic, then only education and technology were needed to bring the margins of the kingdom up to the standards enjoyed in the center.

It is not possible to determine from the sources whether the writers on improvements simply borrowed their notion of Icelandic nature from the natural historians or whether both groups developed similar views at the same time, since the new outlook suited their common interests so well. Both the natural historians and administrative officials traveled within the same social and political circles and belonged to the same associations, and this new conception of Icelandic nature and the proper method to establish knowledge of a territory through direct personal observation were part of a shared set of assumptions within this group. By holding up one region as an example for another, the natural-history and administrative texts both suggested that one region could be transformed into another. In the end, the reader of both genres was presented with a vision of a single North Atlantic nature, which had the potential to be transformed and improved through human intervention.

Many Icelandic historians have treated the reforming projects of the late eighteenth century as ineffectual, apart from perhaps the single example of the reindeer transport. After the first two decades of the nineteenth century, there were no longer any large-scale economic or technological reform projects in Iceland, until the renewed drive toward modernization in the first decades of the twentieth century, especially after World War II. Since the Enlightenment reforming impetus seems to have fizzled out by the 1820s, and the projects were individually dismissed as failures by their instigators, historians have traditionally assumed that the experiments had little long-term effect. Gunnar Karlsson, for example, calls the projects "distressingly unsuccessful" and Harald Gustafsson also evaluates them as essentially failures.[49] But despite their lack of results when considered individually, these efforts did not disappear without a trace. Iceland in the nineteenth century became less isolated and more connected to Europe in many ways—culturally, economically, and intellectually—than it had been previously. The appearance in the mid-eighteenth century of natural histories about Iceland, and especially their translation into the major European languages, certainly played a role in shortening the perceived distance between Iceland and Europe. Although some natural histories still continued to describe "exotic" nature and "primitive" people in Iceland, at least nature and culture were described and investigated according to scientific principles that Europeans held to be objective and rational after the mid-eighteenth century.

Eighteenth-century treatises on improvements reached a much smaller audience than the readers of natural histories. These were not usually printed and were intended to be read only by the officials to whom they were addressed and would not have held much general appeal. However, they too aimed to use rational and scientific principles to describe the situation in Iceland. Both sets of writers used a single language to discuss nature in the North Atlantic, and one of the basic assumptions of this language was the homogeneity of nature throughout the region. While this new idea about North Atlantic and Icelandic nature replaced earlier beliefs in Iceland's exotic qualities, it also established a new basis for the authority of an author: in order to know Iceland after the mid-eighteenth century, one must have lived there. Secondhand reports or short visits were not sufficient. The Enlightenment emphasis on rationality and science, which was manifesting itself all over Europe, had the effect of transforming Iceland into an ordinary place, one that could be managed and regulated like any other region of the Danish kingdom.

This new language was not mere rhetoric in natural histories read by the European elite or by a few Danish officials, but had results and impact on the everyday lives of people in the Danish kingdom. It shaped practices that changed the lives of the lower classes, as the experience of farmers with the reindeer in Iceland illustrates. Changes in scientific language and culture had real political and practical meaning. Even though changes in bureaucratic practices cannot be said to have arisen solely from natural histories, and natural histories were not shaped by the will of the state alone, these two spheres complemented and reinforced each other in Enlightenment Europe. Although many nineteenth-century foreign writers, influenced by Romanticism, tried to make Iceland into an exotic place again, the role of the Icelanders as the voices of authority about their own country, established in the eighteenth century, could not be diminished later.

Furthermore, this new view of North Atlantic nature was not imposed by Danish bureaucrats from above; rather, the powerful Icelandic elite, the "big fish in a small pond" such as Skúli Magnússon and Magnús Stephensen, recognized that it could also be a tool that served their own interests as Icelanders as well as those of the Danish state. Unlike the late-nineteenth-century Icelanders, such as Jón Stefánsson, who sought to link the nature of

Iceland with that of Great Britain as a means of disentangling the connection between their country and Denmark, these Enlightenment Icelanders looked within the Danish state for their tools and voice of authority. There was, in the end, an ironic result of managing nature in eighteenth-century Scandinavia: in establishing themselves as the special authorities about nature in Iceland, native Icelanders ended up transforming their country in European eyes into a more "ordinary" and less exotic place, similar to the other North Atlantic provinces of the Danish kingdom.

The possibility arose of unwelcome contrasts between Inuit and European adaptation to the Arctic. . . . Suppose an inhabitant of Thule or Angmagssalik had studied the background of the painting [Millais's North-West Passage, which portrays an old sailor gazing nostalgically at pictures of British polar expeditions], and said: why are those men pulling the sledge themselves? Where are their dogs? Or: what peculiar snowshoes. Or: those clothes don't look that warm.—*Francis Spufford (1996)*

3 | MASTERING THE WORLD'S EDGES

Technology, Tools, and Material Culture in the North Atlantic

Despite the work of the officials to improve material conditions in the North Atlantic, making a living there was never easy. One of the problems for the farmers, at whom the Icelandic and Danish officials aimed most of their efforts, was the absence of tools, especially plows. Thomas Tarnovius, who lived in the Faroe Islands for five years as a young man in the 1650s when his father was a pastor on the island of Suðuroy, wrote in his description of the Faroes that "not very much can be said about the farmers in the Faroes, since they have only few fields to work, and in these fields they do not use the plow, but must turn over by hand as much earth as they can use, using spades for this, and with great difficulty, since the soil is full of stones."[1] One hundred and fifty years later, the Faroe Islanders had made little progress in this regard, according to Jørgen Landt, who was also a pastor there. In his *Forsøg til en Beskrivelse over Færøerne* (Description of the Faroes), Landt pointed out the multiple difficulties with the introduction of plows to the islands. Even if the farmers had plows, he wrote, there was no wood to repair them and keep them in working condition. And even if they had the wood, most importantly the farmers lacked the knowledge to repair this tool. Although some Faroe Islanders had gone to Norway in order to learn about plowing, this attempt at technology transfer within the Danish kingdom had not yielded results, according to Landt, although he did not report what happened to these individuals.[2]

Although Tarnovius and Landt made the same basic observation about agricultural conditions in the Faroes, there was a shift in the way each thought about the absence of plows. Tarnovius limited his comment to a bare description of the farmers' circumstances, while Landt sought in addition to explain the reasons for this technological deficiency of the islands. Landt's approach is typical of the eighteenth- and nineteenth-century texts on the North Atlantic, which give the impression of reiterating a well-worn and familiar theme. By 1800, these authors were no longer just pointing out long-standing problems, they were also seeking explanations for why the problems of tools and technology in the North Atlantic were so persistent, and why the efforts of reforming officials over the prior half century had failed to take root. The explanations offered usually rested on one or both of two causes: the deficiencies of North Atlantic natural conditions and resources, or the diminished moral and intellectual capacity of the natives of the region.

What did foreigners' observations about material conditions in the North Atlantic lead them to conclude about the people who lived there? How did their evaluation of these material conditions influence their evaluations of the difference between their homes and their fellow countrymen and the people they encountered in the North Atlantic? Throughout the eighteenth and nineteenth centuries, the depressed circumstances in Iceland and the rest of the North Atlantic was a theme in many European travelogues, including those of Uno von Troil in 1772, Ida Pfeiffer in 1845, and Richard Burton in 1872. Although these three had different impressions of Iceland—von Troil was mostly positive, Pfeiffer and Burton rather disparaging—their conclusions on the subject of Icelandic material conditions were similar. The writers tended to portray the North Atlantic as a static place, where technology did not advance beyond "primitive" conditions and the natives continued to struggle with the same problems over the course of centuries.

Although European impressions of North Atlantic nature, as in these texts, were diverse, the conclusions about material and technological conditions there were much more consistent. Individuals who found North Atlantic nature exotic as well as those who found it unexceptional agreed that the region's technology and material state were below expectations. If the traveler measured the North Atlantic against the conditions of his or her home, the North Atlantic appeared deficient, often surprisingly so, given the otherwise high levels of literary and cultural achievement that the travelers also took note of. Was this a contradiction, and, if so, how could it be reconciled?

The North Atlantic narrative of technology, material conditions, and tools parallels the stories of North Atlantic nature. The technological narrative was written by foreign travelers, by natives, and by visitors who settled in the North Atlantic, such as Danish and German missionaries in Greenland. David E. Nye, in his *America as Second Creation: Technology and Narratives of New Beginnings*, discusses "technological narratives" of the settlement of North America.[3] Central tools, such as the axe, the mill, or the railroad, functioned as symbols of American mastery over the new land and the story of this conquest, he argues. In the North Atlantic, although plows and their absence were frequently discussed, no single objects emerge in a similar way, but rather material conditions taken as a whole were read as narratives of the culture. On the North Atlantic frontier, however, the story was considerably more ambiguous than on the North American. Rather than a straightforward tale of progress, the quality and deficiency of material conditions were linked to variable patterns of human history.

"MEASURING MEN AND MACHINES" IN THE NORTH ATLANTIC

Incongruity between literature and technology in the North Atlantic was only surprising once travelers understood the relationship between material conditions and the character of the people who created and lived in them as a general principle of human history. In eighteenth- and nineteenth-century Europe, the narrative of industrial progress promoted by thinkers such as French positivist philosopher Auguste Comte and the Victorian political historian Thomas Carlyle connected the improvement of material culture to the improvement of moral character. Material culture was the outward signifier of the inner character.[4] People who were unwilling or unable to improve their tools showed their deficient moral and intellectual states. By the late nineteenth century, the people designated in this way by European travelers were often the colonized peoples of Africa and Asia, who did not have the intellectual capacity to invent machines, but were instead awed by the Europeans' use of emblematic tools such as guns.[5]

According to this hierarchy, the Icelanders and other inhabitants of the North Atlantic could also be categorized as people who were not, like the Europeans, on the evolving path toward improvement. To many visitors, this stagnation indicated some deficiency of character despite high levels of literary and cultural achievement. According to von Troil in 1772, the Icelanders "continue to work in the manner they are used to, without thinking of useful improvements."[6] Seventy years later, Pfeiffer complained of the lack of hygiene and sanitation in Iceland and the poor condition of the agriculture. She argued that the land was fertile enough; the fault was with its management because Icelandic farmers failed to drain the bogs and clear the fields, as German peasants did.[7] Writing at the end of the nineteenth century about Icelanders and technology, Burton compared the islanders with other "primitive" peoples whom he had encountered in his numerous travels. He also complained about hygiene and lack of accommodations and conveniences in Reykjavík, blaming this on the fact that the "race is thoroughly unmechanical, as we might expect from its social state."[8] To illustrate the point, he told a story about an Icelander misusing a sledge, which the man strapped in front of him instead of dragging it with a load behind him. Burton compared this native misunderstanding of an imported tool to the "negros" of Sierra Leone carrying wheelbarrows loaded on top of their heads. He attributed Icelanders' relationship to machines in part to the educational system that, he wrote, "ignores modern science and especially mechanics."[9] In his reference to their "social state," Burton placed the Icelanders, together with the people of Sierra Leone, at a less evolved state than Europeans, who not only understood how tools should be used but invented the sledge and the wheelbarrow themselves, and were thus able to spread them among more primitive cultures.

Not all visitors who commented on the use of tools in Iceland in the nineteenth century associated their misuse or absence with poor moral character or intellectual and social underdevelopment. Some pointed instead to the environment and a lack of natural resources, as did the German legal scholar Konrad von Maurer, who visited Iceland in 1858. In his travel diary, he interspersed lengthy discussions of saga literature, the condition of Icelandic trade, the church and religious life in Iceland, as well as many other subjects. However, he also noted the lack of building materials in Iceland, which were imported at great expense, and the poor condition of Icelandic gardens.[10] According to him, there were also very few plows, an observation that indicates this deficiency had been regarded as remarkable by visitors for at least two hundred years. Von Maurer mentioned the civil authorities' efforts to set good examples of agricultural practices and correct these problems, but, in contrast to Pfeiffer and Burton, faulted mainly the difficult environmental conditions of the island, and not the inhabitants themselves, for Iceland's state of mechanical development.

THE EUROPEAN RECOLONIZATION OF GREENLAND AND THE ROLE OF MATERIAL CULTURE

The level of North Atlantic material conditions and technology, which was merely irritating or a curiosity for the foreign visitor, was of course a more urgent concern for the Danish government. The narrative of technological decline in the North Atlantic appears not only in travel reports but also in official and semiofficial writings, such as those of Skúli Magnússon and Magnús Stephensen, for whom the reshaping of both North Atlantic nature and tools was part of a single project. The Norwegian Lutheran pastor Hans Egede launched an even more ambitious project of reform and rebuilding in the North Atlantic in 1711. He was concerned with the decline of Norse Greenland, the furthermost outpost of civilization in the North Atlantic. Continuous contact between the Norse settlement there and Europe had been sustained from circa 985 through the High Middle Ages, when Greenland was a source of exotic luxury goods for Europeans, including Greenlandic falcons, narwhal and walrus tusks, polar bear furs, and sealskins.[11] However, a cooling climate over the course of the fourteenth and fifteenth centuries made the European-style subsistence farming practiced in the Greenland settlements increasingly precarious.[12] Although there is much debate about the cause of the

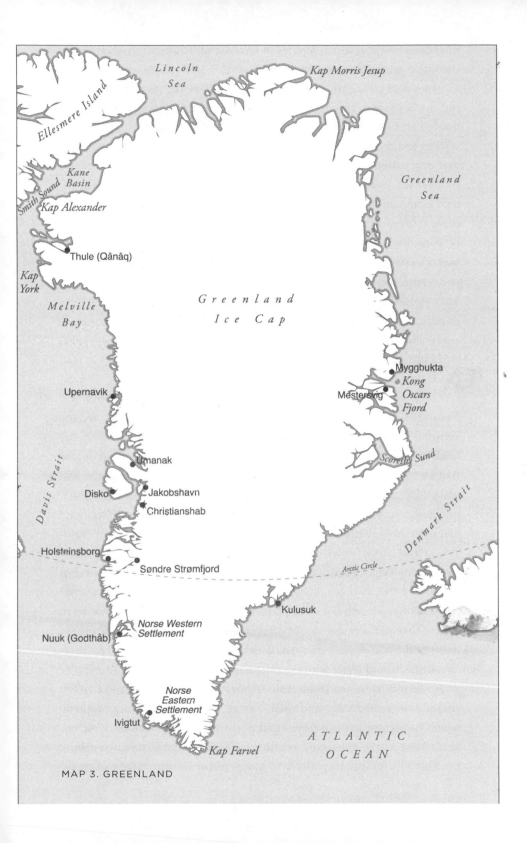

MAP 3. GREENLAND

final demise of the Norse colonies in Greenland, scholars today agree that the settlements ceased to exist before 1500.[13]

More than two centuries later, Egede conceived the plan of reestablishing the Scandinavian Greenland colonies on their original sites, finding the remains of the medieval churches and the descendants of the Norse settlers and restoring the Inuit natives to the Christian flock. He made his first application to the Danish Crown for funds in 1711 but only received support ten years later. In 1721, Christian VI granted the Bergen-Greenland Company monopoly rights to trade in Greenland, outfitted them with three ships, and gave a state salary to Hans Egede, his family, and a handful of workmen and traders. Egede and his family established a colony on the western coast of Greenland in Godthåb, where the capital of Nuuk is today and where the western Viking-age settlement had been located (map 3). They worked as missionaries among the Inuit, whom Egede believed were in part descended from the Viking settlers. He and his sons wrote extensively about many aspects of Inuit life, including their language, social structure, and hunting tools.[14] In the introduction to his major work in 1741, *Det Gamle Grønlands Nye Perlustration eller Naturel-Historie og Beskrivelse over det Gamle Grønland* (The Reemergence of Old Greenland or a Natural History and Description of Old Greenland), Egede connected the spiritual restoration of Greenland with its material revitalization. Greenland, he argued, had once been part of the Christian kingdom, and during that same period it had been rich in natural products such as whales and seals.[15] He claimed that in the beginning of Greenland's European history, that is, during the Norse settlement of the island, the trade from Greenland had been profitable. Thus, Greenland had the potential to become as valuable to the Danish Crown as the other marginalized regions of the Danish-Norwegian kingdom, such as Iceland and northern Norway—Egede's own birthplace. Just as those regions were experiencing economic difficulties in the eighteenth century, so was Greenland, but there was every reason to believe that all the earlier conditions could be restored and that the inhabitants of the island could enjoy the benefits of improved trade and technology, which would arrive with the return of Christianity.

Egede picked up the eighteenth-century European narrative of North Atlantic material decline and used it as an incentive for future progress, which he understood as a restoration of the historic conditions of Greenland.[16] Just as the nineteenth-century Icelandic nationalists saw promise for Iceland's future prosperity and independence in the return of medieval conditions, Egede offered the Danish Crown a similar narrative about Greenland. Looking at the North Atlantic, Egede considered Greenland to have been the final outpost of European civilization in the North Atlantic, which had slipped away with the demise of the Norse colonies. This spiritual and moral decline was recognizable in the material conditions of the inhabitants of Greenland, who during the Middle Ages had practiced European-style animal husbandry and farming—including using plows— but no longer did so in the eighteenth century. Analogous, although less extreme, in Egede's view, was the decline in material conditions in Iceland and northern Norway, but because these inhabitants had remained Christians they were not in such great need of his ministrations as the "lost souls" of Norse Greenland. From these closer dependencies to the Danish Crown, one could reach out to the European Greenlandic past.

Egede's idea of reconnecting Greenland to the Scandinavian mainland, and thereby to the civilized world, with Iceland as a go-between, had already existed in the seventeenth century. Even before Egede, a group of highly placed and influential Icelandic scholars had pointed out the advantages of reestablishing trade between Iceland and Greenland. This, they argued, would bring both material and spiritual benefit to the inhabitants of Greenland. In 1683, Thormod Torfæus, the royal historiographer to Christian V, suggested that Icelanders should sail from Breiðafjörður in west Iceland, the point of Erik the Red's departure, to the Old Norse settlements in western Greenland in order to seek out the descendants of the original land takers and to support the Danish state. Torfæus's ideas were supported by Arngrímur Jónsson Vídalín, whose grandfather had also written about Greenland.[17] In his book, Arngrímur the grandson suggested several ways in which the Icelanders could reestablish their connection to Greenland. If there were still descendants of the Norse settlers there, then the seventeenth-century Icelanders could rescue them; if the settlers had died out, then the Icelanders could bring Christianity to the heathens. This spiritual mission also entailed the duty to investigate the material conditions in Greenland and the products of the country, and to send craftsmen to help improve the tools for fishing and hunting whales.[18] The Icelandic historian Árni Magnússon also promoted the idea of rediscovering "old Greenland" (det gamle Grønland) in Denmark and recommended Arngrímur's book to the king's minister of finance, Joachim von Ahlefeldt.[19] This Icelandic scholarship on Greenland argued that, because of their historic ties, it was the Icelanders' duty and privilege to reestablish the connection to Greenland. Even though the sailing routes suggested by Torfæus and Arngrímur were not used, and Icelanders ultimately played only a small role in the Danish recolonization of Greenland, their notion of "old Greenland" as a place linked to Denmark through Iceland was still influential within the Danish kingdom.

The cultural link between Iceland and Greenland was also supported by the existence of two sagas dealing with Greenland. These two stories, about the Norse settlers in Greenland and the discovery of Vínland, *Erik the Red's Saga* and *The Story of the Greenlanders* (*Eiríks saga rauða* and *Grænlendinga þáttr*), were composed in Iceland sometime in the thirteenth century. Like the other Icelandic family sagas, they are mostly realistic stories, with some elements of fantasy—such as the appearance of a uniped, a one-legged creature who shoots an arrow and kills one of the main characters in *Erik the Red's Saga*. Aside from this sort of incident, both stories reliably recount essentially the same tale, dealing of the adventures of the members of the Eiríksson family, their life in Greenland, and their exploration of Vínland. As they are simple stories with a small cast of characters—especially as compared to the major family sagas such as *Njáls Saga* or *Laxdæla Saga*—they are easy to remember and have long been popular. These stories helped early-modern Scandinavians recall the common medieval past of Greenland and Scandinavia. They also sustained the belief in cultural links between Scandinavia and Greenland and fueled Danish plans for the rediscovery of "old Greenland" as a place properly belonging to the Scandinavians.[20]

These ideas about "old Greenland" thus lay in the background of Egede's project of restoration. More important to his success than such cultural connections, however, was his ability to convince the Danish Crown of its mercantile interests in Greenland and reinforce the idea of Scandinavian history in the North Atlantic. Egede's attention to Greenlandic products and material conditions resembled that of the Icelandic officials and was in a similar manner rhetorically and strategically aimed toward his Danish audience. While he was more concerned with spiritual than material well-being in the North Atlantic, he recognized the interests of the state in the project of reclaiming Greenland, and he also realized that these interests were mainly commercial ones. The Danish state had shown interest in the commercial products of Greenland by financing Egede, and it began to pursue these interests in a more systematic way throughout the eighteenth and nineteenth centuries. When Christian VI assisted Egede and the

Bergen-Greenland Company, he followed the precedent set by his great-great-grandfather, Christian IV (1588–1648), who sent several expeditions to Greenland and attempted to forbid other European nations, particularly the English, French, Spanish, and Dutch, from whaling around Greenland.[21] Christian IV was, however, mainly occupied by the Thirty Years War and his warfare with Sweden during his reign, and he only inconsistently asserted his rights to Greenland. While the Danish king's policy assumed the Scandinavian and Norse heritage of Greenland's inhabitants, and therefore Denmark's right of dominion over them, Christian IV did not fully enforce this claim. In the seventeenth and eighteenth centuries, English and Dutch ships exploited the whale-rich waters around Greenland, and other European countries asserted their right to the Greenlandic trade through the doctrine of the open sea (mare liberum).[22]

Egede's mission also faced spiritual competition from outside the Danish state: Moravian missionaries, many of whom were German speaking, established their missionary station, Neu Herrnhut, in 1733, only half a kilometer away from Egede's, followed by one in Lichtenfels farther south in 1758. Both the Danish and the Moravian missions in Greenland were small in size. During the period from 1721 to 1910, about 150 Danish pastors came to Greenland, while there were only about 50 Moravians there between 1733 and 1800.[23] A study of these missions suggests that Neu Herrnhut was the more successful; the Inuit preferred the simplified church services of the Moravians, with their emphasis on music and song, to those of the Danish Lutheran mission.[24] As there was rivalry and competition between the Lutherans and Moravians—even though on the surface they were both engaged in the same enterprise of bringing the heathen to the Christian flock—it might seem odd that the Moravians decided to build so close to Egede's established mission.[25] The eighteenth-century missionary concentration in a tightly circumscribed area on the west coast of Greenland, however, can probably at least in part be ascribed to interest in the sites of the European medieval past there and the idea of potential "lost Christians." Thus, as eighteenth-century Greenland reemerged as a sphere of interest for Europeans, it was a meeting point for several different European commercial and religious interests as well as between Europeans and indigenous peoples.

Even though Egede placed Greenland in the context of the story of North Atlantic decline, his writings on the whole were sympathetic toward the Greenlandic Inuit and their culture. When captured Inuit had been presented at European courts in the seventeenth century, observers frequently equated their social level with savages from the New World who were presented in similar settings. Adam Olearius, a natural historian and counselor at the ducal court in Gottorp in Schleswig-Holstein, for example, recorded his impressions of the Inuit who were brought there from the Danish court in 1654: they, he wrote, must "really be called savages/for among them there is no understanding of higher things/no decorum/civility and decency/[they] live like animals."[26] For Olearius, the Inuit existed as a people entirely outside of European culture and history. Egede's view, however, stood in sharp contrast with this narrative. He instead placed the Inuit within European history, as the descendants of Norse Vikings. When he described their culture, lifestyle, language, and tools in *Det Gamle Grønlands Nye Perlustration*, he admired their skill with their tools, harpoons, kayaks, and fishing lines, and the pictures in the book feature scenes of Inuit tool use prominently (fig. 9). This impression was confirmed by the report of David Crantz, a Moravian missionary and contemporary of Egede, in his *Historie von Grönland* (History of Greenland), which contains a lengthy account of Inuit tools and particular admiration for the specialization of their spears. Crantz, however, did not adhere to Egede's belief in the European ancestry of the Inuit and considered them a heathen tribe whom the Christian truth had not yet reached. He was therefore disparaging of many of their customs, including the singing and drumming contests. His negative view of Inuit culture did not, however, include their hunting skills and tools, which he compared favorably with those of Europeans. Few Europeans, Crantz pointed out, could manage a kayak even under the calmest conditions, to say nothing of the waters to which the Inuit were accustomed.[27]

THE DEMISE OF "OLD GREENLAND": INUIT TOOLS AND NINETEENTH-CENTURY POLAR EXPLORATION

Although Egede and his family succeeded in establishing their settlement on the Norse site, his vision of the lost Europeans in Greenland ultimately did not prove convincing to other European eighteenth-century writers on Greenland. The physical appearance of the captured Inuit and the incomprehensibility of their language apparently counted as strong evidence against the possibility of European descent. Egede never abandoned the

FIG. 9 Woodcut of Inuit hunting seals on ice, using harpoons, from Hans Egede's *Det Gamle Grønlands Nye Perlustration* (1741). The book also included pictures of Inuit whale hunting in kayaks, a polar bear being killed with a harpoon, and Inuit hunting game (rabbits and reindeer) with bow and arrow.

idea himself: he examined the Inuit language for Old Norse root words and cited the remains of a medieval Norse church at the settlement as support for his theory. However, he was forced to admit that "the endeavors . . . have not had all the success one could desire, yet they have opened the way for new attempts of the same nature . . . not only has the west coast of Greenland, the so-called 'Vesterbygd' been found and resettled, God's word has been preached to those ignorant Heathens, who dwell in those places where

Christianity has been quite extinct and forgot. All this ought to encourage us to continue with full force our efforts to discover the Eastern shore, where the chief colony was located; and hopefully the offspring of our old Norwegian and Icelander ancestors may be found; which is not at all impossible."[28]

Despite Egede's cautious optimism, the idea of rediscovering the Vikings in contemporary Greenland lacked deep resonance in eighteenth- and nineteenth-century Europe. Certainly the Viking past of Greenland was not forgotten in northern Europe, where Vikings were for a long time a source of nationalist and romantic imagery. However, the primary goal of many European explorers in Greenland in the nineteenth century was not to find the remains of travelers who had arrived there before.[29] Rather, their purpose was to venture where no one had been before. For them, the North Atlantic island represented not a European homeland but an unexplored territory to be conquered. Heroic journeys toward the North Pole and to the interior of the island, such as John Franklin's tragic 1845 voyage and the Norwegian polar explorer Fridtjof Nansen's cross-country ski trip over Greenland's interior ice in 1888, gripped the European imagination more strongly than settlements on the southern half of the island did. Rather than portraying Greenland as a place of lost civilization, nineteenth-century explorers tended to see it as a wilderness to be explored. While Viking imagery lent itself well to the ethos of heroic masculinity that emerged, it was used in a less literal and more poetic incarnation than Egede and his contemporaries had intended.[30]

Although the resonance of Egede's concept of the Inuit as a lost Nordic tribe faded after Danish colonization and conversion of the Inuit took hold, other European writings on Greenland and its inhabitants often followed the example set by Egede and Crantz in their estimations of the Inuit as a technologically skillful people. The European presence in Greenland, in fact, depended on their skill, as the products of this labor—sealskins, whale oil, and baleen—built the connection between Europe and Greenland. The preindustrial whale and seal hunt was an activity that required training and practice and could not be casually learned by Europeans, as Egede and Crantz had pointed out. Although the Danish state's interest in establishing reliable trade in these products was clear, the maintenance of these connections was also difficult during the eighteenth century, as it had been during the Middle Ages. Similar to the Danish colonies in the West Indies, Africa, and India, the chief instrument of social policy in Danish Greenland was the trading company. The first private trading companies in Greenland, the Bergen-Greenland Company and the General Company, failed for financial reasons, resulting in the establishment of the public, state-run Den Kongelige Grønlandske Handel (the Royal Greenlandic Trading Company; hereafter KGH) in 1774, which was founded along purely monopolistic lines.

From the onset, KGH pursued a conservative policy with respect to the Inuit. Its main interest was in building an efficient trading network and ensuring the steady flow of Greenlandic products to the mother country. Since the eighteenth-century plans for the settlement of Icelanders or other Danish farmers practicing agriculture in Greenland had not come to fruition, the key economic advantage of Greenland to the Danish kingdom was the Inuit seal hunt. KGH encouraged the continuation of this tradition, at the expense of other industries that the Inuit could have pursued, and insisted that the hunt should be carried out using traditional tools. To ensure this, KGH restricted the numbers of rifles and bullets it allowed to be imported into Greenland.[31] This conservative policy continued even after the liberal reforms in Denmark in the 1830s and 1850s, which gave other provinces of the kingdom representation in parliament and ended the trading monopoly in Iceland and the Faroes. The Danish state policy however, considered the Greenlandic Inuit a primitive people whose culture could not survive contact with modern societies, and such policies were enacted for their protection.

The concept of the "unspoiled primitive" was of course a product of nineteenth-century European Romanticism and not a realistic description of conditions. Contact between Europeans and the Inuit was well underway in the mid-nineteenth century, and KGH was not in a position to control more than a part of it. Nineteenth-century British, American, and Scandinavian explorers were pushing their way up Greenland toward the North Pole or around Greenland toward the Northwest Passage. The mid-nineteenth century also saw the international search launched for the lost expedition of John Franklin, a mystery in which the Inuit report of the fate of the explorers, brought back to England by John Rae, was the subject of much controversy.[32] In the nineteenth century, northern expeditions brought not only international prestige but also new scientific results. John Ross, the first recorded European to come into contact with the polar Inuit living in northwest Greenland in 1818 (whom he called the Arctic Highlanders) was contributing to the magnetic mapping of the globe. His nephew, James Clark Ross, located the northern magnetic pole in 1833.[33] As these nineteenth-century European explorers turned to expanding their horizons beyond where earlier explorers had reached, they became familiar with Inuit techniques of travel and hunting in Greenland—dogsleds, harpoons, kayaks, and ice fishing. Although some polar explorers—most famously Robert Falcon Scott in the Antarctic—were reluctant to adopt Inuit dogsleds,[34] others, such as John Rae, admired Inuit technologies and compared them favorably with European tools and machines.

Some scholars have interpreted this European admiration of and dependence upon Inuit technological skills in polar travel as an indication that perceptions of the Inuit were an exception to the demeaning attitudes that nineteenth-century Europeans had toward people of other cultures. Robert David, for example, claims that British explorers were so impressed by Inuit skills and survival techniques in the Arctic that they credited the Inuit with a higher level of civilization than the peoples they encountered in southern climes.[35] Francis Spufford's study of the nineteenth-century British polar consciousness, however, offers a somewhat different interpretation: noting the privileging of the Inuit within the Victorian tableaux of "primitive peoples," he suggests that the British explorers felt technically incompetent when they compared themselves to the Inuit and therefore omitted the discussion of Inuit tools in their writings.[36] This particular omission seems to have only characterized the British literature, however. Nineteenth-century Danish writings on Greenland often followed the example set by Egede, of praising Inuit tools and hunting skills, although they had by this time dismissed Egede's historical justification for this advancement (that is, his theory of the Inuit's European ancestry).[37]

There are without doubt a significant number of eighteenth- and nineteenth-century European texts that judged Inuit hunting skills favorably and considered that Inuit technological skills set these people apart from other primitive cultures in European classifications of the world. If, however, we look closely at the Danish discussion of Inuit tools and consider it alongside the established narrative of Icelandic and Faroese technological stagnation, then we can read a single narrative in the descriptions of North Atlantic technology. The Danish geographer Hinrich Johannes Rink, who also served on the 1852 government commission in Greenland, wrote several books on Inuit culture, including a collection of Inuit folktales. His work was widely read and translated into English and German. Although Rink had considerable sympathy for the people whom he lived among for some twenty years, and admired Inuit tools and their skills, he placed these tools distinctly at an early stage of human development. Inuit culture, according to him, was not progressing. All Inuit tools had been invented long ago in the distant past, and the Inuit had not changed or improved them since that time. Only the Europeans had introduced mechanical developments and handicrafts into the country. "The art of catching seals," he wrote, "is still pursued in Greenland exactly in the same way as before Europeans had settled there, without the least change or improvement." Furthermore, in his view this stasis was intrinsic and fundamental to Greenlandic culture. The society was incapable of change unless it came from the outside: according to Rink, "there is some reason to believe that the abolition of the ancient manner of hunting seals would prove fatal to the welfare, if not to the existence, of the present race of inhabitants."[38]

Rink's analysis of Inuit cultural levels falls into the standard modes of nineteenth-century European romanticization of primitive people who live in timeless societies undisturbed by historical processes. Inuit culture lacked the internal dynamics that drove Western cultures toward higher levels of development; it only changed in response to the outside forces of European modernity. Everything that Rink admired about Inuit culture belonged to its history. Furthermore, the influence of Europeans in Greenland had caused the decay of Inuit skills in using these tools, as the traditions were being forgotten. As KGH director for two years himself, Rink had to be moderate in this position: he was not able to condemn every aspect of the Europeanization of Greenland. The eighteenth-century missionaries had of course brought the civilizing influence of Christianity. However, according to him, the main goal of the Danish administration in Greenland should be to protect and preserve the native culture against change and modernity, not to alter it. In another paper, published in 1862, Rink investigated "the reasons that Greenlanders and similar people living by hunting decline materially through contact with the Europeans." Here, he argued that the original laws of the Inuit were connected to religious belief and to the authority of the *angakok*, or shamans. By challenging the authority of these individuals, the missionaries had destroyed the internal structure of Inuit life, resulting in the gradual decay of traditional skills.

Rink's recommendations about Danish social policy toward the Inuit followed from his views of their cultural level. The duty of the Danish state, according to him, was to prevent further changes in Inuit culture by restoring Greenlanders to positions of authority in the local councils. These councils were in fact introduced in 1862 upon the recommendation of the commission on which Rink served. For the same reasons, Rink also supported continuation of the monopoly trade in Greenland because it controlled the import of European goods like rifles and bullets. If unchecked, the adoption of these technologies would result in further decay of the use of traditional tools.[39] Of course, the irony of Rink's views was that the social and economic policies that he promoted encouraged those very aspects of Greenlandic culture that he regarded as "intrinsic" to it—its inability to progress technologically.

Rink did not consider Iceland and the rest of the North Atlantic in his analysis of Inuit culture, as the cultural concept of "old Greenland" had lost most of its contemporary resonance by the time of his writing. However, the terms in which he discussed the Inuit relationship to tools, and the cultural meaning of this relationship, bear a striking similarity to the ways in which Richard Burton and other travelers discussed the Icelandic relationship with tools. According to these writers, neither society had developed or improved the tools they had inherited from their ancestors. Both Greenland and Iceland were places untouched by modernity—in both a negative and positive sense, having neither the conveniences of the traveler's home country nor its difficulties. Rink evaluated Greenland and the Greenlanders in much the same way that the Victorian literary scholar William Morris saw Iceland: the North Atlantic represented a refuge from the modern world, a retreat into the past, and it remained a refuge precisely because, unlike at home, nothing did change. Plows were not used two hundred years ago, and—despite all the efforts of the Icelandic modernization advocates—they were still not used after the Industrial Revolution and the steam locomotive had arrived in European countries. For Morris and other writers of his sensibilities, this was a virtue rather than a sign of deficient moral character, as it went hand in hand with the other primitive aspects of Icelandic culture that he admired—the absence of a class system and the freedom from the dehumanizing effects of industrialization.[40]

The shift from the eighteenth-century Greenland of Hans Egede to the nineteenth-century Greenland of Hinrich Rink can therefore be summed up very simply: when Greenland was considered part of Europe, it was possible for its culture to change and progress. Greenland could be restored, both materially and spiritually, to a prior state, and it was also capable of advancement. This narrative of North Atlantic decline and restoration parallels the narrative of the eighteenth-century environmental deterioration of Iceland and the idea of its restoration. By the nineteenth century, however, Greenland and its inhabitants had slipped away from the narrative of European history, and the society was no longer considered to be changing and developing, either materially or spiritually. This developmental stasis set both Iceland and Greenland apart from European societies, where progress, for better or for worse, was closely associated with mechanical innovations. Even though Inuit tools were frequently admired in European texts, few nineteenth-century writers expected European travelers in the Arctic to use them; Rink considered that it would be next to impossible for Europeans to do so. The differences in material culture sharply marked Greenland as a wilderness, and not a homeland, for nineteenth-century European explorers.

POLAR EXPLORERS AND THE ADOPTION OF INUIT TOOLS

This European story of Greenland was firmly situated by the twentieth century. When the Icelandic Canadian explorer Vilhjálmur Stefánsson wrote a history of European polar activities in 1921, he looked back on this nineteenth-century discussion of Greenland and the Arctic and criticized the Europeans for their reluctance to follow the Inuit example and settle in the far North. According to Vilhjálmur, during the nineteenth century, Europeans considered the Arctic climate to be terrible but thought that certain men had such special heroism that they could overcome it. Vilhjálmur thought this theory was utter nonsense: ordinary people could easily live in the Arctic, as long as they behaved as the Inuit did. He praised John Ross at the beginning of the nineteenth century for "borrowing some Eskimo ideas," such as sledges and dogs, but unfortunately he "used them with the ineptness of the novice." To Vilhjálmur it was "extraordinary that no explorer thought of going directly to the Eskimos and borrowing their techniques in toto; that instead of learning native methods they found it necessary to discover for themselves the principles of living and traveling which the Eskimo had discovered centuries before."[41] Vilhjálmur himself was a representative of a latter period in Arctic exploration, in which explorers turned more and more toward native models of exploring and were thus able to live in the Arctic. He positioned himself directly against the idea of nineteenth-century polar heroism, as it was expressed, for example, in the discussions of the search for John Franklin's lost 1845 expedition. He believed that no special courage was needed to live in the Arctic because it was in fact an ordinary place to live, if one adopted an appropriate lifestyle—hence his appellation "The Friendly Arctic," a striking contrast to the previous century's images of a desolate wilderness.[42]

Turn-of-the-century polar explorers did come to adopt Inuit techniques such as dogsleds and ice-fishing harpoons in the way that Vilhjálmur recommended. The Danish explorer Knud Rasmussen, for example, recognized the different cultures of living in polar territories, and he took pride in his mastery of Inuit techniques, which he attributed to his childhood in Greenland and Inuit ancestry.[43] In Rasmussen's view, Inuit and European technologies could be compared on an equal basis in polar travel, although exploration and technological progress—of which he was not at all in favor, for similar reasons as Rink—could only be carried out by Europeans. The American polar explorer Robert Peary—best known for successfully pushing his claim to have been the first man to have reached the North Pole—rhetorically managed his use of Inuit techniques in this endeavor by subordinating their role to that of "cogs in a machine."[44] For Peary, the entire expedition was a factory production, and the dogs, men, sleds, and boats were all "instruments" equally at his disposal. In his book claiming his discovery of the North Pole in 1909, he characterizes "man and the Eskimo dog" as the only two "machines" capable of Arctic travel and the "Eskimos" as "the most effective instruments for Arctic work," whom he "trains in my methods."[45] In this scenario, Peary is the master scientist-engineer who selects the most efficient "tools" for his work, wherever he might find them, but it is his identity as the designer and user of the tools—as a male American of European descent—that is central to polar existence. Within this framework he can easily say in another place in the book that "we speared the fish in the way that the natives taught us, using the regular native spear," without risking his status as heroic conqueror in any way.[46]

Although many twentieth-century Arctic explorers used Inuit tools, this did not fundamentally change their thinking about them or their evaluation of Inuit culture. Peary's language, although extremely explicit in the dynamic of power, is not different from that of nineteenth-century observers.

For them, Inuit tools did not qualify as a technology that enabled advancement and exploration. For Peary, the tools themselves might be useful but were subordinate to his system, which only he as a representative of Western ideology of conquest was able to design and master. Although Peary and his contemporaries valued Inuit tools in Arctic travel, they often still labeled them primitive and looked forward to the day when engine-driven sleds would replace dogsleds as a means of travel. Having finally mastered living in the Arctic environment, and living—or so they believed—on equal footing with the natives there, using their tools, twentieth-century Western explorers continued to look to their own societies, not the indigenous one, for improvements in material culture of Greenlandic life.

In the eighteenth century, the technology and material culture of Greenland showed European travelers how far civilization had declined there and what efforts had to be made to recover it. Through trading companies and missionary work, Europeans tried to draw this North Atlantic island back into the material and spiritual circumstances of the civilized world, by tying it to its medieval Scandinavian history. According to their own estimations, their recovery and improvement efforts were only partially successful. Survival on the northern edge of this world was considered precarious throughout the nineteenth century, and most visitors looked toward further technological improvements, developed in European homelands, to provide the solution to the difficulties of inhabiting the North. Greenland was imagined as a wilderness to be subdued by men and machines. Toward the end of the nineteenth century and the beginning of the twentieth, the Western polar explorers came to consider Inuit tools essential for traveling and living in the Arctic. Their use of these tools, however, did not entail a reevaluation of the culture that produced them. Even for Knud Rasmussen, who was part Inuit himself, the culture was not a dynamic one that produced innovations, and the Inuit knew no such concept as "exploration." For Rasmussen, as for William Morris, this was a positive aspect of North Atlantic life when it was compared to the problems created by European invasions and intrusions into other societies. The story that Europeans told about tools and civilization in the North Atlantic over two centuries of contact shows that this region had for them flexible qualities—it was part of home when this characterization served economic, political, and cultural interests; it was an exotic wilderness when these qualities served other intellectual and cultural needs. In both cases, much of what was said by Europeans about the Inuit and their ways of living was not about a living people but instead described an imaginary Inuit held in the minds of explorers.

NORTH ATLANTIC ISLANDS OF TECHNOLOGY IN A COLD WAR WORLD

The paternalistic Danish colonial policy in Greenland and the romantic images that Europeans had of both Greenland and Iceland came into increasing conflict with the realities of North Atlantic existence. In the first decades of the twentieth century, and with a faster pace following World War II, both Iceland and Greenland became technically modernized Western countries. This occurred especially as a result of the strategic location and role the North Atlantic islands played in cold war politics and with the establishment of the American military bases in both Iceland and Greenland.[47] The establishment of these bases had a dramatic effect on both societies in terms of their cultural and psychological distance from modernity, and the postwar years were times of rapid social change in the North Atlantic. The introduction of technologies such as the radio in Greenland before World War II "brought the world nearer to Greenland," as one historian puts it.[48]

Although substantial parts of the North Atlantic infrastructure, including the building of highways and airports, only came about with postwar foreign imports, the mechanization of the Icelandic fishing industry was already underway between 1900 and 1940. Iron-hulled steam trawlers replaced wooden fishing boats, and motors replaced sails and oars. Following the British and French examples, steam and eventually diesel engines were introduced. The landholding class in Iceland resisted technological modernization of the fishing trade, which they had for a long time held to be a less respectable occupation than farming.[49] Small-scale technological innovation and gradual change characterized the development of the Icelandic fishing fleet. Technological conservatives held a strong political advantage, as the Icelandic system of political representation favored the rural areas. Despite the powerful social forces that stood against them, in the end the small-scale Icelandic fishermen were able to implement these new technologies. The conflict illustrates, however, the ambivalent history of technological improvements in the North Atlantic. There were many voices—both foreigners and natives—who opposed the introduction of modernity through technology into this region. Tools, and their absence, were powerful symbols of social development for the North Atlantic islands.

Unlike many other parts of the world during the nineteenth century, Greenland was an arena where, at least at times, the natives had an opportunity to reverse the European gaze and look condescendingly at how inept the Europeans were at survival in their environment. European discomfort at perceiving themselves as the objects rather than the masters of this gaze was a sensation that had to be managed in one way or another. If, Francis Spufford argues, the British managed this by ignoring Inuit tools, other Europeans managed it by developing condescending and paternalistic attitudes and policies toward tools and the people who used them in the North Atlantic—for example, by allowing the Inuit to have "skill" but denying them "innovation," the creative impulse in design of which only Europeans were capable. Europeans' discomfort about travel in Greenland was a quintessentially North Atlantic experience that went hand in hand with the feelings of being lost and having wandered off the map of the unknown world.

The story of Greenland and its relationship to Europe is a complex one, where the pendulum swings back and forth—from being the last outpost of European Christendom, to a lost heathen wilderness, and then back again. Nor does the story end simply here with kayaks and spearfishing. Linguists and missionaries were the next to take up the European narrative of Greenland. Their tools of exploration were not dogs and sleds but tape recorders and pronunciation guides. Were these better guides in charting a course in the North Atlantic? Were linguists better able to escape the feeling of confusion in the region than explorers were? The discussion of language in the North Atlantic was more theoretical, more imaginary, and in some ways a less pragmatic exercise than the discussion of tools, but it was carried out in some of the same ways that physical exploration of the North Atlantic was.

Those Greenlanders, who are able to express their thoughts in speech and writing, speak and write their language just as the Europeans do.
—*C. W. Schultz-Lorentzen (1951)*

Not one day of my adult life has passed without amazement at how poorly the Danes and Greenlanders understand each other. It's worse for the Greenlanders, of course. It's unhealthy for the tightrope walker to be misunderstood by the person holding the line. And the Inuit's life in this century has been a tightrope dance on a rope fastened on one end to the world's least inhabitable land with the world's most severe and most changeable climate, and on the other end to the Danish state's administration.—*Peter Høeg (1992)*

4 | TRANSLATING AND CONVERTING

Language and Religion in Greenland

The inside of the grocery store in the village of Kulusuk in East Greenland looks like any other Danish grocery store. The jam is a well-known Danish brand (Den Gamle Fabrik), the yogurt also comes from Denmark, and the socks and underwear, like those everywhere else in the world, are made in Mexico and the Philippines. Most of the meat, rather strangely for a place that is still often referred to in tourist guides as a "hunting society," is deep-frozen and shipped in from Denmark. It all costs about the same as it would in Copenhagen—that is, expensive by American standards but not exorbitant, considering how far Kulusuk is from the manufacturing centers. Only in one aisle of the store do you realize that you are not, after all, in Copenhagen: the aisle where they sell the hunting rifles. The prices for these start around 5,000 Danish kronor (just over US $900). The bullets might be kept behind the counter, out of the reach of children and "drunken persons," to whom it is also forbidden, according to the posted sign, to sell alcohol. But where you might find the ammunition was not immediately apparent to me, as the shopkeeper—also in keeping with Copenhagen standards—conversed only taciturnity with the patrons.

Being able to buy a can of Coke in East Greenland is a bit strange, because globalization, which is usually either blamed or credited with bringing Coke from Atlanta, Georgia, to seemingly all other parts of the world, is a very recent phenomenon in Kulusuk. The first foreign travelers to meet the inhabitants of the Ammassalik district, of which Kulusuk—a village of about three hundred people—is a part, were the Danish captain Gustav Holm and his party in 1884.[1] Although a Danish trading and mission station was founded there ten years later, and another Danish expedition came in 1898, European interest in Greenland remained, as it had been since the seventeenth century, focused on the western coast of Greenland. Western Greenland is also where Nuuk, the capital, is today and where the Norse Greenlandic settlement was established by Erik the Red (Eiríkur Þorvaldsson) and his family when they came from Iceland. The historical memory of this Nordic past was so dominant in Europe that settlement and explorations focused on the western part of Greenland, even though the eastern part is actually closer to Europe (although more difficult to travel to because of the sea-ice conditions). As the European encounter with western Greenland predates the European encounter with eastern Greenland by about one thousand years, and the interior ice of Greenland was not crossed until 1888, visitors tend to refer to places like Kulusuk as "untouched"—although clearly this is not the case if you happen to be standing in the grocery store.

This chapter continues the story of Europe's encounter with Greenland and Greenlanders but from a different angle than discussions about tools and technology. Here we look at the classification and codification of the Greenlandic language, which was begun by missionaries living in western Greenland in the eighteenth century and was continued by professional linguists during the nineteenth and twentieth. For this later group, and for the debate that took place among them, eastern Greenland and its inhabitants were of central importance exactly for this untouched quality, because this region was believed to retain more original forms of language and folk culture than those found in the more heavily Danish-influenced areas. Debate centered on the history of the Greenlandic language and its inclusion in the family of Indo-European languages, and so the search for original forms—as elsewhere in European language debates—was key evidence. Thus, the European mental map of Greenland came to include its eastern as well as its western coast and attempted to unite Greenland's history with the European past. Greenland, its people, and their language were reshaped into European models of culture and understood as closer to the known world than they had been before the nineteenth-century linguists took notice of them.

In his 1904 *Phonetical Study of the Eskimo Language*, the Danish linguist William Thalbitzer—a major player in the Indo-European-Greenlandic debate—commented on the differences between a linguist's writings about language and those of amateurs interested in language, mostly, for example, observations by missionaries. Although Thalbitzer acknowledged the useful contributions made by missionaries during the early modern period to European knowledge of the Inuit languages, he held that these contributions were limited because missionaries did not use a consistent method of phonetic transcription, as Thalbitzer did. This meant that their descriptions of Inuit languages were colored by the native language of the individual making the transcription. Thalbitzer explained how this occurs:

> The authors have belonged to different nations, and each one has of course started out from his own language, and made his own native pronunciation and orthography the basis of his auricular impression and his manner of spelling this strange literatureless language. It is natural that each one as far as possible operates with the alphabetical characters of his own language, and only few of them seem to realize how purely accidental it is if these happen to correspond to the sounds of the new language, and how improbable it is that the sound systems of the two languages will in any way cover each other. . . . Therefore if we take the trouble to study the traveler's specimens of the language which he has heard, we must always take into account not only his nationality, but also his own and his interpreters' inaccuracies, misunderstandings, and inconsistencies.[2]

According to Thalbitzer, the observations of the scientist therefore distinguish themselves from missionary writings because scientific observations are not influenced by the personal characteristics, including country of origin, of the author. Missionary writings, on the other hand, take the writer's own characteristics—of language, nation, or religion—as the norm against which to measure all other peoples.

What Thalbitzer claimed about the early modern religiously motivated travelers in Greenland was also true for travelers in the North Atlantic in general, including those whom he would have classified as "scientific": their judgments about the people and nature they encountered were heavily influenced by their own origins. Their translations of language—as well as of nature and of technology—were marked by individual experiences and characteristics. In the case of travelers who were also Christian missionaries, primarily concerned with religious experience, this fact was particularly ironic. As Lamin Sanneh has pointed out, part of the ideology of Christianity is that it is an infinitely translatable faith: the Bible remains the same Divine Word no matter the language into which it is rendered. Thus, Biblical translation into vernaculars was a particularly important part of the missionary project all over the globe, as missionaries thought that the Christian faith would be most easily accepted when it was presented to potential converts in their native language.[3] Missionaries believed that they were presenting the Divine Word in the local idiom exactly as they themselves understood it and likewise believed—perhaps even more strongly than travelers who were less interested in religion—that they were recording the native language, songs, and stories exactly as they were understood by the natives. Of course, as numerous examples of mistranslations of religious and spiritual concepts have shown, translation was considerably more complex than missionaries generally assumed.[4] Recent convents were prone to assimilate Christian concepts into their own religious traditions rather than discarding them in favor of Christianity, as for instance when German missionaries among the Herero people in German Southwest Africa (now Namibia) discovered that converts thought of the Christian Jehovah as a "playmate" to the chief, who was also considered a god.[5] Despite such problems, however, the Christian belief in this ideology of translation remained firm.

Building the knowledge base of language to produce these translations was a long-term project. Among all the different kinds of European travelers, missionaries were generally the individuals who remained the longest in foreign places, and they made some of the most intense efforts to collect native languages and cultures—although some missionaries were also destroyers of the artifacts of non-Christian cultures, most infamously the Spanish missionaries in the Americas. Because of this assimilationist aspect of missionary work, Urs Bitterli, in his classification of different types of cultural encounters between 1492 and 1800, ranks the missionary-native encounter among the least violent types of encounters between cultures, although of course this is only true when considered in context. He also claims that from their intimate relationship with other cultures, which included learning the native language, dressing in native clothes, and living in native dwellings, early-modern missionaries became "the professional group which possessed the fullest information about the alien culture."[6] This analysis stands in sharp contrast with Thalbitzer's early twentieth-century perspective, which accords that honor to the scientist, as someone whose analysis of other cultures was made on the basis of objective standards and not colored by his own language or experiences at home.

For the missionary or Christian traveler, religion was a simple marker of distinction, at least when compared with other markers of difference. Unlike technology, it was usually a binary category: one was either a believer or an unbeliever. It did not, unlike nineteenth-century European racial distinctions, admit a graduated series of distinctions measured by shades of skin color or cranial size. Throughout the period under discussion here, this believer-nonbeliever delineation operated very simply in the North Atlantic, as exemplified in Margit Mogensen's analysis of the Northern Dwellers exhibition at the 1900 World's Fair in Paris. According to her, in the North Atlantic "the hierarchy of civilization was drawn very clearly: first came the old, cultivated Iceland with the church and altar, and one could understand the sad story of how these Northern-dwelling Christians had disappeared from Greenland, and therefore how we must strive to bring them to civilization from this wilderness."[7] In the simplest of presentations, one that could be understood at a glance by the observer in Paris, this was another declensionist narrative in the North Atlantic. In the tenth century, many of the Norse inhabitants of Greenland had been Christians who built and attended services at a church named after Þjóðhildur, the wife of Erik the Red. But now these settlements were part of the hunting grounds of the Inuit, among whom Christian missionaries still labored. As the church of Þjóðhildur (Þjóðhildar kirkja) had been abandoned, Christianity as a marker of civilization had also for a time disappeared from the extreme edge of the North Atlantic frontier, while Iceland and the rest of the North Atlantic remained in this respect part of the European world. It was therefore the duty of modern civilized Europeans to return the Greenlanders to the Christian domain.

Here, we examine the European story of religious life and the relationship between religion and language in the North Atlantic, concentrating particularly on the part of this region where Europeans judged spiritual life to be most endangered, Greenland. Many of the individuals who were concerned with material culture and technology in Greenland were also interested in its spiritual development. In this chapter, however, I focus on the missionaries' relationship to language and translation. In the earliest days of European recolonization of Greenland in the eighteenth century, the study of language was almost completely carried out in the context of missionary work, for which the main concern was Biblical translation. It was not until the final decades of the nineteenth century that the study of the Greenlandic language, linked to the other Inuit languages in North America, came under the domain of professional linguists, as Thalbitzer envisioned. What this meant, I argue, was actually not a break but continuity in terms of how Europeans perceived the Greenlandic language. While the missionaries understood language as a tool that would link the civilized and the uncivilized world by reforming this outmost post of civilization to match a European religious and moral code, the linguists recast a language that missionaries had found in practice to be profoundly different from their native Indo-European languages into the norms of Indo-European linguistics. The missionaries imagined a global civilization under one Christ, facilitated by the transparency of language. Nineteenth- and twentieth-century linguists erected huge language families of relations, showing how the languages spoken in Greenland and North America were linguistically related and even arguing that Greenland and the Euro-Asian continent were linguistically joined. What these processes meant for Greenland, and for the Greenlandic natives who spoke this language, was similar: in both in the missionary and the linguistic mind, Greenland and its people were reshaped into European or Western norms, and they moved increasingly closer to the centers of civilization, as judged from the European standpoint. Thus, this process paralleled those previously described in other parts of the North Atlantic—for example, the attempts to domesticate the Icelandic natural world— but proceeded by different actors and through different modes and measures.

For the study of Greenlandic itself, of course, the missionary approach and the linguistic approach were quite different. The missionaries generally regarded the language as difficult to master and often commented on translation problems. Like many other travelers to the North Atlantic, they emphasized the exoticism of the cultural encounter they were attempting to negotiate. Nineteenth- and twentieth-century linguists admitted that the language was not easy for speakers of European languages to learn, but from the beginning they understood it in relation to other languages spoken by the natives of North America. They used the grammatical features of the language, rather than a common faith, to join the land masses together. Thus, in a broader understanding of Greenland and its people, the missionaries and linguists performed similar work, despite Thalbitzer's 1904 denial of any connection between their viewpoints.

At the same time that missionaries and linguists were producing a body of texts attempting to codify and explain the rules of Greenlandic and its dialects, the Icelandic language and the saga literature were also becoming a major focus of interest for linguists. These were important not only for Icelandic and Iceland as a nation but also for the country's neighbors. One much-discussed topic in Scandinavia in the nineteenth century was how to spell Faroese and Norwegian words correctly and what different spellings of these words meant for the Faroese and Norwegian people (this is treated in depth in chapter 5). The missionary language work in eighteenth-century Greenland was not at this stage of debate, however. The study of Greenlandic began at a more basic level than the study of Faroese, Norwegian, or Icelandic. As there was no written literature in Greenlandic before the missionaries arrived, the words of the language first had to be simply collected. The intentions of these early writings were therefore rather functionalist in nature, as for example the dictionary of Greenlandic words and a Greenlandic grammar produced by Hans Egede's son Poul in 1750 and 1760.[8] Such basic texts were sufficient to meet missionaries' purposes: their aim in understanding the Inuit language was to facilitate biblical translations and Christianization. Gradually, however, scholars became interested in Greenlandic for its own sake, and, aided by the tools of nineteenth-century philology, began to produce more descriptive and complete grammars of this language.

GREENLANDIC AND THE INDO-EUROPEAN LANGUAGES

What were the issues with understanding, translation, and classification of Greenlandic? Greenlandic is not one of the Scandinavian or Germanic languages, nor is it now considered to be part of the Indo-European language family to which the Scandinavian and other Germanic languages belong. The language is usually divided into two main dialects, North and South Greenlandic, which can then be further divided into Polar Greenlandic, the Upernavik dialect, Bay Greenlandic (or West Greenlandic), Middle Greenlandic, South Greenlandic, and East Greenlandic. In relating these dialects to each other, Finn Gad compares the differences among them to the difference between Icelandic and Danish: from the same origin, and with many common words, but not necessarily mutually intelligible.[9] Most European writings on Greenlandic, especially in the eighteenth and nineteenth centuries, treated these dialects as a single language, which, from the point of view of grammatical descriptions, was appropriate. In the remainder of this chapter, therefore, I use the term "Greenlandic language" for the overall language in comparisons with "Indo-European" or "Germanic" languages.

One of the most basic differences between Greenlandic and the Germanic languages is in the way that words are formed. This fact accounts for what is perhaps the main reaction of a native English speaker when faced with a Greenlandic text for the first time: why do Greenlandic words have to be so long? Greenlandic words are long because Greenlandic is an agglutinative language, and four or five suffixes can be connected to a root word. The Germanic languages, including English, on the other hand, are classified by linguists as inflective languages—that is, words change their meanings by changing their endings, or inflections: *I jump, I jumped, he or she jumps*. The change of endings—*ed, s*, or no ending—to the root verb "jump" tells us that the verb is in the present or past tense, in the first or third person. In Greenlandic, words change their meanings by adding affixes onto a root word, and these affixes can also be used as independent words in their own right.[10] In his essay on the Greenlandic language, Christian Wilhelm Schultz-Lorentzen gives the example of the construction of the word *eqalugssuarniariartorqussaugaluagaugut*, meaning "we have received firm orders to go out and catch sharks," which is composed of the root word *eqalug* (fish) with nine suffixes added.[11] Furthermore, each affix in an agglutinating language only carries one meaning. In English and other inflectional languages, such as the example of the verb "jump" above, a single affix can carry several meanings. The final *s* in "he jumps" gives us three pieces of information about the verb—namely, that it is in the third person, the singular, and the present tense. In agglutinating languages this would have to be expressed by three separate affixes. Thus, inflectional languages can pack many meanings into one affix, but agglutinating ones do not.

Schultz-Lorentzen cites the example of *eqalugssuarniariartorqussau-galuagaugut* as an extreme case of Greenlandic agglutination. Not every Greenlandic word is that difficult. Still, judging from the perspective of a speaker of a Germanic language like English, Greenlandic seems undeniably convoluted. The modern reader will probably judge the first efforts of the eighteenth-century missionaries to find similarities between Greenlandic and Germanic words a rather quixotic enterprise, but these early attempts must be understood in the context of the same actors seeking to identify Scandinavian physiognomy in Inuit bodies.

Certainly the eighteenth-century European settlers in Greenland, including Hans Egede and his sons, did not primarily interest themselves with the Inuit language for its own sake. Rather, Egede, in keeping with his mission of finding descendants of the Norse settlers of Greenland, examined the language for Old Norse root words.[12] As these proved as scarce on the ground as the elusive Scandinavian settlers were, the missionaries' attention turned to the practical matter of learning the Greenlandic language as quickly as possible in order to facilitate the conversion of natives to the Christian flock. The texts produced by Poul Egede and Otto Fabricius can be best described as handbooks toward this end. In their treatment of Greenlandic, they always compare it to European languages, namely to Danish and Latin, in explaining the grammatical points. This was not because of any presumed natural connection between Greenlandic and European languages, however, but merely a means of relating unknown constructions to the languages they assumed their readers knew best. In this respect, Thalbitzer's criticism of the early missionary efforts had some basis; these texts did indeed have an orientation toward individuals from specific linguistic, as well as spiritual, backgrounds.

For the European understanding of Greenlandic, Samuel Kleinschmidt's pioneering work in the 1800s can be seen as a definitive break with the missionary tradition of considering the Greenlandic language only in relationship to European languages. Kleinschmidt was the son of a Moravian missionary, Johann Conrad Kleinschmidt, and grew up in Greenland until the age of eight, when he was sent to school in Germany. At age twenty-six, he was called by the Moravians to the mission at Lichtenau in Greenland, where he remained for the rest of his life, also working at the missions in Lichtenfels and Neu Herrnhut.[13] Kleinschmidt had a thorough working knowledge of Greenlandic; in his private writings he mixed Greenlandic words in with German text and also, especially later in life, with his writing in Danish.[14] In many respects, he felt himself to be Greenlandic and able to express a Greenlandic viewpoint, as he had lived the majority of his life in Greenland. This inclination reveals itself in his major linguistic work, the 1851 *Grammatik der grönländischen Sprache mit teilweisem Einschluß des Labradordialekts* (Grammar of the Greenlandic Language with an Inclusion of some Discussion of the Dialect of Labrador).

Here, Kleinschmidt laid particular emphasis on the fact that his was the first grammar of Greenlandic that sought to describe the language on its own terms, without comparing it to European languages.[15] In his description of Greenlandic, Kleinschmidt followed certain general principles of Indo-European linguistics, as the study was being formulated at that time in European universities in Berlin, Leipzig, Göttingen, Paris, and Oxford. Kleinschmidt's book was published in Berlin and, through Samuel's brother, Emmanuel, who was a Moravian pastor there, *Grammatik der grönländischen Sprache* came to the attention of the Orientalist Wilhelm Schott and Franz Bopp, one of the founders of comparative linguistics. Schott was extremely impressed by Kleinschmidt's linguistic work and wanted to have more information about the "Labrador dialect," about which Kleinschmidt had learned most of what he knew from his acquaintance with the Moravian missionary Ferdinand Kruth. Kruth had been sent to Labrador before he came to the mission at Lichtenau and was therefore able to the compare the Inuit languages spoken in both places based on his personal experience.[16] The Moravians' status as a transnational missionary society, therefore, from the beginning played an important role in facilitating comparisons between Greenlandic and other Inuit languages.[17] Because these missionaries were typically sent to new regions every ten years or so (although Kleinschmidt remained in Greenland until he left the order in 1859), and their vocation compelled them to have a good working knowledge of the native language, they were uniquely suited to make comparisons among the various Inuit or Native American languages. In this respect, they played the missionary role in cultural contacts as Urs Bitterli has described it quite well. Such transcontinental linguistic comparisons also helped strengthen the impression of Greenlandic as a language that could be described and understood by using the regular and systematic rules of language study—those which had been developed to understand the relationship among the Indo-European languages such as Sanskrit,

Greek, and Latin—rather than as an exotic and complex language impossible for outsiders to grasp. The language of the North Atlantic, along with its nature, could also be ordered and managed.

One of the principles of Indo-European linguistics that Kleinschmidt followed in his grammar was the stress on developing a systematic orthography for the language, for which Kleinschmidt adhered to Bopp's principle that each sound should be represented by a separate letter.[18] Kleinschmidt used an entirely Latin alphabet in his grammar, except for choosing the Greek *K* (Kappa) to represent the Greenlandic *kra* sound. Furthermore, Kleinschmidt paid attention to the historical development of the Greenlandic language and took the morpheme as the basic unit of language, as Bopp had. Like most Indo-European linguists of his time, he was not very concerned with dialectical variation or differences in pronunciation; rather, he tried to create a common spelling that could be understood by all the Inuit living in Greenland.[19] This aim went hand in hand with his religious work of biblical and psalm translation, as the production of texts that could be read by all Greenlandic Inuit was clearly the most practical and useful accomplishment of studying the language, as seen from the Moravian perspective. In this respect, Kleinschmidt's Greenlandic orthography—which became a point of dispute between him and several Danish colleagues in the 1860s and 1870s—was a major step in the direction of making the Greenlandic language appear familiar to students of European languages.

BUILDING THE LANGUAGE FAMILIES: ESKIMO-ALEUT AND INDO-EUROPEAN STUDIES

The generations of scholars following Samuel Kleinschmidt were in part defined by William Thalbitzer's attempt to establish a firm boundary between professional linguistic work and the language study that had preceded it. While acknowledging Kleinschmidt's contributions, along with those of Poul Egede and other missionaries, Thalbitzer made it clear that "modern and future philologists . . . will find other problems to solve and will require other means of solving them than those which were at Kleinschmidt's disposal."[20] In other words, he wanted to ensure that the study of Greenlandic would be in the future be the domain of professional philologists, not of missionaries. Ironically, however, several of the linguistic discussions in which Thalbitzer engaged during his career owed a great deal to missionary knowledge of languages and in fact can be best understood as a continuation of themes in Kleinschmidt's work.

One of the questions for Thalbitzer's generation of linguists was the possible connection between the "Eskimo languages" and the Aleutian languages, on one hand, and the Indo-European language family on the other. Kleinschmidt himself had never asserted these connections and, indeed, had never worked in Aleut or Indo-European linguistics in general. His dictionary and grammar, however, did lay the foundation for that of Thalbitzer and his students, linguists such as Louis L. Hammerich, Knut Bergsland, and Erik Holtved, Thalbitzer's successor to his chair of Eskimo Culture and Language at the University of Copenhagen. Thalbitzer and Hammerich in particular tried to make connections between Inuit languages—both the Greenlandic and North American languages— and the Indo-European language family. It was a very large step to find a connection between Greenlandic, indigenous North American languages, and Indo-European ones. The original Indo-European language, which is today believed to have been spoken by people in the fifth millennium BCE, originated perhaps around the Black Sea area. The Indo-European family includes most of the languages of Europe, like German, Spanish, Italian, and Greek, as well as those of Asia, including Sanskrit and Iranian. The original language of the fifth millennium, called Proto-Indo-European, was an inflected language, so at the most basic level of structure it was difficult to make a case connecting Greenlandic to it. Nevertheless, this was exactly the aim of Thalbitzer's circle of linguists, beginning with work in the first half of the twentieth century.

As Hammerich was able to admit, knowledge of Greenlandic and native North American languages sufficient to make his case for these relationships only came though the work of missionaries in these regions.[21] Kleinschmidt's 1851 grammar, supplemented by his information from his fellow Moravian, Kruth, supplied the first link in connecting North American Inuit and Greenlandic languages to each other. Kleinschmidt's contemporary and sometime collaborator, Hinrich Rink, suggested that the Inuit culture originated at a single point on the Arctic coast and then spread along it, although he did not precisely locate his proposed point of origin.[22] Although not a linguist himself, Rink referred to linguistic evidence as one of the points of his argument: the similarities of the verbal endings among the Inuit and Siberian languages. Further work, including that of the French linguist Victor Henry,[23] eventually led to establishing a relationship among

Inuit languages spoken in North America, the so-called Eskimo-Aleut language family, which bridged the North American and Asian continents via the Aleutian Islands.[24] This language family stretches along the northern and western coasts of Alaska, from Kodiak in the south to Point Barrow in the north; it then continues along the northern coast of Canada, along Cape Parry, Victoria Island, and Churchill, all the way to Labrador, from which point the language group is believed to have migrated to Greenland. The hypothesis was first formalized by Thalbitzer but was based on some unpublished ideas of the well-known Danish linguist Rasmus Rask. He held that the Inuit had originated in Asia and moved westward across the North American continent, with Greenland being the furthermost point of their settlement.[25] It was not until Knut Bergsland's work in the following generation, however, that it was proven that the Inuits had used the Aleutian Islands as a bridge between Asia and North America at the end of the ice age.[26] The research of both Rask and Bergsland echoed David Crantz's eighteenth-century contention about the Asian (Mongolian) origins of the natives of Greenland, although Crantz had based his ideas on the physical appearance of the Greenlanders alone.[27]

Following this work on the Eskimo-Aleut language family, a Dutch linguist, Christian Cornelius Uhlenbeck, attempted to build connections between language families and to claim a relationship between Eskimo-Aleut languages and the Indo-European language family.[28] Uhlenbeck drew upon the Rask-Thalbitzer hypothesis about the Asian origin and westward movement of the Inuit, but he himself was not a specialist in Eskimo-Aleut languages; his main work outside of studies in Indo-European languages was with the language of the Blackfoot of North America. Nevertheless, in a series of works from 1907 to 1941, he laid out an increasing number of sound correspondences between word pairs in Indo-European and Eskimo-Aleut in which the two words were also identical or related in meaning. For example, Uhlenbeck problematically asserted that *nutăq* (new) in Eskimo was related to the Latin word for "new" (*novus*) and the Indo-Germanic word *nu*.[29]

Thalbitzer took up Uhlenbeck's theory in his 1945 *Uhlenbeck's Eskimo-Indo-European Hypothesis: A Critical Revision*. Although he was skeptical of a certain number of Uhlenbeck's sound pairs, Thalbitzer concluded that there was still "a great deal left which will serve to support [the] argument."[30] Furthermore, he could not satisfactorily resolve the details of the phonetic changes (namely, concerning the laryngeal consonants in Indo-European and the uvular consonants in Eskimo-Aleut) that must have occurred if Eskimo-Aleut and Indo-European were related. Nevertheless, Thalbitzer still thought there were enough viable sound pairs that the theory could not be rejected. The question was, what did all this mean for the history of the relationship between the Eskimo-Aleut and the Indo-European peoples? When and where did the Eskimo-Aleut who were Indo-Europeans live? Uhlenbeck held that the original homeland must have been in Siberia about five thousand years ago, a contention that some archeological evidence supported.[31]

Thalbitzer was less willing to specify when and where he considered the homeland to have been, but he did lay out additional evidence for the Siberian theory. In a manuscript published at the height of his career, *Eskimo Religious Rituals and Beliefs*, he turned his attention to the religion and mythology of the Inuit. In this text, he discussed a book written by the Norwegian polar explorer Fridtjof Nansen, *The Life of the Eskimo*. There, Nansen had resurrected the idea—more popular in the eighteenth century—that pieces of the mythology of the Greenlandic Inuit had been borrowed from Icelandic settlers in Greenland.[32] The evidence Nansen was able to muster for the theory was rather amorphous— a series of stories in the Inuit and Icelandic corpus with similar elements, and the tradition of naming a newborn child after a recently deceased family member, for example. In his comment on Nansen's work, however, Thalbitzer did not entirely dismiss the idea of Nordic-Inuit connections, but he did point out that Nansen's route of transmission was likely wrong: "Nansen's conception is not without interest . . . but a probability of a direct connection between Icelandic and Greenlandic is very weak, if not entirely absent. . . . The route of transmission of this mythology is certainly not from Iceland and Norway to Greenland, but rather through Siberia, across the Bering Strait, where the transmission of the Greenlandic language carried it still further east."[33] Rather than a line of direct Nordic descendant, Thalbitzer argued that the customs came to Greenland the long way around. He based his arguments on the shamanistic traditions in Greenland compared to those in pre-Christian Scandinavia and Siberia.

When we compare this argument with Thalbitzer's critique of missionaries before and after this writing, an interesting theme emerges. Thalbitzer was suggesting that the spiritual world of the Inuit, Europeans, and Asians was already unified, even before the missionaries appeared on the scene in Greenland. The global unity of belief sought by the Christians was therefore nothing new; only the beliefs themselves were different. Although the missionaries perceived Greenlandic beliefs and customs as "exotic" and "foreign," in fact they might have been similar to those in pre-Christian Europe. Since eighteenth-century European thought often associated the exotic with Europe's own past, this would not actually have been a novel line of thought for the missionaries.[34] What is worthy of notice is the parallel that Thalbitzer draws between language and religion and the way in which he sees both as connecting points between Greenland and Europe, passing through Asia and North America.

Thalbitzer's younger colleague and student, Louis Hammerich, confined his work more narrowly to linguistic material and did not address the possible connections of belief. Hammerich argued for the relationship between Eskimo-Aleut and Indo-European based on what he called "irrational correspondences" between the languages families; that is, similarities that were too significant to be coincidences and could be explained in no other way except by a familial relationship between the languages. Among these similarities is the fact that both language groups use the same letter to represent both the plural of nouns and the second-person singular in verbs (this letter is *t* in Eskimo-Aleut and *s* in Indo-European). Secondly, neither language family has an essive case; that is, a case used to demonstrate being or existence (a case that exists in other language families, for example, the Finno-Ugric languages). Hammerich argued that the Indo-European system of nominative, accusative, dative, and genitive cases had developed from an older system of super- and subordination (that is, adding affixes), which had been retained in the Eskimo-Aleut languages. This theory would furthermore explain the appearance of a so-called thematic vowel—a sound that does not have meaning attached to it—in the verbs and nouns of Indo-European languages. This thematic vowel was a relic of the older case system of super- and subordination that no longer served its original purpose. Hammerich postulated that both language families, Indo-European and Eskimo-Aleut, originally had this case system and therefore neither needed the essive case, since the state of being would be encompassed by the functions of super- and subordination.[35]

Another, more general point that Thalbitzer and his students took up was to argue against the characterization of the Inuit languages as primitive. Here, too, they followed in the footsteps of Kleinschmidt, who saw Greenlandic as equally sophisticated as European languages. Once the grammatical structure of the Greenlandic and the other Inuit languages had been understood and described, as was the case by the end of the nineteenth century, it was difficult not to appreciate their complexity. Both Thalbitzer and Hammerich argued that it was merely certain superficial characteristics of the Inuit languages that had caused eighteenth-century writers to think of them as primitive—for example, that Greenlandic does not have any words for numbers greater than twenty.[36] However, such words were not needed in the Greenlandic environment, as the word for "many" would suffice to describe any village or herd of caribou larger than twenty.[37] Against this paucity of numerical expressions, Thalbitzer and Hammerich noted the capacity of Greenlandic to express abstract ideas. This was accomplished mainly through the feature of the language that most obviously differentiated it from European and Indo-European languages, namely the use of affixes. Through the addition or alternation of affixes to produce different nuances or shades of meaning, Inuit storytellers were able to alter the folktales they performed for the tape recorders of linguists and anthropologists. Stories that were told to audiences of native speakers became more intricate and detailed through the use of affixes than those recited for European or American scholars.

Commenting on the high degree of abstraction possible in Inuit languages, Hammerich opined half-jokingly that "we might surmise that it would be rather easy to translate a philosophy of existence like that of Heidegger into Eskimo."[38] These twentieth-century linguists also agreed that the missionaries had been mainly responsible for the characterization of Inuit languages as primitive. Because so many other aspects of Inuit life appeared primitive to the missionaries—especially their religious life and material culture—it seemed natural to assume that their language was also underdeveloped, particularly when one could point to such obvious examples as a lack of words for numbers and the fact that they read the time on European watches by describing the spatial arrangement of the clock hands. By pointing out the sophistication of Greenlandic and other Inuit languages, Thalbitzer and Hammerich also thus set themselves professionally apart from the missionaries, as they considered that it was only through their linguistic training that they were able to recognize how Inuit affixes functioned. This sophistication, however, was in fact one that Kleinschmidt had already recognized in his 1851 grammar.

In 1951, the centennial of the publication of *Grammatik der grönländischen Sprache*, Hammerich laid out the fullest argument he ever made for the relationship between Inuit and Indo-European languages.[39] Aside from the two reasons already mentioned above, Hammerich listed a number of sound correspondences between Inuit and Greek, Latin, Sanskrit, and the Old Germanic languages—that is, words or roots of words that sound the same and also have similar meanings. Hammerich estimated that there were about sixty such correspondences in all, which he held was an "amazing similarity."[40] However, even this most complete mustering of the available evidence was insufficient to make a persuasive case; Indo-European linguists generally do not base cases for language relatedness on sound correspondences alone, which are regarded as too subject to change to be really reliable evidence. Morphology, or analysis of word structures, is thought to be a far better indication of language relations than phonology. Ultimately, the theory, although never explicitly disproved, never gathered enough support to become established in the literature either. Knut Bergsland continued to work on the Eskimo-Aleut languages, while Hammerich shifted his professional interests to Alaska and northern Canada.[41] The broad scope of the theory, which in effect attempted to link many of the peoples who lived north of about fifty degrees latitude, from Siberia to Greenland, could not avoid drawing skeptical reactions among the linguists.

Despite the lack of a conclusive theory linking Inuit and Indo-European languages, the Eskimo-Aleut family is well-established in the literature, and the general result of the work of Thalbitzer's group of linguists was to establish closer connections between Greenlandic, the languages of North American Inuit peoples, and the Aleutian and Siberian languages. This result can be best interpreted as a continuous line of development from the earliest studies of Greenlandic by eighteenth-century missionaries up through the development of the professional discipline of linguistics in the nineteenth and twentieth centuries. The missionaries and the linguists both brought Greenland—its language and also its people—into closer connection with the European and American continents. While the missionaries sought to transform this frontier of civilization into a global civilization, the linguists reinterpreted a people and their language into the norms of European linguistics. What this meant for Greenland, and for its people, was similar: they were reshaped into European and Western norms and understood as closer to the known world than they had been in the past. The story of their language therefore parallels the story of North Atlantic nature and North Atlantic technology: the exotic was made familiar.

This is not to argue, however, that there was no difference between the missionaries' and the linguists' understanding of Greenland and no changes in the European perception of Greenland between the eighteenth and the twentieth centuries. In the late nineteenth century, the previously unknown region of East Greenland became part of the European picture of the country. For linguists of Thalbitzer's and subsequent generations, East Greenlandic was significant because of its isolation and lack of contact with Danish and other European languages. Thalbitzer and Hammerich made their arguments about the connection between Indo-European and Eskimo-Aleut languages by citing examples from East Greenlandic as well as West Greenlandic. In the east was where original word forms could be discovered that showed the primary linguistic relationships, not in later borrowings, which could be misleading. Eastern Greenland also occupied a similar role in the studies of folklorists and anthropologists—as a source of "pure" culture.

For missionaries, the contact with East Greenland was naturally also of interest, as here was another opportunity to bring souls to the Christian flock. However, they could not regard it as the chief location of their interest in Greenland; it had fewer inhabitants than western Greenland in a land where population density was low to begin with. Furthermore, the people of East Greenland had no history of contact with Christianity, and there had never been any European settlements there. One could only assume that conversion would proceed even more slowly than it did in the west. Eastern Greenland therefore appeared marginal to the spiritual story of the country, whereas it occupied a central role in the linguistic and cultural one in the late nineteenth century.

In the story of their language classification, the native speakers of the Greenlandic were mostly passive figures. Although missionaries, linguists, anthropologists, and folklorists clearly worked closely with native informants, in both the scientific and religious accounts of these endeavors the natives only functioned as helpers toward a larger goal and were only understood that way. This story thus differs from the one about Greenlandic tools and technology, in which the Inuit were at many points regarded as the experts with knowledge that European and American explorers had to learn. While this passive role into which the Greenlanders were cast by linguists and anthropologists is unfortunate from a modern perspective, it is hardly unusual in the history of such encounters in the colonial context. We turn now to another story of language change, this time in the Faroe Islands. But the main actors in that story, the Faroese, were able to shape the codification of their language to a much larger degree than the Greenlandic Inuit were. The reasons for this difference are quite obvious: the Faroe Islanders spoke (although did not write) a language whose Indo-European descent and relationship to Icelandic, Danish, and German were never in question. Only the details of this relationship, not its broad outlines, had to be negotiated. In the end, it took until the middle of the twentieth century before Europeans allowed Greenlanders even a claim to the cultural inheritance that the Faroese (and Icelanders and Norwegians) already possessed in the Middle Ages.

Gudfinna: We need only think of the sagas. Where have we men now like
Skarphjedinn and Grettir Asmundsson? There are none such
in these days. . . .

Arnes: He must have been a great man, but that brings to my mind
what the leper said the other day, when the talk turned to the
old sagas.

Halla: And what did he say?

Arnes: Distance makes the mountains blue and mortals great.

—*Jóhann Sigurjónsson (1916)*

5 | READING BACKWARD

Language and the Sagas in the Faroe Islands

L anding in the Faroe Islands is not very comfortable for people prone
to airsickness. Of the eighteen islands that make up the Faroes,
only one of them, the westernmost of the larger islands, Vágar, has
enough flat ground to build runways. The airport at Vágar was built by the
British during their occupation of the Faroes during World War II, since
all of the other islands were judged too mountainous for the construction
project. Even at Vágar, the descent is like being dropped out of the sky
between cliffs. The sensation is somewhat similar to a helicopter landing,
climbing down levels of the atmosphere stage by stage, especially at night
when it is windy. Although the pilots are skilled and the safety record at
the airport is in general good, accidents do occur, as in August 1996, when

the Danish chief of defense, Jørgen Hans Garde, his wife, and seven others were killed when their plane slammed into one of the cliffs near the Vágar airport.

Since Vágar was chosen for the international airport because of its geographical suitability and not for social reasons, like proximity to a large city, most travelers arrive and get in a bus immediately at the airport for an hour's drive to Tórshavn, the capital of the Faroes. Tórshavn, which is the smallest capital city in the world, is located on the neighboring island of Streymoy.[1] Until Vágatunnilin, the underwater tunnel between Leynar and Fútaklett, was completed in 2002, travelers had to get off the bus, board a ferry, and then get on another bus on the other side in order to get to the capital (map 4).

This slight inconvenience for the traveler at the end of the journey is actually an inconvenience that has been imposed by the modern technology of travel. For most of the history of the Faroes, travelers landed exactly where they usually wanted to be: at the port at Tórshavn, getting off a boat from Denmark or from the British Isles. Even if their real interest was in bird-watching or other nature-oriented travel, Tórshavn was still, like Reykjavík in Iceland, the first logical stop to equip themselves. Ferry lines still run, but—unless you want to take a car to the islands—most people now arrive in the Faroes by air. The result is that Denmark is no longer the dominant intermediary, the necessary passage point to the Faroes. Rather, the Faroe Islands are now much more connected to Scandinavia, and even to Europe as a whole, by air. They are not yet really connected to the North American continent in the way that Iceland is, but that time may be coming.

This development is a modern one. Much of Faroese history, from the thirteenth century on, can be understood in terms of its relationship with Denmark and a relationship with Europe that was largely mediated through Danish interpretations of the Faroes. The story of Faroese language politics is the story of how some Faroese intellectuals at the end of the nineteenth century tried to break this tradition but, in their efforts to do so, ended up mediating Faroese identity through its North Atlantic neighbor, Iceland. Although this might seem in retrospect like a strange decision in the atmosphere of nineteenth-century European nationalism, for one people to attempt to establish their own identity by arguing how similar their language was to that of others, by the late nineteenth century, the cultural status of Iceland within the Danish kingdom was such that this approach seemed a reasonable strategy to a group of Faroese intellectuals. Therefore,

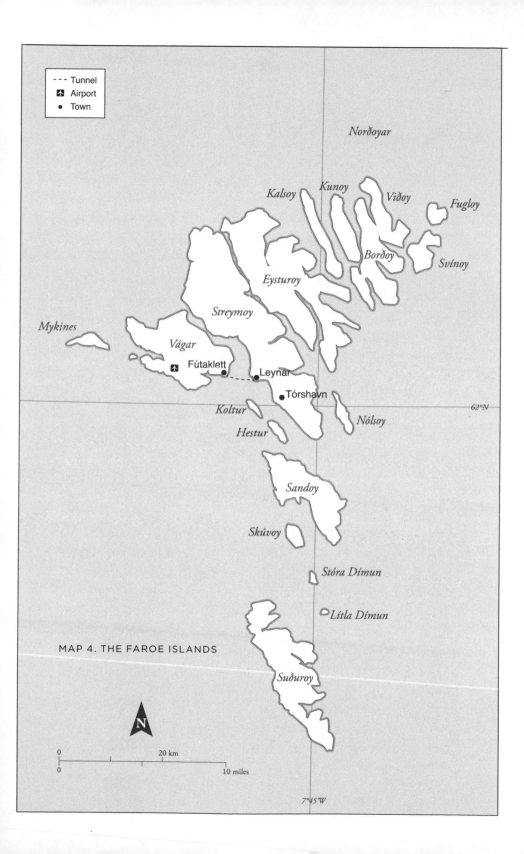

Kalsoy

Kunoy

Viðoy

Fugloy

Borðoy

Svínoy

Eysturoy

Streymoy

Mykines

Vágar

Fútaklett ✈

Leynar

Tórshavn

Koltur

62°N

Hestur

Nólsoy

Sandoy

Skúvoy

Stóra Dímun

Litla Dímun

MAP 4. THE FAROE ISLANDS

Suðuroy

N

--- Tunnel
✈ Airport
● Town

0   20 km
0   10 miles

7°45′W

in order to understand the Faroese language debates, it is important to spend some time contextualizing the position of Iceland and Icelandic language and literature within the European cultural milieu in the nineteenth century. Although there are some technical details of Faroese alphabets in this story, the key point is that the proponents of the two main spelling proposals used different logics to promote different ideas of Faroese identity. The choice was between two versions of being Faroese: either Faroese within the North Atlantic, or Faroese with a Danish heritage.

LITERARY HERITAGE IN THE NORTH ATLANTIC

In a book with an unexpected coupling of two different parts of the world—*Egypt and Iceland in the Year 1874*—the American scholar and literary figure Bayard Taylor described riding on horseback from Reykjavík toward Mount Hekla accompanied by Geir, a seventeen-year-old Icelandic boy. Although they spoke in English, occasionally Geir hesitated over an English word, and so he asked Taylor what the word was in Latin. When the conversation turned to literature, Geir asked Taylor's opinion of Lord Byron and Shakespeare, whom he had recently read. The young Icelander was also enthusiastic about the German Romantics, especially Schiller, and then switched from speaking English to German in order to discuss them in greater depth. Taylor was deeply impressed by this linguistic and scholarly virtuosity, all the more so because Geir had never visited an English- or German-speaking country, in fact, had never left Iceland.[2]

Despite the visitor's amazement, the quality of this exchange was not unusual, nor was Taylor's reaction to it out of the ordinary. Since the visit of Joseph Banks in the late eighteenth century, foreign travelers had been regularly astonished by the linguistic abilities of Icelanders. When eighteenth- and nineteenth-century travelers presented themselves to local Icelandic officials upon their arrival on the island, they were frequently greeted in their native languages—English, Danish, German, or French. Other Icelanders they encountered, especially the local priests, spoke to them in Latin, which was often more embarrassing than reassuring to the struggling traveler, and evoked self-critical appraisals of the travelers' own Latin proficiency.[3] To communicate with the farmers they lodged with throughout the country, the visitors were at last forced to employ the services of a bilingual interpreter. Despite living in turf houses (often described as "earthen huts") with dirt floors, these farmers were generally literate and able to tell the travelers stories from the early settlement period of Icelandic history, that is, the stories of the medieval Icelandic sagas, which had attracted so many visitors to Iceland in the first place, especially during the latter half of the nineteenth century.

In explaining this experience, which travelers found to be quite different from what they had encountered in other foreign travels and among their own farmers at home, the visitors often referred to the long literary tradition in Iceland, dating back to the writing of the medieval sagas in the thirteenth century. Icelandic saga literature is a composite tradition of many different genres. Some of the stories are legendary and fantastic in nature and feature warriors with superhuman strength, battles with giants, and journeys to the Far East, India, and even to imaginary lands. The largest number of sagas, however, fall into a genre known as the family saga, which deals in a mostly straightforward and realistic manner with stories of the early settlement of Iceland in the ninth and tenth centuries. Feud is the main subject of these sagas—disputes of honor between families. They recount stories, often over multiple generations, of families falling out with each other over stolen property, marriage arrangements, or insults to one member. Typically, the dispute begins with a relatively small incident—for example, the unauthorized riding of a favorite horse in *Hrafnkels Saga*—and escalates to involve more and more participants on each side, with the stakes increasing with every exchange of blows. Ultimately, mediators and men with legal knowledge are brought in to resolve the conflict, which could have brought death even to distant cousins of the original disputants by the time it had run its course.

These stories, which are supposed to have been based on even older oral traditions from the settlement period,[4] had been rediscovered by Europeans, mostly by scholars in Sweden, Great Britain, and Denmark, beginning in the sixteenth and seventeenth centuries. These scholars claimed that the sagas were recited aloud or read at isolated farmsteads during the long Icelandic winter nights, thus keeping the traditions of literary and historical knowledge alive among the ordinary folk of Iceland. Nineteenth-century travelers concluded that the farmers they met were the direct descendants of these medieval bards. The history of the North Atlantic, preserved in its landscape and material culture, was also to be found in these stories.

Early modern historians used the Icelandic sagas as part of their documentation of a unified northern people, the "Goths," whose existence was supported by classical scholars such as Jordanes and Tacitus. Since the sagas, while written in Iceland, take place not only in Iceland but also in Norway, Sweden, and Denmark, historians of this school used them as evidence of linguistic and cultural unity between Iceland and mainland Scandinavia. European Gothicism advanced a twofold image of these people: on one hand, they were considered a people of great primitive genius arising from the pure environment of the North; but on the other, they were also the barbarians who destroyed the remnants of the decaying classical world.[5] This understanding divided the world symbolically between a northern freedom and purity and a southern tyranny and corruption, a myth repeated later by Montesquieu in his *L'esprit des lois* in 1748. Some scholars went so far as to claim that Scandinavia, the "womb of nations" according to Jordanes, was the original birthplace of classical learning. The exemplar of this school of scholarship was the Swedish scholar Olaus Rudbeck, who published his four-volume *Atland eller Manheim* between 1679 and 1702, in which he exhaustively proved that all the classical myths had Scandinavian antecedents. The myth of a Nordic past in seventeenth-century Sweden also took on contemporaneous political significance when Sweden entered the Thirty Years War, fighting battles in the Holy Roman Empire under Gustavus II Adolphus, nicknamed "The Lion of the North," in 1630. The seventeenth-century Swedes were retracing the steps of their Gothic ancestors.

In seventeenth-century Denmark and England, saga scholarship proceeded along more sober and philological lines, with the work of Thomas Bartholin, Ole Worm, and Árni Magnússon in Denmark and Henry Spelman and William Temple in England. Their focus was on collection, codification, and translation of the sagas, with relatively little emphasis on historical interpretation. Still, romantic enthusiasm for Viking heroism was not absent from this work. For example, it was a mistranslation of skaldic verses by Worm and his associates that led to the popular but inaccurate image of bloodthirsty Vikings drinking mead from the skulls of their defeated enemies.[6] The European enthusiasm for Icelandic literature continued throughout the eighteenth century, with Bishop Percy's translation of *Five Pieces of Runic Poetry* (1763) in England, Paul-Henri Mallet's *Edda, ou monuments de la mythologie et de la poésie des ancien Scandinaves*

(Edda, or Monuments of Ancient Scandinavian Mythology and Poetry; 1781) in France, the Ossianic poems fabricated by James Macpherson in Scotland in the 1760s, and the German poets Friedrich Gottlieb Klopstock and Gotthold Ephraim Lessing, who used themes from Norse mythology and modeled their works along Gothic lines. In eighteenth-century Denmark, Adam Oehlenschläger and N. F. S. Grundtvig, a theologian and founder of the Danish folk high school movement, also drew upon Norse mythology as catalysts for their poems. The Scandinavian example also inspired the Swiss scholar Johann Jakob Bodmer to codify Middle High German heroic literature. Indeed, the German literary corpus and the Scandinavian shared large numbers of common elements and themes. Low and High German legends were the original sources for the story of Sigurd the Dragon Slayer, whose story became one of the most popular in both German and Scandinavian literature. The myth forms the core of the Middle High German poem *Nibelungenlied* from the twelfth century, the Old Norse *Völsunga Saga* in the thirteenth, and the nineteenth-century Ring Cycle operas of Richard Wagner. One of the most important figures of eighteenth-century European intellectual life, Johann Gottfried Herder, translated Old Norse verse himself. He also published a treatise in 1796 advising German poets to make use of themes from Norse mythology in their poetry, rather than looking to Greek, because he believed that Norse mythology was closer to German language and culture and that modern German literature could be revitalized by returning to these roots. Many of his fellow poets were in fact already taking this advice.

When nineteenth-century European travelers arrived in Iceland, therefore, they were well prepared by their reading to discover gravestones engraved with runes, Viking ship burials, and evidence of sacrifices to Óðinn. Somehow, although none of these has ever been found in Iceland, many of the travelers, like Taylor, still managed not to be disappointed by the experience, as they were well able to imagine for themselves a past they could not see.[7] Indeed, in the nineteenth century the imagery surrounding Iceland as a mysterious place of origins was even extended into more popular literary works such as Jules Verne's *Voyage au centre de la terre* (*Journey to the Center of the Earth*; 1864) and Pierre Loti's (Louis Marie Julien Viaud) *Pêcheur d'Islande* (*Iceland Fisherman*; 1886). In Verne's novel, the narrator, aided by the discovery of a sixteenth-century Icelandic manuscript written in code, embarks on a journey to the center of the earth though the Snæfellsnes glacier. Traveling from Hamburg to Copenhagen, from Copenhagen to Reykjavík, and from Reykjavík to the glacier into the earth, he metaphorically travels back in time, seeing on the way both the primitive peoples of Europe and the origins of the earth. The leader of the expedition, the uncle of the narrator, is a professor of geology, and the novel is interspersed with geological passages as well as descriptions of Iceland borrowed from travel books.[8] In Loti's *Iceland Fisherman*, the sea and the fog surrounding Iceland give the narrative its sense of mystery. The landscape of Iceland, seen as the fishing boats approach it, is "chimerical" and "illusory," qualities mirrored in character of the Icelandic hero Yann and his mercurial treatment of the devoted Gaud.[9]

Throughout the nineteenth century, saga literature remained the primary focus for well-known visitors to Iceland such as the German legal scholar Konrad von Maurer in 1858, the Victorian socialist William Morris in the 1870s, and even W. H. Auden, who came to Iceland in 1937.[10] According to these scholars, it was the very remoteness of Iceland in the North Atlantic that had preserved the "native genius" of the Icelanders as a literary people and their heritage of the sagas (although the manuscripts themselves had resided in Copenhagen since the early eighteenth century),[11] and that left the language in such an unaltered state that the farmers who hosted the travelers could, and did, read the medieval sagas for pleasure.

It was, however, not only romantic travelers who idealized the Icelanders and their literary abilities; modern language scholars have also singled out Iceland for its remarkable language history. For example, Lars S. Vikør writes that "Iceland is practically the only example in Europe (and possibly in the world) of a linguistically homogeneous nation-state. One hundred per cent of the Icelanders speak Icelandic as their first language and use it as a dominant language in all spheres of life, while it is not spoken anywhere outside Iceland. The language is even without dialectal variation. . . . Thus language is one of the prime ingredients of Icelandic nationhood, besides the old literature and culture, and the geographical isolation of the island."[12] This characterization of Icelandic relies on a number of motifs created by visitors to the North Atlantic since the eighteenth century. "Geographical isolation," "homogeneity," and "the old literature and culture" have been for hundreds of years the lens through which foreigners saw the country. During the nineteenth century, these concepts were not only used descriptively but also carried considerable weight in discussions of language politics in Scandinavia, not only in Iceland, but also in the surrounding and adjacent areas, such as the Faroe Islands, Norway, Finland, and even Schleswig and Holstein, the southern end of the Danish state. Scholars who discussed the "isolation" of Icelandic in nineteenth-century language debates in Scandinavia often had opinions about how words should be spelled or how cases should be declined, even when the language under discussion was not even Icelandic. The "purity" and unchangingness of Icelandic as a Scandinavian *Ursprache* was often held up by participants in several Scandinavian countries as an ideal to which they should aspire in their reforms. Modeling their reforms, they argued, on Icelandic norms of spelling or grammar lent their own language—for example, Norwegian or Faroese—some of the prestige of Icelandic. With this prestige came a cultural capital that could be deployed in arguments for political representation and independence in nationalist struggles.

Opponents of the "Icelandisation" process, on the other hand, resisted looking to another language as a model for their own and thereby implicitly accepting that Icelandic was superior to their own language, which had its own cultural tradition. Furthermore, they objected that this narrative about Icelandic portrays Iceland as a timeless society that does not develop. Icelandic may have had the prestigious cultural heritage of the sagas, but it was a heritage that was dead, since no one composed sagas or poetry in the medieval style anymore. Like the Latin reportedly spoken in nineteenth-century Iceland, it was impressive from a scholarly point of view, but it excluded the Icelanders from entering the modern age and left them permanently at an earlier stage of historical development. In his study of African language politics, Derek Peterson has described the implications of British and German orthographic codification of the African languages, arguing that this standardization "locked [the Africans] into the pattern of tradition," after which the African languages lost the flexibility and versatility that Swahili speakers had in the nineteenth century and Gikuyu speakers struggled to preserve in the first decades of the twentieth.[13] Although the degree and type of power and influence that European visitors had over the Icelanders is very different than the situation in colonial Africa, a similar process took place in the North Atlantic, albeit with the full agency of the Icelanders in establishing this standardization of their language and, in so doing, the narrative about its timelessness and purity.

One of these language conflicts in which Icelandic and its status played a role took place in the Faroe Islands in the nineteenth century. This struggle illustrates how the Faroe Islanders, through their debate on language reform, engaged with the questions of modernity, tradition, and timelessness. By choosing sides in the debate between two different orthographies for Faroese, they tied themselves to different visions of the history of their people and country. The historical narrative of their country was a key factor in debates over political representation within the Danish kingdom, as it was also for the Icelanders and Schleswig-Holsteiners. Writing their language, putting the words on paper, shaped the Faroese community, not by demarcating the difference between Faroese and non-Faroese, but by determining who the Faroese were among the Scandinavian peoples. Writing their language told them their history and their position within the North Atlantic. The two different Faroese spelling systems introduced in the nineteenth century juxtaposed two visions of Faroese history and identity. One understood the Faroese people as part of a common, Pan-Scandinavian tradition shared by other North Atlantic countries, particularly Iceland. The other placed emphasis on the uniquely Faroese experience of history and a cultural heritage, represented by the medieval ballads and ring dances, which were not part of the Icelandic tradition. Implicit in the debate over orthography, although rarely overtly expressed, was a careful weighing of the political advantages and disadvantages of both schemes. What was gained and what was lost for Faroese identity, and thus for Faroese autonomy and representation within the Danish kingdom, by following an Icelandic language model? Did Icelandic offer the Faroese the best weapon to contest the hegemony of the Danish language? Or, as some argued, did it also threaten Faroese identity just as much as Danish did?

Unlike the situation in many European countries, the Faroe Islanders, as subjects of the Danish composite monarchy, were situated among multiple centers and multiple language standards, of which the Icelandic model was one. These different norms carried with them specific cultural and political meanings that language scholars, reformers, and politicians were obliged to take into consideration as they sought to establish new standards for various Scandinavian languages in the nineteenth century. As the example of the Faroe Islands shows, these various norms manifested themselves in the use of different letters or different spellings but were conceptually much more significant, carrying with them political implications for the position of the Faroes within the Scandinavian region. Choosing orthographic representations of sounds was an expressive political statement about a vision for the future of this island nation in the tumultuous environment of nineteenth-century Scandinavian language politics.

NATIONALISM AND REGIONALISM IN NINETEENTH-CENTURY SCANDINAVIAN LANGUAGE POLITICS

As the Danish-Norwegian state shrank during the nineteenth century, expressions of regional and national identity became more pronounced in some quarters. The need to defend the national identity against perceived threats emerged, particularly in border areas such as Schleswig and Holstein, two provinces that were majority German-speaking, although with a minority Danish-speaking population in Schleswig. These two provinces experienced three years of civil war after the end of Danish absolute monarchy in 1848 over the question of whether the duchies properly belonged to the German or the Danish nation. At the end of the war, they remained in Danish hands and were subjected to a strong "Danification" policy until their loss fifteen years later to the combined forces of Prussia and Austria.[14]

Language politics also played a major role in Norway after its separation from Denmark and incorporation into the Swedish state in 1814 with the Treaty of Kiel. After centuries of union, the official language of Norway was Danish, although with considerable regional differences in pronunciation. During the 1830s, Norwegian nationalists such as Henrik Wergeland and Ivar Aasen deliberately sought to construct a Norwegian language that was perceived as "not Danish." For this new standard, Aasen relied heavily on the dialects of western Norway, which were remote from the capital and had not been corrupted by contact with Danish. This language, first called Landsmål, and then Nynorsk after 1929, became established as a separate standard alongside Bokmål (called Riksmål before 1929), the language of the capital, which is closer to Danish in its written form.[15]

The process of establishing these two standards was a lengthy and fiercely fought debate that did not die down until the 1960s. As was the case elsewhere in European language debates, the major issues were the notion of purism and the question of what language could be considered authentically Norwegian after centuries of domination by foreign powers. Generally speaking, the supporters of Nynorsk adopted what I have called here the Icelandic model, by introducing archaic structures into the language such as the feminine gender for nouns, which no longer existed in Danish. The supporters of Riksmål were also concerned with language purity but most often took the contemporary spoken language as their guide for spelling. For example, in 1907, two years after gaining independence from Sweden, the Committee on Riksmål recommended to the Norwegian Ministry, as part of a language reform package, that the voiced lenis stops *b*, *d*, and *g* be replaced by the unvoiced fortis stops *p*, *t*, and *k* in the postvocalic position. This proposal was accepted immediately for two main reasons: firstly, it made orthography consistent with pronunciation, since words like *løb* (race), *vide* (to know), and *sag* (case) had always been pronounced with unvoiced fortis stops in Norway. Secondly, it fit in with the ideal of being "un-Danish," since standard Danish is unique among the Scandinavian languages for its voiced postvocalic stops. Therefore, this reform met both the linguistic standards and ideological requirements of the new nation, and it established that Norwegian speech, not Danish writing, should be the model for language.[16] However, it was not always easy in this context to determine what being pure or Norwegian actually meant. In another debate in the 1950s, a proponent of Bokmål argued that the productive nominal suffix *-else*, which was thought to have been introduced into Norway by German Hanseatic traders, actually had developed in Norway in the late Middle Ages.[17] As a consequence, modern Norway has developed two language standards: a minority Nynorsk representing the independent nation and its idealized, preunion past; and a majority Bokmål representing an existing literary tradition and Pan-Scandinavianism.

THE FAROESE CASE: BETWEEN THE LINES OF LANGUAGE

In the case of the Faroes, language reform was also closely connected with political developments and movements for independence within the Danish kingdom. As elsewhere in Europe, following the views of Johann Gottfried Herder, the identification of a distinct people, a *Volk* (or, in Danish, *folk*) with a distinct language and with political rights spread throughout the kingdom, especially after the convening of consultative assemblies to the parliament for various regions of the realm in the 1830s. In this context, language was central to the question of political representation. But what constituted a language, and what constituted a dialect? What was native to a language and what was foreign to it? The answers to these questions for the nineteenth-century Faroe Islands depended upon their historical narrative, which in turn was a key factor in the islanders' struggles for political representation. Thus, debates over orthography were not only scholarly matters but were also strategic disagreements about politics. Both sides in the Faroese language debate saw their orthographical system and historical narrative to which it was attached as protection for their country against the dangers of the modern world. They shared a common goal of not only finding a standard orthography for Faroese but also defending the language, and its speakers and readers, against foreign importations that would damage this traditional culture and cause it to be forgotten. But they differed radically in how these traditions could best be defended and what exactly these traditions represented—a Pan-Scandinavian heritage or a uniquely Faroese one?

In their struggles to resolve these questions, the Faroe Islanders were disadvantaged compared to the Icelanders or even to the Norwegians. In contrast to the rich literary heritage of the medieval sagas and poetry that brought European travelers to Iceland and led them to marvel at the literary prowess of the natives, in the eighteenth-century Faroe Islands there was no native written language at all, and the only medium for written communication was the official language of the kingdom, Danish. As Tom Nauerby points out in his excellent study of the Faroese language conflict and national identity, the linguistic situation in the Faroes has been for a long time and continues to be multilayered.[18] It was not simply that the officials spoke Danish and the common people Faroese. Rather, the highest social classes, such as the church vicars, spoke Danish as it was spoken in Denmark. In the late nineteenth century, one Faroese writer rather provocatively—and almost certainly with political motivation—claimed that about a third of the common people could not understand this language, despite four centuries of its use as an official church language and six centuries of Danish domination. The language that they understood and spoke instead with officials and in the church was a particular Faroese form of Danish, in which the words were pronounced exactly as they were written.[19] Since standard Danish (then as today) displays strong differentiation between the pronunciation of a word and its spelling, these two tongues, a "Copenhagen-Danish" and "Faroese-Danish," sounded quite different, although they both would be written as standard Danish. In addition, there was also an oral Faroese, spoken among the islanders themselves, for which no standard written form had ever existed, because Danish (or Latin) had always been used as official languages since the islands' incorporation with Denmark under the Kalmar Union of 1397. Nauerby suggests that this linguistic situation served to maintain cultural divisions within Faroese society: since Faroese had no written form, it was used as an oral, private language within small social groups of locals; and since Copenhagen-Danish and Faroese-Danish shared the same written form, they were used as the public language of official discourse.

While a tripartite linguistic situation in a region is not unusual, the relative status of the three languages of the Faroe Islands was also complicated. This question was important because the relationships of languages to each other, and their relative status, complexity, and age, were major research problems in the new study of linguistics in the nineteenth century. Since the comparative study of languages undertaken by Sir William Jones, a British judge stationed in India in the 1780s, who noticed the similarities among Latin, Greek, and Sanskrit, the fundamental assumption of language study had been that older forms were the perfect ones and that languages devolved rather than evolving to higher forms. Jones claimed not only that the languages he studied were grammatically and phonetically related but also that Sanskrit was more complex and more perfect than the others and that all three languages must have come from a common source. His work was taken up, especially in Germany, by scholars such as August and Friedrich von Schlegel. Together, these researchers established the existence of the Indo-European language family. During the first decades of the nineteenth century, scholars such as Rasmus Rask and Franz Bopp, as well as Jakob Grimm and Wilhelm von Humboldt, worked at refining their understandings of the similarities and differences among these languages.[20] Their common assumption was that languages tended to simplify and lose their formal structure over time.[21]

Throughout the nineteenth century, linguists generally held that more grammatically complex languages were older and that simplification of languages took place over time. Latin, for example, originally had seven cases (nominative, accusative, dative, genitive, ablative, locative, and vocative), but speakers reduced these to six by using the ablative case for the locative. The Germanic languages then further simplified this case structure, absorbing the functions of the ablative and vocative into other cases, leaving German speakers today with a four-case system. Although this often remained merely implicit in the discussion, nineteenth-century linguists tended to place cultural value on the older forms of languages as more pure and on languages preserved only in texts over the ones spoken. There was not much emphasis on oral or contemporaneous language in early linguistics, and the little there was tended to have a specifically historical orientation. For example, when Rask traveled to Iceland, he saw his visit as an opportunity to reconstruct the Old Norse elements still found in the Icelandic language. He did not show any interest in modern developments and believed the language was doomed to extinction and would be replaced by Danish in a hundred years.[22] As for the language spoken in the Faroes, he labeled it "a dialect . . . of little interest, since it has no literature."[23]

Rask's evaluation of Faroese was not universally shared, however. Jens Christian Svabo, a naturalist who traveled around the islands making collections in 1781–82, was the first to describe the Faroese language, although his prognoses for the future state of this language was the same as Rask's about Icelandic.[24] Svabo also started work on a Faroese dictionary and on a collection of Faroese ballads. The ballads, which became important as evidence of Faroese culture and literary creativity in the later nineteenth century, became known in Denmark due to the efforts of several individuals, including Svabo, P. E. Müller, and Jóhan Henrik Schröter, a Faroese pastor. In 1822, Hans Christian Lyngbye, a pastor from Jutland visiting the Faroes, published a complete cycle of the ballads about Sigurd the Dragon Slayer.[25] In 1846, another pastor and Faroese linguist, Venceslaus Ulricus Hammershaimb, published several articles on Faroese language and literature.[26]

While the first few decades of the nineteenth century saw the beginnings of publication of materials about the Faroese language and in Faroese, the odd situation was that a standard written Faroese did not actually exist. When Lyngbye published the Faroese ballads, which tradition held originated in the Middle Ages, he could only attempt to phonetically transcribe the sounds he heard, and there was no standard method for phonetic transcription at this time. In 1823, Schröter translated the Gospel of Matthew into Faroese, by following the classical rule that a language should be written as it was pronounced. This rule, however, ran against the theory of most nineteenth-century language scholars that a language should be written so that its original, historical morphemes could be seen. These two principles clashed directly in the dispute over Faroese orthography.

THE POLITICAL CONTEXT OF FAROESE LANGUAGE STUDY

This small group of Faroese religious men and language scholars were working in a situation that differed in two important respects from the other, much more famous nineteenth-century language scholars located in the German and French metropoles. First, and most obviously, they were geographically remote and outside of the intellectual milieu of the philological seminars and university life. Most of the participants in the Faroese language debate were pastors or local officials, only one of them held a doctorate, and they were in no position to obtain professorships or receive state funding for their linguistic work. More importantly, however, their chief concern was an oral language without a written tradition. While other language scholars busied themselves with Sanskrit, Greek, Latin, Gothic, or Old Norse texts, this group worked with a language that, by the standards of many other European language scholars at the time, did not exist at all, or, if it did, was not of any interest. This circumstance oriented the concerns of the Faroese group quite differently from their more privileged continental colleagues, and it lent the Faroese language debate a specifically practical dimension, grounded in immediate political realities.

Considering the political circumstances in which the Faroe Islanders found themselves in the nineteenth century, their concern with protecting their language and culture should not surprise us. Compared to Iceland, or even to Norway, the Faroes were marginalized within the Danish kingdom. Following the Danish loss of Norway to Sweden in the Treaty of Kiel in 1814, the Faroese Løgting (a local representative council similar to the Icelandic Alþingi) was abolished in 1816. At the representative councils convened in Copenhagen in 1835, a Danish official nominated by the king represented the Faroe Islands, although native Faroese officials were elected to serve there after 1844. And in the Education Act passed in 1845 (Provisorisk Reglement for Almueskolevæsenet paa Færøerne), a system of board schools was introduced in the Faroes, in which Danish would be the language of instruction. During the discussion in the councils preceding the passage of the act, Faroese was defined as a language dialect (*mundart*), rather than an independent language (*kultursprog*), because of the lack of a written literature.[27] When the new Danish constitution was adopted in 1849, following the revocation of absolutist monarchy in 1848, the Faroe Islands were incorporated into the Danish state as an inseparable province like any other in Denmark. At the same moment, Iceland enjoyed a status outside the constitution with a separate assembly, the Alþingi, reestablished by special royal order in 1843. Although language was not the only factor contributing to the unequal legal and political status of the North Atlantic islands, it was clear that no one during this period disputed the fully independent status of Icelandic as a language and its well-attested literary heritage, and that few in the Faroes could muster comparable evidence for literary traditions there.[28]

Mid-nineteenth-century political developments within the Danish state were not entirely negative for the Faroe Islanders, however. In 1852 they received a local representative body, a county council with some advisory rights in lawgiving matters, under the old name Løgting, although it had diminished powers. Furthermore, in conjunction with the general movement toward liberalization of trade in the kingdom, the monopoly trade company that had exercised semifeudal control over the islands since 1709 was abolished. In the cultural arena, the Education Act was widely unpopular, proved impossible to enforce, and was withdrawn after popular resistance in 1854.[29] After 1844, however, it had become the official position of the Danish state that the Faroese language was no more than a dialect and not a fully developed language.

At the same moment, language politics on the southern edge of the Danish kingdom, in Schleswig and Holstein, were also troublesome. Danish feelings of national sympathy had been aroused by the suppression of Danish in the schools by German-speaking majorities in Schleswig. In his pamphlet *Dansken paa Færøerne: Sidestykke til Tysken i Slesvig* (Danish in the Faroes: A Parallel to German in Schleswig), Svend Grundtvig questioned the genuineness of these feelings of Danish patriotism. If the publicly expressed sentiments about the spirit of the Danish people were sincere, then the Danes ought to turn their attention to the "weapon" with which an "unjust and indifferent [Danish] brother" acted to "overpower and destroy a weaker [Faroese] sister."[30] This "weapon" was the Education Act, claimed Grundtvig, which replaced the "natural" and "traditional" methods that Faroese parents used to teach their children with a system of state schools in which the Faroese language was only to be used as an aid to teach children correct Danish. This was, wrote Grundtvig, "just the same that the Germans have done and continue to do in Schleswig. There people use the Danish language in order to teach children German and argue, in just as naïve and circular a manner, just as a trotted-out excuse: this is necessary, because German is now the language of the Church! . . . To describe Faroese as a dialect of Danish, one could just as well describe Anglo-Saxon as a dialect of English, Latin a dialect of Italian, and so on, with no end to this nonsense."[31] Grundtvig's rhetoric of linguistic family relationships in this essay sprang from the work of Rask and the German nineteenth-century language scholars. He appealed to the sympathy of his Danish audience by pointing out that their own language was also threatened by southern hegemony in the same way that Faroese was. If the official Danish position insisted that Faroese "cannot be called a language, it is rather only a manner of speaking or a dialect, which is a mixture of Icelandic and Danish," one might, on just as good a scientific basis, "call Danish a mixture of German and the Nordic language."[32]

Grundtvig's argument, in the context of mid-nineteenth-century Danish-German relations, made the political implications of language policy explicit. Set in this context, the creation of Faroese orthography came to be seen as an urgent necessity by many Faroese intellectuals by the latter half of the nineteenth century. The preservation of their cultural heritage, including the transcription of the ballad songs, required a method of writing. The Nordic language family should remain intact, not divided, and each family member should claim his rightful heritage and position within it. The concern of the group of Faroese intellectuals and linguists was for the preservation of Faroese culture through language. A society for the promotion of Faroese literature, Føringafelag, was founded in 1881 among students in Copenhagen, publishing its own newspaper, *Føringatíðindi* (News of the Faroes), starting in 1890. The orientation of this society was similar to that of the Icelandic literary society, which Rask founded in Copenhagen in 1816, followed by Carl Christian Rafn's Society for Northern Antiquaries in 1825.

REPRESENTING TRADITION AND MODERNITY IN TWO FAROESE ORTHOGRAPHIES

Venceslaus Ulricus Hammershaimb, who published the Faroese etymological dictionary, took the principles of nineteenth-century historical linguistics and of Rask's work on Icelandic close to heart in his 1846 orthography for Faroese.[33] Stressing the close kinship between Faroese and Icelandic gave Faroese a claim to authenticity or purity higher than that of Danish, since Faroese would then be closer to an original Old Norse, which Rask assumed to be fundamentally identical to modern Icelandic. Faroese words should not be spelled in Danish ways, as Danish had been corrupted by contact with other languages, especially German. Rather, one should use Icelandic spellings, which had remained isolated and therefore pure and gave Faroese a connection to the saga literature.[34] In one of the moves designed to strengthen these connections, Hammershaimb used the letter ð (pronounced as a voiced *th* in Icelandic, as in the English word "then") in his orthography, which made written Faroese look similar to Icelandic and more distinct from Danish, which does not have this letter. If the goal had been to transcribe a spoken Faroese, this letter would have been unnecessary. (It is never pronounced as *th* in the Faroes, but most often as a *g* sound.) That was not a consideration for Hammershaimb, however, as he spoke of one of the successes of his orthography as clearing up the "distorted" pronunciation of the language, which had moved away from its historic, that is, its Norse roots.

In this work, Hammershaimb also followed guidelines for Faroese suggested by the Icelandic nationalist Jón Sigurðsson, who had criticized Schrøter's phonetically based orthography.[35] Thus, one of the strategies of the Faroese for claiming their own identity was to follow the model of the Icelanders. Turning to the literary heritage invoked by Icelandic gave them the authority of tradition sufficient to combat a Danish heralded as the official language of education and scholarship. A 1888 poem "Málstrev" (Language Toil) by Jóannes Patursson, a member of the Føringafelag from one of the wealthier farming families, reflects this view. In this poem, Patursson refers to "foreign ways" being borne away from the Faroese "like soap bubbles" by a "north-west wind." Although Patursson denied this interpretation, it is clear from the map of the North Atlantic that a "north-west wind" would come to the Faroes from Iceland and push "foreign ways" toward Denmark.[36]

The linguist Jakob Jakobsen, who studied French and Scandinavian languages at the University of Copenhagen and wrote his doctoral thesis (the first by a Faroe Islander) on the Norn language of the Shetland Islands, emerged as the major opponent to Hammershaimb's historical linguistics. Before embroiling himself in the language politics of his day, Jakobsen had already thought at length about the historical development of language. In his dissertation, Jakobsen showed that the Norn language, which was dying out in his time and is now extinct, was not a dialect of Low Scottish, as had been assumed, but was related to the Scandinavian languages.[37] Since these islands, along with the Orkneys, were once part of the Danish kingdom but had been given as part of a dowry to Scotland in 1469, the historical roots of this language had been obscured and its use abandoned in favor of English. To Jakobsen, the death of this language was a tragedy and a cautionary tale for the Faroe Islands, where the native language was also in danger of being swallowed up by a colonial tongue.

Jakobsen's casting of the Shetland Islands as an example of "history gone wrong" was an interesting break with traditions in the North Atlantic. Earlier in the nineteenth century the Danish governor of the Faroe Islands, Christian Pløyen, a strong supporter of the Faroese cultural traditions, had written an influential book in which he pointed to the Shetland Islands as a model for the Faroese to emulate. In Pløyen's view, the technology and economic condition of the Shetland Islands were so far advanced by comparison with the Faroes that the best thing to do would be to send the Faroe Islanders to the Shetlands to learn new methods of fishing and agriculture.[38] The Shetlands quite literarily represented the future of the Faroes. Jakobsen, however, read the history of the region from the opposite direction. "Improvements" carried out in the cause of modernity had carried the Shetland Islands so far away from their historical origins that the fundamental element of their identity that rooted them in the North Atlantic region—their language—had been lost. Looking to the Shetlands as a model for Faroese existence was therefore, for Jakobsen, simply inappropriate. Furthermore, the very connections between the North Atlantic and Europe which Pløyen had most praised—the shipping and fishing trade—were for Jakobsen the cause of the problem, since it was exactly at these points of connection that the necessity of using English as a lingua franca had obliterated the use of Norn.

But, as far as Jakobsen was concerned, a reaction that sought refuge in the archaic usages of Icelandic was equally misguided and destructive to the true spirit of the Faroe Islands. If Faroese were modeled after Icelandic, it would become a dead language whose existence was justified by centuries-old manuscripts rather than by the words in the mouths of living people. In addition to rejecting the ð from Hammershaimb's orthography, Jakobsen used the letters å, ä, and ö in the positions where Hammershaimb generally preferred *o* (or *á*), *æ* (or *a*), and *ø*. Since the Danish vowel set contained *å* (spelled at that time as *aa* and pronounced as a long *o*, as in the English "or"), *æ*, *o*, and *ø* (identical to *ö*, and also sometimes written this way in the nineteenth century), and the Icelandic vowel set contained *o*, *á*, *æ*, *a*, *ö*, and *ø*, these differences meant that Jakobsen's written Faroese appeared on the page as significantly different from Danish and was probably not easily legible for a native Danish speaker, while Hammershaimb's written language could be read by a native Icelander with only a little difficulty. To give an example of the differences, the line of a Faroese story that Jakobsen wrote as "*Mikjenes hevur ættir manna sögn vere flotåiggj*" was written in Hammershaimb's system as "*Mikines hevir efter manna søgn verið flotoyggj*" (According to legend, Mykines was once a floating island). The words *efter* and *verið* in Hammershaimb's system make the Faroese sentence appear similar to Icelandic, in which these words are spelled *eftir* and *verið*.[39]

In his views, Jakobsen echoed Svend Grundtvig, who argued that the Faroese ballads were actually a higher cultural art form than the Icelandic manuscripts, because they represented a living rather than a dead culture.[40] Since the Faroe Islands were fortunately still in possession of this heritage, substituting Icelandic cultural hegemony for Danish through artificial spelling was nonsensical—"This could easily lead to the Faroes becoming an Icelandic province, to our having to address our annual requirements to the Icelandic Treasury instead of the Danish, and, as a consequence of this, our having to send our representatives to the Icelandic Alþingi instead of the Danish Rigsdag," opined a supporter of Jakobsen's spelling system, Jóhann Hendrick Schrøter. In Faroese politics, Schrøter was a fierce opponent of Jóannes Patursson, who, as he expressed in his poem "Málstrev" quoted above, looked to Iceland for the force that would drive Danish out of the Faroes.[41]

According to Jakobsen's configuration of the North Atlantic countries, the Icelandic language represented the distant past, a past that did not offer guidance for the Faroese present. Additionally, Jakobsen claimed that Hammershaimb's spelling did nothing to resolve the tripartite linguistic situation in the Faroes, because it simply meant that the Faroe Islanders would be forced to learn Icelandic, Danish, and the new Faroese as their mother tongues instead of the Faroese, Copenhagen-Danish, and Faroese-Danish that had been in place earlier.[42] To put it another way, Jakobsen and those who favored his spelling reform claimed that Hammershaimb and his supporters had not changed the linguistic and cultural paradigm of the Faroe Islands in the late nineteenth century. They had just exchanged the roles of the languages and substituted Icelandic into the category previously occupied by Danish. This substitution left the islands still in a vulnerable, colonized, and culturally devalued position. In their response, the supporters of Hammershaimb's spelling rejected this politically orientated argument. Those matters had nothing to do with language reform, they maintained, and the issues were mainly cultural, not political. In the Middle Ages, when all the North Atlantic islands were self-governing, they had spoken a common Norse tongue. After the end of their medieval independence, this Norse language had changed in the Faroe Islands through considerable contact with Danish. Spelling reform restored the Faroese language to its original state, which had been better preserved over the centuries in Iceland. This did not mean that the restored Faroese was Icelandic; rather it was the indigenous language of the Faroes before foreign influence crept in. If the result was that Icelanders could read and understand Faroese, so much the better, but Hammershaimb's followers rejected the argument that there would be any connection between which letters to write and where to send the government's bills.

Supporters of both spelling systems played a kind of game of deliberate political naïveté, claiming that their reforms were scientifically grounded in principles of language study and that they were not enemies of the Danish language, all the while manipulating letters within a social context where language and politics were impossible to separate from each other. Both sides in this debate were well aware of the Norwegian language reform debate, which had assumed an openly nationalist tone by this time, and of the struggles over Danish and German and their political implications in Schleswig and Holstein. While the Faroese parties at times made political references to this context—such as Patursson's "north-west wind" poem— they also fell back on the logic of scientific principles of linguistics in order to portray themselves as politically dispassionate language scholars.

It would not be going too far to say that the supporters of the two proposals were in fact speaking different languages, as they each maintained a different logic of language reform. Both sides insisted that their systems were based upon scientific principles, but they had different models for this science in mind. The Faroese of Hammershaimb could be supported by the principles of nineteenth-century linguistics, which held that one could follow patterns of regular changes over time back to an original form. His

Faroese was a recovered relic of the past, like animal bones dug up by naturalists or rock strata unearthed by geologists. When Jakobsen created his spelling, on the other hand, he based it on a spoken language, choosing the dialect of Tórshavn. The capital was undergoing rapid population growth during the nineteenth century, as were the rest of the islands, after centuries of a relatively stable level of about 5,000 people in all of the islands. By 1920, there were 2,500 people living in Tórshavn, which was 12 percent of the total population of the Faroes.[43] Naturally, it was the inhabitants of this town who had the most contact with Danish officials and merchants at the port and who spoke in a manner that was thought to be the most Danish-influenced in the Faroes. According to Jakobsen, it was reasonable to base the written form on this variant because all dialects in a region compete with each other and the strongest one—which he judged was the Tórshavn—would emerge victorious and be raised to the status of a written language. Jakobsen's spelling, therefore, followed the natural progression and development of language. He was simply standardizing what would happen anyway of its own accord, following a logic of natural selection. This was exactly the opposite of what Hammershaimb and Patursson desired, since "it was not the task of the written language to seal the advance and victory of the 'Danification' process once and for all, but, on the contrary, to fight against it."[44] By choosing different definitions of what they meant by "natural processes," both sides grounded their systems in scientific reasoning and borrowed different pieces of the language of nineteenth-century evolutionary biology, a science that other European linguists had already adopted as a model for their emerging field.[45]

Both sides, however, whatever their differences, saw language reform as a conservative project of cultural preservation, undertaken as a bulwark against modernity. Hammershaimb admired the Icelanders for having been able to protect their language against change, while Jakobsen saw the language change that had followed in the wake of the technological modernization of the Shetland Islands under British rule as a call to action and a warning for the Faroes. This basic commonality was symptomatic of language study in Scandinavia in general. Already in one of the very first scientific writings on the Icelandic language, by Arngrímur Jónsson in 1609, he praised Icelandic for its purity and warned against the dangers that had occurred in Denmark and Norway, where this original, common Norse tongue was changed through the influence of foreigners.[46] Later language scholars tended to follow in Arngrímur's footsteps in this respect.

Language politics in Scandinavia, as often in the German-speaking lands, centered on the image of an idealized past state of the language, which it was possible to recover or return to by following the principles of the scientific study of language, just as evolutionary biologists could reconstruct past forms through tracing lines of descent.

In the history of Scandinavian language politics, it was taken for granted by all parties that language was the significant measure of culture. The different areas of Scandinavia, or of the North Atlantic islands, could then be arranged hierarchically by language scholars, based upon the degree to which these different regions had been able to preserve the Old Norse language and culture. In the language debates about the nineteenth-century Faroe Islands, the cultural mapping of the North Atlantic proceeded along two axes, one geographic and one temporal. Although they ended up in basic agreement about the appearance of this map and the cultural ordering of the islands, the logic behind the schemes of these two groups of language reformers was different. Seen geographically, as Jakobsen's supporters saw them, the Faroe Islands were located closer to the center of civilization than the Shetlands or the Orkneys, where Norse dialects had died out in favor of English, and closer also than Greenland, where the eighteenth-century Danish efforts to find Norse words in the Inuit languages had long since been abandoned.[47] Iceland, where there was a better-developed written literature and less influence from Danish than in the Faroes, was on the other side of the scale, at the center of civilization (although, as noted above, there was not complete agreement about relative cultural merits of saga manuscripts and ballads). The central position occupied by Iceland did not mean that the Faroe Islanders should emulate Icelandic usage, however. Each island, or island group, in the North Atlantic was geographically and culturally distinct. Each had its own proper history, culture, and language. Unfortunately, these culturally distinct patterns were sometimes interrupted or interfered with by outsiders, as in the Shetlands and the Faroes. When this happened, it was the duty of citizens to return their country to the path of its own language and history. For this reason, Jakobsen and his followers were able to argue that changing Faroese in the direction of Icelandic should be resisted, since this was no better for the islands than the Danish usages that had been introduced.

Hammershaimb's supporters, on the other hand, arranged the North Atlantic according to a temporal logic. Icelandic was esteemed because it had retained the largest share of the common medieval Norse culture, while the Faroes and the other North Atlantic islands had all, to varying degrees, suffered some degradation of this heritage. Iceland, then, represented the purest, oldest state of this culture, and the correct reform would be a modeling of language on all the islands to the norms of Icelandic or Old Norse. None of the islands were ever culturally distinguished from one another at any point in their history; they were only positioned at different points in a downward spiraling temporal path. To regain their autonomy, they had to climb their way up this path, backward into the past.

These positions both fit into the larger patterns of thinking about the North Atlantic. For both sides of the spelling debate in the Faroes, the North Atlantic was in danger of losing its language and cultural heritage and descending into the state of unknown and unintelligible wilderness. Just as spiritual life and the natural world presented dangers on these outpost islands, so too did language. Little could be more fundamental to maintaining a connection to the civilized world than language. Without the connection of the shared heritage of Latin, Henry Holland claimed that his ability to understand the emotions of the Icelandic student visiting Scotland would be reduced to interpretations of his facial expressions. Although Hammershaimb and Jakobsen might have disagreed about how to solve the problem, they recognized the danger that the Faroe Islands were in. Against this danger, one might try to erect fences against reindeer in Iceland, restrict the importation of bullets to Greenland, or publish newspapers in the Faroes—all three manifestations staked claims in debates about North Atlantic history and culture and the region's relationship to European traditions and modernity.

THE FAROESE CONSENSUS ON PURISM AND POLITICS

Thus, devising different spellings for the Faroese language in the nineteenth century implied particular positions on the nature of Faroese, and North Atlantic, history and culture. Such divisions were much more fundamental, and more difficult to solve, than the problem of how to spell words in the newspapers. Given that these two different positions were at stake in the Faroe Islands in the late nineteenth century, how were the language disputes ever resolved? Although compromises over the technical details could be hammered out, as they were in the Faroe Islands, in another sense the issues never went away, and discussions about language and language purity are still a major topic of public dispute in the North Atlantic. Gísli Pálsson, an Icelandic anthropologist, has argued recently that the nineteenth-century Icelandic nationalist movement placed an emphasis on social equality, cooperation, and consensus, even claiming that social equality had existed in Iceland in the early Middle Ages. Icelanders were encouraged to minimize difference among themselves; thus, different class, gender, or regional norms for language, while acceptable in English, are regarded as illnesses in Icelandic.[48] Language is not only a marker of identity but also an indication of the health of society. In Iceland, for example, one particular type of grammatical mistake, the substitution of a dative pronoun for a nominative in certain constructions ("*mér* [dative] *hlakka til*" instead of the correct "*ég* [nominative] *hlakka til*," meaning "I look forward to"), became known as the "dative disease" (*þágufallssýki*).[49] Standard language is called "pure" (*hreinn*), the same word as "clean." With these metaphors, a single standard language is invoked, with those who speak it being classed as healthy and those who make mistakes as sick or, in other metaphors, as wild and ignorant (from *hljóðvilla*, "wrong sounds"). These metaphors enforce a single standard language that is an artificial ideal—the ideal cited by Lars Vikør earlier in this chapter. Despite an intense focus on language education toward this single standard in the North Atlantic, language is there, as everywhere else in the world, marked by class and gender distinctions, especially as Iceland began to include a larger immigrant population in the final decades of the twentieth century.

In order to reach this point of establishing a single standard language as a reference by which to measure deviation, as the Icelanders have done, a consensus on the modern standards for Faroese had to be reached by people who interpreted the history of the North Atlantic islands fundamentally differently. In 1893 the Føringafelag appointed a committee, with both Hammershaimb and Jakobsen on it, to find a solution. Two years later, they put forward their proposal, called Broyting (Changes), a compromise system that favored Hammershaimb's position considerably. Although Broyting was adopted in 1897, Patursson continued to push for spelling that was closer to Hammershaimb's, leaving the membership of Føringafelag and his post as editor of *Føringatíðindi* in protest over Broyting. In 1899, the group returned to using Hammershaimb's orthography, but many members had left by that time and Føringafelag disbanded in 1901.[50]

Modern Faroese orthography remains substantially as it was invented by Hammershaimb in 1846, although the notion that some usages are "half-Danish" or "half-Icelandic" persists. This means that considerable differentiation between the spoken and written languages still exists in the Faroes. Modern Faroese is legible to Icelanders on the page but not easily understandable in conversation, while the Danish spoken in the Faroe Islands is often pronounced more literally, as it is spelled, than the Danish spoken in Copenhagen. Often, it is more understandable to nonnative speakers of Danish than is standard Danish.[51]

The victory of the Icelandic model in the Faroese language arena set in place a pattern that later political discussions about autonomy and independence for the Faroe Islands have tended to follow. In political discussions between Denmark and the Faroes about independence, comparisons are often drawn with the independence process of Iceland between 1870 and 1918. In 1918, Iceland and Denmark drew up a contract, renewable after twenty-five years, making Icelanders responsible for their own affairs. The contract expired while Denmark was under German occupation during World War II, and the Icelanders, encouraged by the American authorities, declared full independence, which the Danish government recognized. In recent years, the Faroese Landstyre (the home-rule government of the Faroes within the Danish state) and the Danish government have agreed to examine this Icelandic model as a path toward independence for the Faroes, although the question of the ability of the islands to achieve economic self-sufficiency is the major point of difficulty.[52] Such a path offers both pragmatic advantages and a resolution of the question of identity. In their inclination to follow an Icelandic political model, the Faroe Islanders seem to have resolved for themselves the question of how they map the North Atlantic and where they see themselves in it. By choosing to follow the Icelandic linguistic and political example, they in effect concluded that the North Atlantic was a common zone of culture, distinguished by time rather than space. But, by following this model, they also disagreed with the Icelandic nationalists whom they followed. These politicians and scholars succeeded during the nineteenth century in convincing their own countrymen and other European nations that their island was unique, distinguished by their culture and nature from every other place on earth. This was a result that the Faroese were unable to propagate internationally as successfully as the Icelanders were. One way of interpreting the outcome of the language debates in the Faroe Islands is to see them as a pragmatic, strategic move of relying on existing models of both language and politics to achieve concrete political goals.

The history of language policy in Scandinavia also shows how standardization of language does not always take place from political centers; it can also proceed from within marginalized regions themselves. There was not one single language in the Danish realm, trying to establish itself and standardize the peripheries. Rather, there were two centers, offering different linguistic and cultural models in the Danish kingdom: a political-cultural center in Copenhagen, representing a literary life of cafés, newspapers, and the theater and a connection with the European centers in London, Paris, and Berlin; and a cultural center in Reykjavík, offering a version of the Scandinavian past based on the Old Norse sagas of the thirteenth century. Even though the Danish state had developed since the seventeenth century under Christian IV into a strongly centralized state with a single administrative center in the political capital, the cultural status of peripheral regions such as Iceland was not diminished in the eyes of the capital. Danish cultural leaders, in fact, never tried to downplay the cultural significance of the Icelandic past for their own culture. For most nineteenth-century Danish literary figures, Iceland was esteemed as the land of the sagas, the repository of the great Pan-Scandinavian cultural heritage, the heritage that was drawing the European and American visitors to Iceland to try to converse in Latin with the natives. That nineteenth-century Icelanders did not see this as a Pan-Scandinavian legacy but as uniquely Icelandic was a cultural disagreement that ended in a political solution. The maintenance and rhetorical power of this cultural center in Reykjavík, which also had relevance for the Norwegian language debates, meant that Faroese language politics were, seen in one way, more complex than they might otherwise have been: they had two standards against which to distinguish themselves, rather than one. In another sense—and the viewpoint that that Faroese language politicians seem to have finally agreed upon with the Broyting solution—the existence of the Icelandic model made their own struggle easier, since there already existed a well-established corpus of literature on North Atlantic culture to support their case, one whose worth state leaders were willing to accept without question.

The different positions the Faroe Islanders took about spelling their language in the nineteenth century entailed different historical narratives and identities for them within the Scandinavian region. A distinct *folk* not only had its own language, it had its own history. A firm knowledge of this language and history protected them against foreign encroachments that brought undesirable forms of modernity to the islands. This belief then sought refuge in the Icelandic model, firmly established in the past. By modeling themselves on a timeless society,[53] the Faroe Islanders could reject the corrupting connections with modern Europe and everything that came with them: the industrialization of the fishing trade, the move from rural to urban life, and the Danish that represented colonial power and Faroese marginalization. Of course, this attempt to resist modernity and fix their national identity permanently at a certain, determined point in history was, like the Latin "spoken" in nineteenth-century Iceland, an illusion. As soon as the Faroese accepted the equation of *folk*, language, and history and entered into discussion with the Danish government over the school language and political representation, they began to become part of modern Europe, from where these ideas originated. Simply by looking to Iceland as a model for their own linguistic and political development, by placing themselves within the other nineteenth-century Scandinavian language debates, the Faroe Islanders created the connections whose influence they wanted to resist. This uneasy position between tradition and modernity is fundamental to North Atlantic history.

We are in fact refugees from Europe, and the question is
whether we want to return.—*Jón Baldvin Hannibalsson,*
Iceland's Social Democratic foreign minister, speaking to
Icelanders living in Copenhagen (March 1990)

EPILOGUE | WHALES AND MEN

Contested Scientific Ethics and Cultural Politics
in the North Atlantic

I t is difficult, for outsiders anyway, to think about Iceland without dealing in metaphors and symbols. Whenever Iceland surfaces in the international press, journalists are apt to explain whatever the issue at hand
might be in terms of sagas, Vikings, volcanoes, glaciers, earthquakes,
poetry, or independence. Although these writers frequently acknowledge
that visiting the geysers and the Blue Lagoon (Bláa Lónið) resort, and writing about the landscapes of volcanic rock surrounding the Leifur Eiríksson
International Airport, have become clichés, it is nearly impossible to omit
these obligatory stops on the Icelandic tour. And once the foreign traveler
has stopped at the Blue Lagoon, sat in its muddy waters, looking up at the
steam released by the geothermal plant, his or her mind seems to fixate

on concepts of Icelandic purity and nature-respecting technology that the spa appears to represent. The travel article that results then relates the spa experience or sighting of a puffin or a trip to a Reykjavík nightclub as being the key to understanding everything about Iceland.

Depending on symbols to imagine Iceland, as tempting as it is, is also distorting. It tends to fit all Icelandic events into preexisting categories. Everything that happens in Iceland—and everything that will ever happen there—becomes predetermined by these signs.[1] With this in mind, and having surveyed the historical origins and development of some of these symbols in the preceding chapters, I want to return to my point of departure for this story: Iceland at the close of the twentieth century. Around the same time that I was beginning to study and travel to Iceland, two native sons returned to the country. Kári Stefánsson, founder of the controversial biotech firm deCODE Genetics (Íslensk erfðagreining), worked at Harvard University and the University of Chicago before returning to Iceland in 1997. Keiko, the orca who stared in the three *Free Willy* movies, returned in September 1998 to the Icelandic waters where he was born, after his sojourns in Canada, Mexico City, and the Oregon coast.[2]

These two arrivals—occurring at the moment that I was paying increasingly more attention to the idea of "Icelandic arrival"—juxtaposed different understandings of Icelandic nature.[3] The two controversies that unfolded around them—over deCODE's proposed Health Sector Database (HSD) and North Atlantic whaling politics—brought issues of conflicting scientific standards and ethics to international attention. At the high points of these debates, Iceland became a site of international media attention, where foreign journalists camped out to make television documentaries about the developments. The return of these two travelers at the end of the millennium, and the international debates that surrounded them, drew upon the historic images and debates about Iceland and the rest of the North Atlantic. Although biotechnology and animal protection are issues of the twenty-first century, the cultural history of the different versions of Icelandic nature in these issues is now well over two hundred years old. When Kári declared that Iceland was a perfect laboratory for biotechnological experimentation and returned with promises of multimillion-dollar profits for its citizens and subjects, and when Keiko's human companions claimed that the waters off Iceland were a nature preserve for him, these stories were convincing because they already existed. The promoters of these projects were not inventing new stories about the North Atlantic but were repeating old ones.

In both the deCODE and the whaling episodes that I discuss in this chapter, the Icelandic government took a position that was perceived by some to contradict international conventions. Supporters argued that the government's position was justified due to certain historical contingencies that set Iceland apart from other nations and regions. The standards that some international observers wished to apply to the Icelandic case did not fit, it was argued, because the realities of scientific research in Iceland had not been correctly understood. The allegedly objective standards had been developed for more mainstream cases that did not fit the unique Icelandic reality.

Claiming to be special and claiming to be misunderstood by foreigners are of course not uniquely Icelandic responses to criticism. In their arguments, however, the supporters of whaling and of the HSD drew on the long history of the development of metaphors and narratives about Iceland. The opponents of whaling and of the HSD—which included many Icelanders and other natives of the North Atlantic, as well as foreigners—also drew on other strands of metaphor and contesting narratives about Iceland rooted in the history of travel and exchange in the North Atlantic. The point of contention in both debates was an accurate description and understanding of nature in the North Atlantic and whether that nature should be understood as unique and remarkable or whether it in fact was similar to nature in other regions of the world—the same question that occupied naturalists in the eighteenth century. What happened in Iceland at the end of the millennium was, in effect, a restaging of its early modern history.

Narratives about the North Atlantic, whether they were told about landscapes, animals, tools, or language, developed and came to their conclusions in similar ways. Each of the preceding chapters has traced a debate about the characteristics of this feature of the North Atlantic, in which the debate ranged over the question of whether the North Atlantic, as it was measured by these aspects, should be considered an exotic place very far from European norms, or was a place that was essentially part of Europe and European history. The results of these conflicts were mixed, but the general conclusion was that the North Atlantic, at least most parts of it, became less exotic and moved closer to Europe in the time frame from the eighteenth century until about the end of World War II. This movement was not steady or consistent, and it did not apply equally to all parts of the North Atlantic. The normalization of technology in the North Atlantic was a much slower and more tangled process than religious conversion in the region. With respect to material culture, Greenland remained outside of European norms at the beginning of the twentieth century, while Iceland had already begun technological modernization. However, the general pattern is that the North Atlantic became "not exotic" over this period. It got "electricity and central heating and cars and buses . . . telephones that work and supermarkets and electric milking machines and tractors . . . high-rise apartment buildings . . . modern single family homes . . . credit cards, money machines, color TV . . . an alphabet the same as we use for English." The North Atlantic countries became "thoroughly modern."[4]

One does not have to accept these standards of modernity, of course. They are themselves an artifact of writing at the end of the twentieth century; they mostly describe technology and deal with machines. But it is equally important to realize that technology was never the only standard. The classification and the management of nature, religion, and language were also significant foci of this larger debate. At the beginning of this process in the eighteenth century, the North Atlantic was marked as a territory outside Europe. Gradually, through scientific investigation, classification, and discussion of the North Atlantic landscape, nature, technology, material culture, religion, and language, the lines of demarcation on the map moved. By the 1950s, both Europeans and natives of the North Atlantic generally saw the region as belonging to Europe and conforming to European norms of the measurements that had been previously under debate.

In this process of transformation, travelers from different European states pursued their own intellectual, economic, and cultural interests in the North Atlantic and helped to shape competing visions of the region as domestic or as exotic. Natives of the North Atlantic also participated in this process by resisting, contesting, or allying themselves with the stories and agendas of foreigners. In part, this process was accomplished through actual transformation of the region, for example, by the adoption of new farming and fishing technologies. Another piece of this story, however, consists of the changing perceptions of the North Atlantic, such as the artistic renderings of nature and landscape.

While some debates about the North Atlantic were decisively resolved—few linguists today would seriously consider the Greenlandic language to be a member of the Indo-European language family—others were less clear in their outcomes. Discussion continues within Iceland and in other parts of the North Atlantic about how nature should best be utilized and controlled. Two additional recent debates surrounding the North Atlantic illustrate how the region remains a kind of borderlands—uncertain about its location with respect to centers of measurement. Both the issues of human genes and whales involved two of the major themes of the eighteenth- and nineteenth-century debates: nature and technology. They both begin with some artifact of nature that has contested scientific status—the uniqueness of the Icelandic genetic pool, or the health of whale populations. They then extend to call into question the technologies of human utilization of this nature—computer databases and blood samples, or whaling ships and harpoons.

Although the deCODE and whaling controversies owe their existence to advancements in biotechnology and genetic research, the availability of international venture capital, international money markets, the global environmental movement, and an international press to draw attention to the plights of endangered animals, only the trappings of the stories are modern. The narratives invoked were old news. The modern controversies retold stories about the North Atlantic that travelers had written in the eighteenth and nineteenth centuries, but they told them in the international press and on the Internet rather than in travel books and expensive natural histories designated for an elite and select audience. The North Atlantic narrative has spread even more broadly in the twentieth-first century. As it became a mass commodity, it offered age-old material to a larger consuming public.

When this larger public, composed of diverse elements such as whale enthusiasts and bioethicists, heard the North Atlantic narrative for the first time through the stories of Kári and Keiko, they did not generally recognize it as a narrative. Although the metaphoric elements of the story—the sagas and the Vikings—were acknowledged as clichés, the story as a whole was accepted as the literal truth. This is what made the narratives of the modern controversies even more powerful and convincing—that they were told to an audience who, while well-read and highly educated on many subjects, knew little or nothing of North Atlantic history. Without any context in which to place these stories, they seemed to emerge from nowhere, immediately gripping in the plights of the protagonists but slippery in their details. DeCODE and whaling have been frequently discussed with respect to ethics and moral decisions. This chapter, however, does not take a moral position on the deCODE and whaling controversies.[5] Here, I simply want to explain, by analyzing the history of North Atlantic narratives, why these issues became controversies with such moral significance.

deCODE AND THE WHALES: A BRIEF HISTORY

In 1996, deCODE Genetics registered as a corporation in Delaware and opened a laboratory in Reykjavík. Two years later, the Health Sector Database bill was introduced in the Icelandic parliament (Alþingi) during the spring session. Following protests, and an intense public discussion within Iceland during the summer months of 1998, the Alþingi passed a new version of the bill in the fall session. This HSD bill became a law on December 17, 1998.[6] Following this, the controversy opened outside the boundaries of Iceland and became an international discussion.

What made deCODE and the HSD law so controversial and what distinguished the company and its plan from other biobank projects underway in Great Britain, Estonia, and Newfoundland was the Icelandic position on the principle of informed consent of medical subjects. The general standard of informed consent is that a donated sample of blood or body tissue must be done with the consent of its donor, who must also be informed which tests will be performed on the specimen. According to the HSD law, however, medical information about all Icelandic citizens would be included in the database unless they registered their objections and explicitly refused to allow their doctors to transfer their information to deCODE. Along with this information, deCODE would receive the "presumed" or "assumed" consent of the patient to perform any tests on this information that it deemed necessary in the future, without asking the express permission of the patient. In other words, the law enacted an opt-out rather than an opt-in principle. This was perceived in some quarters as contradicting acceptable standards for biobanks and human research. For example, the Helsinki Declaration of the World Medical Association, passed in 1964, states that the patient has the right to withdraw consent from participation in research at any time without reprisal.[7] Under the HSD law, once the information was entered into the database, it would be impossible to remove it.

In answering the international protest that followed the passage of the HSD law, supporters justified this unusual aspect of the project by referring to Icelandic history. In an interview, Kári Stefánsson stated that, "formerly, our nation has suffered because of its isolation. Now, it is an asset. Modern science will enable us to take advantage of our isolation."[8] According to his view, the circumstances of Icelandic history of limited immigration, a small, "genetically homogeneous" population, with written records of family relations going back until the settlement period, had made the medical and genetic information of the Icelanders an exceptionally rich and desirable source for constructing the database.[9] The database, however, would be a powerful tool only with the participation of all Icelanders, and it was impractical for deCODE to ask each individual Icelander to consent to every experiment the company might wish to perform in the future. Thus, the history of Iceland, taken together with its present circumstances of universal national health care, a generally well-educated public with a high literacy rate, and democratic forums and institutions, were all used as arguments by the supporters of deCODE to justify the version of the bill that passed in December 1998. Because the forces of Icelandic nature through hundreds of years of catastrophes and disasters had shaped the genetic heritage of the population to make it such a suitable subject for genetic research, the legal circumstances in Iceland for deCODE should also be exceptional.

Such special pleading did not impress the critics of deCODE, who quickly emerged within the country as well as internationally. The non-profit group Mannvernd (literally "protection of people," formally known as the Association of Icelanders for Ethics in Science and Medicine), along with the Icelandic Association of Physicians—whose members as doctors would be obliged under the law to transmit information on their patients to the database—joined to express their opposition to the HSD law. One of the major themes in the opposition's discussion was the image—which became ubiquitous in journalistic writing about deCODE—of Iceland and its inhabitants as a "laboratory" for biotechnological research.[10] For the opponents of deCODE, this was a troubling metaphor because, not only did it suggest the use of one set of individuals for the benefit of others, it was also a metaphor that had been applied to Iceland by foreigners during the period of the island's marginalization and dependence. It recalled the island's colonial past and a time prior to its emergence into modernity.

This reference to a premodern, colonial past then underwent a further development in the international deCODE debate. Opponents of the project compared Iceland to third world countries, suggesting that the Icelanders had been exploited by international or foreign concerns and that the Icelandic government was failing to protect its citizens. The colonial past of Iceland was being reenacted through the tools of a new science. For example, in a critique of the regulatory framework that the Icelandic government enacted for overseeing the operations of the HSD, including questions of privacy, population geneticist Richard Lewontin wrote that Iceland "begins to sound like Mexico" in its values and ethical standards, and not like "a northern European nation."[11] His language was then sharply rebuked by the anthropologists Gísli Pálsson and Paul Rabinow, who used the Icelandic *Sonderweg* argument in their reply, accusing the critics of deCODE of holding colonialist attitudes themselves in their assumption that the inhabitants of a small northern island are not capable of establishing adequate human-rights protections. Gísli Pálsson and Rabinow claimed that a majority of the Icelanders supported deCODE, and it was arrogant of citizens of other countries to attempt to dictate the conditions under which the Icelanders were allowed to conduct medical research.[12] For the critics of deCODE, bioethical standards—like whale populations—had to be monitored by the international community to be meaningful, while Gísli Pálsson and Rabinow saw the potential reenactment of old power and privileges in these standards.

At about the same time that the HSD bill was being discussed in the Icelandic parliament, Keiko arrived home in Iceland. Although he had experienced a difficult residence abroad, having become very ill during his captivity in Mexico City, by 1998 he had won friends worldwide through the three *Free Willy* movies highlighting his plight. Following the success of the first film in 1993, he had been moved for rehabilitation to the Oregon Coast Aquarium in 1995, with the financial support of Warner Bros., the makers of the film. The Free Willy/Keiko Foundation was established to oversee his recovery. In 1997, the foundation announced the goal of returning Keiko to the North Atlantic waters, and this was accomplished on September 9, 1998. When Keiko arrived in Iceland, he was placed in a pen off the Westman Islands in order to transition to living independently of humans. After nearly four years of training, including learning how to catch fish on his own, he left the pen in the summer of 2002 and swam to the Taknes fjord in Norway.

Although the project of returning Keiko to the wild seemed to be one of simple humanitarianism, it was in fact more complicated. Releasing Keiko into the North Atlantic waters, returning a captive animal into the wild, stirred up the standing debate over Icelandic and Norwegian whaling and the differences between the North Atlantic native understanding of whales and those of outsiders to the region. On one hand, the Icelandic public, bemused at the idea of foreigners' spending upwards of nine million dollars to return an animal that had already lived half of his natural life span in captivity to the wild, cheerfully received Keiko as the celebrity he had become, with commercial promotions tied in to his release. According to a poll taken shortly before Keiko's arrival, 54 percent of Icelanders supported his return, while only 24 percent were opposed to it.[13] However, there was also a more problematic undercurrent to the Keiko debate than Icelandic amusement at American sentimentality and the Americans' ability to invest substantial economic resources in their particular ideal of nature. Returning Keiko to Icelandic waters actually violated Icelandic law against the import of living animals. Six years earlier, the Icelandic Ministry of Fisheries had refused to allow Sea World to return another killer whale, Tillikum, to Icelandic waters on the grounds that there was a risk that the animal could be carrying undetectable infections acquired during captivity. This orca was not, however, an international media star but had contributed to the death of a trainer in an accident. In the negotiations with the Ministry of Fisheries preceding Keiko's return, many marine biologists cited the earlier case to support their contention that a whale who had grown to adulthood in captivity had not learned the skills to survive in the wild and that the entire plan was a flawed, sentimental idea based on a Hollywood script rather than good science.[14]

Furthermore, while Iceland had ceased whaling in 1989 in accordance with the International Whaling Commission (IWC) zero-catch quota that had gone into effect in the 1985–86 whaling season, the Icelandic government had repeatedly lobbied for the resumption of whaling. The government contended that whaling was a long-standing practice in Iceland that should therefore be culturally protected and that the minke whales hunted were not in fact endangered, unlike other larger whale species. Some Icelandic protesters against the Keiko decision believed that the ministry was acquiescing in some sense to the American cultural view of whales in allowing the return of the animal, when the Icelandic position on whaling had not been respected by the United States, a major player in the IWC. Although one protester signaled his opposition by threatening to kill and eat Keiko,[15] many Icelanders seemed to see the return as an easy way of winning international goodwill on the whaling issue (fig. 10). The Norwegians also welcomed Keiko after he left Icelandic waters and allowed him to be buried in Norway after his death in December 2003, although it would have been traditional to bury the whale at sea (and environmental experts, concerned about mercury contamination of the soil from the body, actually recommended this). Both the Norwegian and Icelandic governments seemed to see the Keiko episode as a means of demonstrating that they were not—contrary to the bad press they had received on this subject in the previous twenty years—unfeeling barbarians toward whales. Rather, they were protecting one whale that had been damaged, not by North Atlantic peoples, but by the anti-whaling nations such as Mexico and the United States.

In Keiko, the debate over North Atlantic whaling was crystallized by the figure of one internationally famous, charismatic killer whale, just as the debate over Icelandic genes and property rights came to focus on Kári, who has been often described as charismatic in the international media.[16] Both issues of course had longer histories than these two figures. The Icelandic Blood Bank (Blóðgefafélag Íslands) and the Icelandic Cancer Society (Krabbameinsfélag Íslands) had been collecting medical data in databases since the 1930s and 1950s. Both societies kept this medical data under informed consent procedures. In 1965, a larger project for a medical database was established at the University of Iceland with funding from the U.S. Atomic Energy Commission. The main purpose of this database was to investigate the effects of radiation on the human body. Using information from the Icelandic Blood Bank, the Genetic Committee at the University of Iceland envisioned genetic information on Icelanders serving as a useful control group to compare with populations affected by atomic radiation.[17]

As Gísli Pálsson points out, these projects were generally well-supported by the Iceland public and went hand in hand with the long-standing cultural interest of the Icelanders in heredity and genealogy. He dates this interest back to the Middle Ages, with the writing of the *Book of Settlements (Landnámabók)* and the *Book of the Icelanders (Íslendingabók)* in the twelfth century, the histories of Iceland that listed all of the original settlers, their families, and landholdings. Since 2003, an online, publicly accessible version of the *Book of the Icelanders* has been available on the deCODE Web site. This version has been brought up to date using a number of historical sources, such as censuses, to include genealogical information on 700,000 Icelanders living in Iceland since the Middle Ages. There are of course gaps in this historical record, and no one can be sure exactly how large these gaps are, although deCODE claims a 95 percent "connectivity rate" of documented connections between individuals and their parents for the database. Gísli comments that looking up one's own relatives and establishing family connections to others became something of a party

FIG. 10 Sigmund Jóhannsson's cartoon from *Morgunblaðið*, a large Icelandic daily newspaper, October 4, 2001. The cartoon is linked to a letter to the newspaper by Helgi Geirsson, "Let's Eat Keiko and Begin Whaling Right Away." A chef serves Keiko up to Kristján Loftsson, the owner of the only Icelandic whaling company, chastising him, "But you have to promise to eat all your food first, Kristján." Kristján should take care of what is already on his plate—Keiko—before he goes out to catch more whales. Cartoon courtesy of Sigmund Jóhannsson.

game, with amusing, and occasionally emotionally distressing, results in the days after the database was launched. (The public version of this database, unlike deCODE's encrypted version, is egocentric; one can only look up personal family relations, not all Icelandic families.)[18]

The whaling controversy also has a decades-long history: it began in the 1970s with the "save the whales" movement, leading up to the IWC moratorium (technically, a zero-catch quota) on commercial whaling in 1982, which took effect in the 1985–86 hunting season. Much of the conflict over the moratorium—the most controversial action this multinational organization had taken since its establishment in 1946—has centered on the "indigenous whaling" clause, an exception to the zero-catch quota.[19] Under this clause, whale hunting classified as "indigenous" is permitted with strict quotas, while those hunts that are classified "commercial" or "industrial" are not. In the North Atlantic, the result of the IWC regulation is that whaling for consumption is specifically allowed in Greenland but not in Norway or Iceland. (The pilot whale hunt in the Faroes does not fall under IWC regulations but has also, like the Norwegian and Icelandic hunts, been the target of international protest and critique.) Many natives of the North Atlantic argue that whaling has also been practiced for centuries in these countries and that their practices do not necessarily endanger the whale populations any more than "indigenous" ones do.[20] Critics of this policy have also suggested that the IWC's reasoning behind the zero-catch quota and its regulation is not scientifically grounded in knowledge of whale populations but rather is based on the tradition of Western romanticization of indigenous peoples—a tradition that defined these peoples as using only primitive tools and not industrialized technologies. Hunting by these peoples was therefore considered to be benign toward whale populations as a whole, whereas hunting by industrialized Western nations was thought to harm them. Thus, the regulations recapitulate the historic marginalization and disenfranchisement of the North Atlantic peoples, reiterating a romantic stereotype that privileges indigenous tools and the people who use them.[21]

These two sides—the pro-whaling and anti-whaling factions—are recent manifestations of the much longer debate about North Atlantic nature. The philosophical position of the anti-whaling faction emerged from the environmental movement of the 1970s and the "save the whales" campaigns. According to some of the popular environmentalist literature produced about whales from the 1970s on, whales have a "mystique" that "inspires wonder and exhilaration among people from all races and all nations in a way that no other non-human species has equaled so widely." In addition, whales "have a special affinity for human beings" and a "universal appeal."[22] This way of thinking about whales is identified by some critics as the logic of "charismatic megafauna": that a class of large animals, also including elephants and panda bears, have been anthropomorphized into poster children for the environmental movement and receive attention and protection because of their perceived humanlike nature. In a 1983 conference, sponsored in part by the IWC and Greenpeace, the organizers acknowledged that whales, in addition to being of interest in their own right, function as "powerful symbols of environmental concern." As symbols of endangered animals and threatened environments par excellence, their main role in popular environmental discussions in recent years has been to draw attention to general environmental concerns about a range of causes rather than to engage in specific debates over the health of certain species of whales, the issue in which the North Atlantic pro-whaling advocates are most interested.

The pro-whaling faction in the North Atlantic did not respond immediately to the "save the whales" campaigns of the 1970s with an articulation of their own philosophical viewpoint. At that time, the supporters of whaling in Iceland, Norway, the Faroes, and Greenland did not perceive the anti-whaling movement as fundamentally hostile to their activities. They believed that such protests were mainly aimed against the larger whaling nations such as Japan and the Soviet Union and did not affect the kind of small-scale whaling they were engaged in. They assumed that it was the larger nations who were responsible for most of the environmental problems in the world. The largest Icelandic daily newspaper, *Morgunblaðið*, reported in 1980 that Japan caught ninety-nine of every hundred whales in the world, and before 1985 its articles more often discussed the effect that a whaling ban would have on the Japanese economy than the Icelandic economy.[23] Furthermore, since the United States and Great Britain were at the front of the anti-whaling movement and two of the major whaling nations were the Soviet Union and Japan, the anti-whaling sentiment was often interpreted in the North Atlantic as an expression of political opposition to the Soviet Union and economic fear of Japan rather than as an environmental issue at face value. Nations such as the North Atlantic ones who were friendly to the interests of the United States therefore had no reason to be concerned.

In addition, many citizens of North Atlantic whaling nations opposed whaling themselves. An Icelandic nature-protection group, Skuld, protested against whaling in Reykjavík in 1979 and 1980.[24] They pointed out that killing whales was antimodern, as well as unnecessary, now that that scientific research had made us aware of the intelligent and sympathetic nature of whales.[25] A reporter for Morgunblaðið traveled with a Greenpeace boat on some of their actions in Spain and wrote articles sympathetic to Greenpeace in the early 1980s.[26] The paper never editorialized about the whaling issue until 1985, appearing to regard the impending commercial ban as not sufficiently worthy of particular Icelandic interest.

After the zero-catch quota went into effect, a new element came into this debate. In the North Atlantic, this often was cast in terms of the "rights of small nations." For example, in July 1985, Morgunblaðið wrote that "no nation, especially a small nation, can afford to build international agreements on such a two-faced morality." By "two-faced morality" the author meant that the IWC regulations permitted the indigenous whaling of about two hundred whales yearly in Greenland, while the Icelandic minke whale catches, roughly the same number in the years before 1985, were forbidden.[27] The Faroe Islanders also reacted to the mid-1980s international campaigns against pilot whale hunting with surprise and indignation. They replied that whaling practices in the Faroes were traditional, deeply rooted in the culture, and should therefore qualify for an exemption under the indigenous rights clause. Since the Faroese Islanders were under the rule of the Danish state but had a different set of cultural traditions, especially cultural traditions associated with whaling, they should qualify for the indigenous exemption as an "isolated population," reasoned the pro-whaling advocates in the Faroes.[28]

In independent Norway and Iceland, the case for such an exemption was weaker. Instead, pro-whaling advocates often referred to alternative scientific data on North Atlantic whale populations, which appeared to demonstrate that they were not in fact endangered by Norwegian and Icelandic whaling. However, Norwegians and Icelanders also began in the mid-1980s to defend whaling as an expression of their cultural values and national sovereignty. The language in which this argument was often phrased was very similar to that of the indigenous rights claim: Icelanders and coastal Norwegians have historically experienced a struggle for survival against the harsh realities of nature. Having experienced this struggle, they have a different relationship with nature than foreign urban dwellers who are removed from the realities of life and death. Therefore, a person's national identity as an Icelander or Norwegian—although he or she lives in a major city, buys meat from the supermarket, and has never fished or whaled—endows this individual with certain rights, including the right to eat whale meat when it is served at a restaurant in Oslo.

Furthermore, the opposition to the internationally accepted position on whaling became an important piece of this North Atlantic identity in the political realm. It is, according to this rationale, necessary for smaller nation states to take strong stands against unfair pressure from larger nation states through the domination of the IWC, otherwise they would appear manipulable and their national sovereignty would be at risk. It was even more essential, according to this perspective, not to give in to so-called terrorist attacks like those of the Sea Shepherd Conservation Society in Iceland in 1986 and in Norway in 1992 and 1994, where whaling boats and equipment were sabotaged.[29] The economic value of whaling—which never amounted to more than a few percent of either the Icelandic or Norwegian economies—was not the significant point. It was the small nations against the large nations. In this spirit, the Norwegians controversially declared their support in 1997 for Botswana, Namibia, and Zimbabwe in their efforts to get elephants removed from the endangered species lists. Just as the Norwegians claimed about minke whales, these African nations argued that elephants were not endangered but were destroying farmers' crops and had to be hunted. After a trip to Africa, the Norwegian whale commissioner denied that Norway was in the business of "trading whales for elephants." Rather, he claimed that Norway and the African countries found themselves in the same boat, allies from mutual interest against the larger political powers, stating that "we have a relationship with animals that 'everyone' thinks are endangered, but in reality these populations are highly sustainable."[30]

The pro-whalers of the North Atlantic also formed their own organizations to counter the authority and influence of the IWC, Greenpeace, and the Sea Shepherd Conservation Society, founding the High North Alliance (HNA) in 1991, the North Atlantic Marine Mammal Commission (NAMMCO) in 1992, and joining the World Council of Whalers (WCW). Both NAMMCO and HNA envision themselves as regional alternatives to the IWC's global authority. NAMMCO conducts its own scientific research on North Atlantic whale populations in cooperation with Canada, while HNA functions mainly as a lobbying organization. WCW is primarily a group advocating for the rights of whaling peoples and borrows much of the rhetoric of the indigenous rights movement.[31] Although this is rarely made explicit in the programs of these organizations, much of the pro-whaling literature has tended to treat groups like the Faroe Islanders, Icelanders, and Japanese and Norwegian small-scale whalers as a kind of indigenous people by referring to them as "coastal communities," "traditional cultures," "remote communities," "artisanal whalers," or "minorities." This language seeks to blur the categories of Western/commercial whaling and indigenous/subsistence whaling fundamental to the IWC's current policy. While arguing along the same lines as the IWC policy that "some people are special" (and should therefore be allowed to eat whales), these groups have also attacked the "whales are special" notion by claiming that all whales are not particularly intelligent or nurturing, and, in any case, all animals are special in one way or another—there is no reason to single out whales for humanlike status.

What has therefore emerged from the latest phase of the whaling debates is a series of alliances built on symbolic oppositions—some of which appear quite odd, such as the idea that oil-rich Norway could perceive itself in solidarity with postcolonial African nations. Another unlikely convergence of opinion in this debate is between pro-whaling groups and animal rights organizations such as People for the Ethical Treatment of Animals (PETA). Both oppose the speciesism of whale enthusiasts that holds that some animals are more equal than others.[32] What seems most at issue, and most managed and regulated under the current system, are not only whales, or the tools and techniques of hunting them, but the identity of the people involved and the conflict between local knowledge and scientifically objective knowledge about whales. Whatever the merits of the current system, such a regulation of identity is difficult in principle. It is easier, for example, to regulate the tools used in hunting than the identity of the person who carries them. And the moment for this type of regulation seems inauspicious, as it is being formulated in international agreements at the same time that identity is being reconceptualized or broken down in various ways, such as by virtual identity in online worlds or by notions of hybridity in cultural studies. Given these circumstances, some legal experts have come to regard the IWC's 1986 regulation as impossibly broken.[33]

deCODE AND THE WHALES: THE END
OF THE DEBATE?

The whaling and deCODE episodes reprise many of the themes from the earlier chapters of this book: indigenous versus modern, colonialism and postcolonialism, the unique and the general laws of nature. Although the two sides do not necessarily map neatly onto each other—for example, if someone is anti-deCODE, it does not imply that he or she is therefore also pro-whaling—the general positions and arguments taken by both sides in these debates are versions of eighteenth-century discussions about North Atlantic nature. The deCODE issue seems to have now run its course, however. Opponents to the HSD law challenged its legality in the years after 1998. The central legal issue was the rights of the deceased, who were unable to opt out of the database, nor were their heirs empowered to do so on their behalf. The plaintiffs in the lawsuits alleged that this violated the Icelandic right to privacy, based on the article of the Icelandic Constitution guaranteeing citizens the "privacy of life, home, and family." Although lower courts had upheld the HSD law, on November 27, 2003, the Icelandic Supreme Court sided with Ragnhildur Guðmundsdóttir over the transfer of her father's data and struck down the HSD law as unconstitutional.[34] By late 2003, other problems had also emerged with the construction of the database. More than twenty thousand Icelanders had chosen to opt out, or nearly 6 percent of the population, which would have created a significant gap in the database.[35] The encryption of the data had created complicated technical problems, and the economic fortunes of deCODE had declined along with a substantial drop in the price of its shares on the stock market. The company decided to scale back the project and work to construct a database with the samples and information it had already collected, concentrating its research on heart disease and diabetes.

The whaling debate remains active: at the 2006 IWC meeting, the 1986 decision was due to expire. After a contentious meeting in St. Kitts and Nevis that year, the IWC decided not to change its policy, as there was still no scientific consensus among the members on the health of various whale populations. Several months after this meeting, Iceland resumed scientific whaling, and whale meat is, as of this writing, again available in restaurants in Reykjavík. After the Icelandic economic crash in the fall of 2008, many Icelanders looked to tourism as a means out of their economic predicament, as tourists could now travel to what had been one of the world's most expensive countries for around two-thirds of what the trip had cost before the crash. Icelandic nature, therefore, could be the anecdote to the "irrational exuberance" of which the deCODE enterprise now seemed a part. A new focus on Icelandic tourist attractions, including whale watching, naturally raised concerns that Icelandic whaling might injure this industry, either by chasing the whales away from the tourist boats or by inspiring a boycott of Iceland by environmentally minded tourists, as had happened in the past. In response, the Ministry of Fisheries has designated specific areas for whaling and for whale watching in order to try to keep these two industries from interfering with each other.[36]

Whenever and however these two controversies are eventually resolved, what the deCODE and whaling episodes show is that the central questions about the North Atlantic that I have posed have not been entirely answered. Where is Iceland and what sort of place is it? Is it a modern country or a traditional one? What is its relationship to the rest of the North Atlantic and its distance from both Europe and the United States? This series of questions are not, on the one hand, as open as they were in the mid-eighteenth century, as they have been worked through with respect to the themes of landscape, nature, technology, material culture, religion, and language. On the other hand, they are not completely closed either, as it is still possible to assert that at least some of the North Atlantic natives are "traditional whaling peoples" and that scientific and ethical standards there are ones that cannot be understood or evaluated correctly by outsiders.

This fact leaves, at the beginning of the twenty-first century, a sensation that travelers in the eighteenth century would have found familiar: a sense of confusion, of disorientation bordering on illness, when arriving in Iceland for the first time. This confusion is one of the ways in which the traveler realizes that he or she has arrived in the borderlands, a place that is just slightly off the edges of the map of the known world. The journey through the borderlands is the struggle to establish fixed points of measurement and location that then form the cultural relationship between the North Atlantic and Europe. This journey does not begin and end in the same place. Some points in the North Atlantic can be located on the map, measurable in terms of tools or language. Others remain elusive. At the beginning of the third millennium, this elusive quality is one that con-

tinues to draw travelers to the North Atlantic, with Iceland and Greenland being promoted by tourism companies as "Europe's last wilderness"
and the "last unspoiled" or the "last untouched" places on earth. Although
the tours offered under this marketing rhetoric may be exciting and well
worthwhile in their own rights, readers of this book will at least not be
tempted to take them at face value. Through studying the history of images
and debates over North Atlantic nature, we can see that visiting the North
Atlantic takes place in the mind even as it takes place on top of a glacier or
in a Reykjavík night club. This has been the case for as long as foreigners
have been visiting the North Atlantic—even before they could reach the
tops of glaciers or visit night clubs.

NOTES

Epigraphs: W. H. Auden, with Louis MacNeice, *Letters from Iceland* (London: Faber and Faber, 1937), 26; William Ian Miller, *Bloodtaking and Peacemaking: Feud, Law, and Society in Saga Iceland* (Chicago: University of Chicago Press, 1990), 13.

1   Quoted in Alex Ross, "Björk's Saga," *The New Yorker*, August 23, 2004, 49. Apparent connections between Björk's music and the Icelandic landscape have been a theme in many articles and books about her; see, for example, Evelyn McDonnell, *Army of She: Icelandic, Iconoclastic, Irrepressible Björk* (New York: Random House, 2001), 20–24.

2   The historian of science Skúli Sigurðsson has commented on the cultural

constructions of remembering and forgetting in Icelandic life. In his view, Icelanders suffer from a technological amnesia that obscures the story of their rapid technological modernization after World War II and the large amounts of foreign aid received by the country, in favor of a preoccupation with the distant past when Iceland was independent and saw itself as isolated from the world. See Skúli Sigurðsson, "The Dome of the World: Iceland, Doomsday Technologies and the Cold War," in *Aspects of Arctic and Sub-Arctic History*, ed. Ingi Sigurðsson and Jón Skaptason (Reykjavík: University of Iceland, 2000), 463–73, and "Electric Memories and Progressive Forgetting," in *The Historiography of Contemporary Science and Technology*, ed. Thomas Söderqvist (Amsterdam: Harwood Academic Publishers, 1997), 129–49.

3   Since my first visit to Iceland, the Saga Centre (www.njala.is/en) has opened nearby this site in Hvolsvöllur, about twenty-five kilometers to the north. The center bases itself heavily on the story of *Njáls Saga* and includes a Saga Hall where one can arrange a Viking Feast, complete with storytelling and staff in period costume. Thus, the museum appears to fill the perceived gap between the tourist expectations and the actual site at Bergþórshvoll.

4   There are, of course, historical and archaeological explanations for the general absence of preserved structures from the medieval period in Iceland. Turf, or sod, houses with wood frames were the usual building materials at this time. Well-built turf walls can last from about thirty to a hundred years, depending on the upkeep. Due to the rapid deforestation and soil erosion in the years after settlement, medieval Icelanders never moved from turf to wood construction, as people did in mainland Scandinavia. Furthermore, because Iceland lacked an aristocratic upper class that would build castles and possess rich grave goods of precious metals, there were no medieval buildings and only a few artifacts comparable with those of continental Europe during this time period.

5   The history of the term is discussed by Arturo Esobar in his *Encountering Development: The Making and Unmaking of the Third World* (Princeton, N.J.: Princeton University Press, 1995).

6   For discussion, see Eric R. Wolf, *Europe and the People without History* (Berkeley: University of California Press, 1982).

7   Although Iceland suffered from hyperinflation from the 1970s until the mid-1980s (reaching a high of more than 80 percent in 1983), for several decades before the crash of the Icelandic economy in October 2008 the inflation and unemployment rates were low by western European standards: 4 percent and 2.6 percent, respectively, in 2005. Hagstofa Íslands (Official Statistics of Iceland), www.iceland.org/us/index.html. In the fall of 2008, the Icelandic economy plunged sharply, with the Icelandic króna losing about a third of its value on the international markets. Icelandic banks were nationalized and the

trading in the króna was suspended in an effort to control the financial crisis. Trading resumed after Iceland obtained a loan from the International Monetary Fund, the first time a Western nation had done so since 1976. Economic conditions were largely thought to be responsible for the change of government in the January 2009 Icelandic elections, when the long-ruling Independence Party was ousted by a Left-Green and Social Democratic coalition.

8   Fredrik Barth, ed., *Ethnic Groups and Boundaries: The Social Organization of Culture Difference* (Bergen, Norway: University of Bergen Press, 1969).

9   A few references to the very large literature on this topic include Edward W. Said, *Orientalism* (New York: Vintage Books, 1979). See also Said's *Culture and Imperialism* (New York: Knopf, 1993); and Benedict Anderson's *Imagined Communities* (London: Verso, 1991). On the Americas as the quintessential European other, see Peter Mason, *Deconstructing America: Representations of the Other* (London: Routledge, 1990); and Stephen Greenblatt, *Marvelous Possessions: The Wonder of the New World* (Chicago: University of Chicago Press, 1991). On the European viewing of the South Pacific, see Bernard Smith, *European Vision in the South Pacific* (New Haven: Yale University Press, 1985), and *Imagining the Pacific in the Wake of the Cook Voyages* (Miegunyah, Australia: Melbourne University Press, 1992). Another approach is Francois Hartog, *The Mirror of Herodotus: The Representation of the Other in the Writing of History*, trans. Janet Lloyd (Berkeley: University of California Press, 1988). Within the Scandinavian context, see Elisabeth Oxfeldt, *Nordic Orientalism: Paris and the Cosmopolitan Imagination* (Copenhagen: Museum Tusculanum Press, 2005), on the Danish viewing of the Orient; Mark Davies, *A Perambulating Paradox: British Travel Literature and the Images of Sweden, c. 1770–1865* (Lund: University of Lund, 2000), on British travelers in Sweden; and Sverrir Jakobsson, "'Black Men and Malignant-Looking': The Place of the Indigenous Peoples of North America in the Icelandic World View," in *Approaches to Vínland: A Conference on the Written and Archaeological Sources for the Norse Settlements in the North Atlantic Region and Exploration of America,* ed. Andrew Wawn and Þórunn Sigurðardóttir (Reykjavík: Sigurður Nordal Institute, 2001), 88–104.

10 Harold B. Carter, *Sir Joseph Banks 1743–1820* (London: Natural History Museum, 1988), 468. See especially pages 458–70 for an account of Banks's personal relationship with Iceland and his role in guiding British official policy toward Iceland. Various episodes illustrating how British and Danish interests manifested themselves in the North Atlantic are discussed in Björn Þorsteinsson, "Henry VIII and Iceland," *Saga Book of the Viking Society* 15 (1957–61): 65–101; and Derek McKay, "Great Britain and Iceland in 1809," *The Mariner's Mirror* 59, no. 1 (February 1973): 85–93. The first article details the Danish Crown's attempts to enforce its legal claim to the fishing waters

around Iceland and its efforts, under Christian II, to sell Iceland to England. The second discusses the so-called Icelandic Revolution of 1809, when control of the island was briefly seized by a British merchant and Danish adventurer who imprisoned the Danish governor and claimed the island as a protectorate of Great Britain. The British government quickly disavowed this claim, and leading Icelanders acted to return the country to Danish hands. These episodes are but two illustrations of the ongoing British-Danish negotiation over domination of the region during this period.

11 Since Iceland and the Faroes were legally part of Norway at the time of the Kalmar Union, not of Denmark, they should have been passed along with Norway to Sweden when Denmark lost Norway in 1814. The existence of the islands, however, seems to have been overlooked by the framers of the Treaty of Kiel; Iceland, the Faroes, as well as Greenland, remained part of the Danish kingdom after 1814. In 1924, Norway made a claim to Greenland, but the international court in The Hague decided the case in Denmark's favor. Since 1920, Norway has had jurisdiction over Spitsbergen (Svalbard) and Jan Mayen Island. For a legal history of this claim, see Geir Ulfstein, *The Svalbard Treaty: From Terra Nullius to Norwegian Sovereignty* (Oslo: University of Oslo Press, 1995).

12 See "Decolonising the Arctic: Nearly Independent Day," *The Economist*, June 21, 2009.

13 For more details of the political history of the North Atlantic, see W. Glyn Jones, *Denmark: A Modern History* (London: Croom Helm, 1986); Frances J. Shaw, *The Northern and Western Isles of Scotland: Their Economy and Society in the Seventeenth Century* (Edinburgh: J. Donald, 1980); Sverre Bagge and Knut Mykland, *Norge i dansketiden* (Copenhagen: Politikens Danmarkshistorie, 1987); Björn Þorsteinsson, *Island* (Copenhagen: Politikens Danmarkshistorie, 1985); and Finn Gad, *Grønland* (Copenhagen: Politikens Danmarkshistorie, 1984).

14 Jared M. Diamond, *Collapse: How Societies Choose to Fail or Succeed* (New York: Viking, 2005), 178–276. Diamond generally exaggerates the extent of the Norse cultural taboos against fishing. Passages from the sagas make it clear that the stockfish was an important staple by the twelfth century, although sheep and cattle were primary protein sources.

15 See Jette Arneborg, "Det europæiske landnám-Nordboerne i Grønland, 985–1450 e.v.t.," in *Grønlands forhistorie*, ed. Hans Christian Gulløv (Copenhagen: Gyldendal, 2004), 264–65. Thorkild Kjærgaard points out Diamond's misinterpretation in his "'Én enda ofantlige ödegard': Den europæiske ødegårskrise og nordboernes forsvinden fra Grønland," in a special issue, ed. Andras Mortensen, Alf R. Nielssen, and Jón Th. Thor, *Innussuk* 2 (2006): 121–28.

16   Christian Pløyen, *Erindringer fra en Reise til Shetlandsøerne, Örkenøerne og Skotland i Sommeren 1839* (Copenhagen: C. W. Reizel, 1840), 9–12.

17   Carl Julian Graba, *Tagebuch geführt auf einer Reise nach Färö im Jahre 1828* (Hamburg: Perthes and Besser, 1830), 5.

18   Richard F. Burton, *Ultima Thule; or, A Summer in Iceland*, vol. 1 (London: William P. Nimmo, 1875), 169.

19   Margit Mogensen, "Nordboudstillingen i Paris 1900: iscenesættelse af kolonimagten," in *Danmark og verdensudstillingerne i 19. århundrede: de store udstillinger i politisk, økonomisk, teknologisk, og kulturelt lys* (Copenhagen: University of Copenhagen, 1997), 8.

20   The negative reaction of some Icelandic students to a 1904 exhibition in Copenhagen that placed both Iceland and Greenland in the category of "New Countries" is discussed in Kristján Sveinsson, "Viðhorf Íslendinga til Grænlands og Grænlendinga á 18., 19. og 20. öld," *Saga* 32 (1994): 168–70. The Icelanders particularly objected to being classified with the "barbarous" Greenlanders.

21   Mogensen, "Nordboudstillingen i Paris 1900," 8. For a general look at Danish self-presentations at the World's Fairs, see Mogensen's *Eventyrets tid: Danmarks deltagelse i Verdensudstillingerne 1851–1900* (Copenhagen: Landbohistorisk Selskab, 1993). Bruun explains his conception of the exhibition in *Færøerne, Island og Grønland paa verdensudstillingen i Paris 1900* (Copenhagen: Nielsen and Lydiche, 1901). Anders Ekström, *Den utställda världen: Stockholmutställningen 1897 och 1800-talets världsutställningar* (Stockholm: University of Stockholm, 1994), is a more theoretical look at the meaning of exhibitions, still focusing on Scandinavia. On the connection between exhibitions and colonialism, see Timothy Mitchell, *Colonising Egypt* (Cambridge: Cambridge University Press, 1988).

22   Mogensen, "Nordboudstillingen," 14.

23   Gad, *Grønland*, 100–3. See also Mogens Bencard, "Two 17th-Century Eskimos at Rosenborg Palace," *Meddelelser om Grønland: Man and Society* 12 (1989): 47–55; and Michael Harbsmeier, *Stimmen aus dem äußersten Norden: Wie die Grönländer Europa für sich entdeckten* (Stuttgart: Jan Thorbecke Verlag, 2001).

24   Winfried Weißhaupt, *Europa sieht sich mit fremden Blick. Werke nach dem Schema der "Lettres persanes" in der europäischen, insbesondere der deutschen Literatur des 18. Jahrhunderts*, 2 vols. (Frankfurt: Peter Lang, 1979). See also Michael Harbsmeier, "Schauspiel Europa: Die außereuropäische Entdeckung Europas im 19. Jahrhundert am Beispiel afrikanischer Texte," *Historische Anthropologie* 3 (1994): 331–50. Kirsten Thisted, "'Dengang i de ikke rigtigt gamle dage': Grønlandsk fortælletradition som kilde til 1700-tallets kulturmøde," in *Digternes paryk: studier i 1700-tallet*, ed. Marianne Alenius et al.

(Copenhagen: Museum Tusculanum Press, 1997), 73–86, evaluates the European-Inuit encounter in Inuit folktales in order to understand the Inuit role and participation in the historical process.

25 On the connections between travel descriptions and colonialism, see Mary Louise Pratt, *Imperial Eyes: Travel Writing and Transculturation* (London: Routledge, 1992).

26 See Michael Hechter, *Internal Colonialism: The Celtic Fringe in British National Development, 1536–1966* (Berkeley: University of California Press, 1975); also Charles Withers, "The Historical Creation of the Scottish Highlands," in *The Manufacture of Scottish History*, ed. I. Dounachies and C. Whatley (Edinburgh: Polygon, 1992), 143–56. Eugen Weber discusses the civilizing of the French peripheries, although without using the term "internal colonialism," in his *Peasants into Frenchmen: The Modernization of Rural France, 1870–1914* (Stanford, Calif.: Stanford University Press, 1976); and Nicholas Canney looks at the example of Ireland in *Kingdom and Colony: Ireland in the Atlantic World, 1560–1800* (Baltimore, Md.: Johns Hopkins University Press, 1988), as does Nicholas Whyte in his *Science, Colonialism, and Ireland* (Cork: Cork University Press, 1999). An overview of the concept of internal colonialism from a theoretical perspective is Robert J. Hind, "The Internal Colonial Concept," *Comparative Studies in Society and History* 26, no. 3 (July 1984): 543–68. See also *Internal Peripheries in European History*, ed. Hans-Heinrich Nolte (Göttingen, Germany: Muster-Schmidt, 1991).

27 Hechter, *Internal Colonialism*, 31.

28 The idea of oceans as extensions rather than barriers of coastal societies is argued by Michael N. Pearson in his article, "Littoral Society: The Concept and the Problems," *Journal of World History* 17, no. 4 (2006): 353–73.

29 The idea that binary oppositions are particularly central to European identity is argued by Gerard Delanty in his *Inventing Europe: Idea, Identity, Reality* (New York: St. Martin's Press, 1995), 5.

30 Larry Wolff, *Inventing Eastern Europe: The Map of Civilization on the Mind of the Enlightenment* (Stanford, Calif.: Stanford University Press, 1994), 9. Wolff applies this same model in his *Venice and the Slavs: The Discovery of Dalmatia in the Age of Enlightenment* (Stanford, Calif.: Stanford University Press, 2001). Other books that apply the concept of Orientalism to nearby regions are Jane Schneider, ed., *Italy's "Southern Question": Orientalism in One Country* (New York: Berg, 1998); and Nelson Moe, *The View from Vesuvius: Italian Culture and the Southern Question* (Berkeley: University of California Press, 2002).

31 Harald Gustafsson, Einar Hreinsson, and Christina Folke Ax are among those scholars who have used Icelandic administrative records as a source for ethnographic and social history about class and power in eighteenth-century Iceland. See Harald Gustafsson, *Mellan kung och allmoge: ämbetsmän,*

beslutsprocess och inflytande på 1700-talets Island (Stockholm: Almqvist and Wiksell, 1985); Christina Folke Ax, "De uregerlige: den islandske almue og øvrighedens reformforsøg 1700–1870" (Ph.D. diss., University of Copenhagen, Department of History, 2003), and "At gøre en forskel: opfattelse og anvendelse af danske og islandske genstande og sprog i Reykjavik i sidste halvdel af 1700-tallet," *1066: Tidsskrift for historie* 31, no. 4 (2002): 3–13; and Einar Hreinsson, *Nätverk och nepotism: den regionala förvaltningen på Island 1770–1870* (Gothenberg, Sweden: University of Gothenberg Press, 2003).

32 For more details of these projects and their background, see James Fea, *The Present State of the Orkney Islands Considered, and an Account of a New Method of Fishing on the Coasts of Shetland, Published in 1775* (Edinburgh: W. Brown, 1884). A brief overview is provided in Hance D. Smith, *The Making of Modern Shetland* (Lerwick: Shetland Times, 1977), 12–26.

33 Jürgen Osterhammel, *Kolonialismus: Geschichte-Formen-Folgen* (Munich: C. H. Beck, 1995), 22, 25–26. The English translation is by Shelley L. Frisch, titled *Colonialism: A Theoretical Overview* (Princeton, N.J.: Marcus Wiener, 1997).

34 Michael Adas, in *Machines as the Measure of Men: Science, Technology, and Ideologies of Western Dominance* (Ithaca, N.Y.: Cornell University Press, 1989), examines the European evaluation of technology in China, India, and Africa and how European evaluations of this technology contributed to Europe's sense of cultural superiority. Robert G. David, *The Arctic in the British Imagination, 1814–1914* (Manchester, U.K.: Manchester University Press, 2000), applies and critiques Adas's model in the Arctic region.

35 The classic study of Norwegian language politics is Einar Haugen, *Language Conflict and Language Planning: The Case of Modern Norwegian* (Cambridge, Mass.: Harvard University Press, 1966). Some newer research includes Gregg Bucken-Knapp, *Elites, Language, and the Politics of Identity: The Norwegian Case in Comparative Perspective* (Albany: SUNY Press, 2003). On Norwegian national identity, see Øystein Sørensen, ed. *Jakten på det Norske: Perspecktiver på utviklingen av en norsk nasjonal identitet på 1800-tallet* (Oslo: Gyldendal, 1998).

36 A general history of this period in Iceland is Valtur Ingimundarson, *Í eldlínu kalda stríðsins: Samskipti Íslands og Bandaríkjanna, 1945–1960* (Reykjavík: University of Iceland Press, 1996).

37 The tensions and place of the military base in Icelandic society during the cold war is the subject of Einar Kárason's black comedy *Þar sem djöflaeyjan rís* (Devil's Island), made into a film by Friðrik Þór Friðriksson in 1997.

38 E. Paul Durrenberger, "Epidemiology of Iceland on the Brain," in *Icelandic Essays: Explorations in the Anthropology of Modern Life*, ed. E. Paul Durrenberger (Iowa City: University of Iowa Press, 1992), 3.

39 For an overview of this story, see DeNeen L. Brown, "Trail of Frozen Tears:

The Cold War Is Over, but to the Native Greenlanders Displaced by It, There's Still No Peace," *Washington Post*, October 22, 2002, C1.

1 | ICELANDIC LANDSCAPES

Epigraph: Peter Stark, *Driving to Greenland* (Springfield, N.J.: Burford Books, 1994), 120–21.

1   Uno von Troil, *Brev rörande en Resa til Island* (Uppsala: Magnus Swederus Bokhandel, 1777), 49.

2   Ida Pfeiffer, *Visit to Iceland and the Scandinavian North*, translated from German (London: Ingram, Cooke, and Co., 1852), ix.

3   Mary Wollstonecraft Shelley, *Frankenstein, or The Modern Prometheus*, ed. James Rieger (Chicago: University of Chicago Press, 1982), 9–10. The myth of the open polar sea has a very long history in Western thought. Mercator pictured an open polar sea on his 1569 map of the polar regions. The idea persisted throughout the nineteenth century and was supported by authorities such as the German cartographer August Petermann and the American oceanographer Matthew Fontaine Maury. The mid-nineteenth-century American expeditions of Elisha Kent Kane, Isaac Hayes, and Charles Hall searching for John Franklin's lost 1845 expedition all assumed the existence of the polar sea free of ice and even claimed to have seen it or found evidence for it. It was not until Charles Daly, president of the American Geographical and Statistical Society, expressed skepticism of the idea in his address in 1870, and the Austrian geographer Karl Weyprecht and the British explorer George Nares failed to find any evidence of such a sea on their expeditions in the 1870s, that the myth finally fell out of favor. For a brief history of the idea, see Charles Officer and Jake Page, *A Fabulous Kingdom: The Exploration of the Arctic* (Oxford: Oxford University Press, 2001).

4   The view that the laws of physics reversed themselves in the North Atlantic was explicitly rejected by a group of eighteenth-century naturalists, for reasons discussed in more detail in chapter 2.

5   For a discussion of the differences in the environmental history literature, see Simon Schama, *Landscape and Memory* (New York: Knopf, 1995); and William Cronon, *Changes in the Land: Indians, Colonists, and the Ecology of New England* (New York: Hill and Wang, 1983). See also the discussion in vol. 1, no. 1 of *Environmental History* (1996), articles by William Cronon, "The Trouble with Wilderness: or, Getting Back to the Wrong Nature," 7–28; Samuel P. Hays, "Comment: The Trouble with Bill Cronon's Wilderness," 29–32; Michael P. Cohen, "Comment: Resistance to Wilderness," 33–42; Thomas R. Dunlap, "Comment: But What Did You Go Out in the Wilderness to See?"

43–46; and Cronon again, "The Trouble with Wilderness: A Response," 47–55. The classic study of wilderness in American society is Roderick Nash, *Wilderness and the American Mind* (New Haven: Yale University Press, 1973).

6   Mark Nutall, *Protecting the Arctic: Indigenous Peoples and Cultural Survival* (Amsterdam: Harwood, 1998).

7   Henry Holland, letter to his father, Peter Holland, August 2, 1811, Lbs. 4925 4to, 21, Landsbókasafn Íslands. Ingi Sigurðsson disagrees somewhat with Holland in his "Viðhorf Íslendinga til Skotlands og Skota á 19. og 20. öld," *Saga* 18 (1980): 115–78, arguing that many Icelanders actually found Scottish landscapes familiar and thought that farming in Scotland was similar to Iceland, although conducted more efficiently than at home. On the motif of "wonder" as part of perceptions of alterity, see Stephen Greenblatt, *Marvelous Possessions: The Wonder of the New World* (Chicago: University of Chicago Press, 1991). The linguistic relationship between Europeans and the natives of the North Atlantic is discussed in chapters 4 and 5.

8   The literature on scientific collection in Europe and its effects includes Paula Findlen, *Possessing Nature: Museums, Collecting, and Scientific Culture in Early Modern Italy* (Berkeley: University of California Press, 1994); Lorraine Daston and Katharine Park, *Wonders and the Order of Nature 1150–1750* (New York: Zone Books, 1998); Richard Drayton, *Nature's Government: Science, Imperial Britain, and the "Improvement" of the World* (New Haven, Conn.: Yale University Press, 2000); and Jorge Cañizares-Esguerra, *How to Write the History of the New World: History, Epistemologies, and Identities in the Eighteenth-Century Atlantic World* (Stanford, Calif.: Stanford University Press, 2001). On the specific example of the Kew Botanic Gardens and collection, where many of the British Icelandic specimens ended up, see Lucile H. Brockway, *Science and Colonial Expansion: the Role of the British Royal Botanic Gardens* (New York: Harcourt, Brace, Jovanovich, 1979).

9   Banks also befriended the Danish-educated Icelandic elite and actively encouraged and funded the trips of other Britons to Iceland, including the 1809 visit of William Jackson Hooker, who would later become director of the Royal Botanic Gardens at Kew in London. See the articles on Banks in the David Philip Miller and Peter Hanns Reill collection, *Visions of Empire: Voyages, Botany, and the Representation of Nature* (Cambridge: Cambridge University Press, 1996): David Philip Miller, "Joseph Banks, Empire, and 'Centers of Calculation' in late Hanoverian London," 21–37; and David Mackay, "Agents of Empire: the Banksian Collectors and Evaluation of New Lands," 38–57. See also John Gascoigne, *Joseph Banks and the English Enlightenment: Useful Knowledge and Polite Culture* (Cambridge: Cambridge University Press, 1994). Banks's Iceland diaries are incompletely published as Roy Rauschenberg, "The Journals of Joseph Banks's Voyage," *Proceedings of the American Philo-*

sophical Society 113 (1973): 184–216. Anna Agnarsdóttir has done considerable research on Banks and Iceland; see her "Sir Joseph Banks and the Exploration of Iceland," in *Sir Joseph Banks: A Global Perspective*, ed. R. E. R. Banks et al. (Richmond: Royal Botanic Gardens, 1994), 31–48, and *Great Britain and Iceland 1800–1820* (Ph.D. diss., London School of Economics, Department of International History, 1989). Older, but still useful, is Halldór Hermannsson, *Sir Joseph Banks and Iceland* (Ithaca, N.Y.: Cornell University Press, 1928). Some of the Banks manuscript material is contained in *New Source Material on Sir Joseph Banks and Iceland*, Occasional Papers, Manuscript Series 5 (San Francisco: California State Library, Sutro Branch, 1941), and Neil Chambers's edition of *Scientific Correspondence of Sir Joseph Banks, 1765–1820* (London: Pickering and Chatto, 2007) also contains some material on Iceland.

10 Benjamin Franklin commented on the dense fog experienced in North America in the summer of 1783. Like many of his contemporaries, he incorrectly attributed its cause to an eruption of Hekla rather than Laki. See Benjamin Franklin, "Meteorological Imaginations and Conjectures," in *Memoirs of the Literary and Philosophical Society of Manchester* 2 (1784): 357–61.

11 This investigation of nature was also carried out on other frontiers of the European periphery. As Brian Dolan's study of E. D. Clarke's travels in Scandinavia and eastern Europe points out, Enlightenment travelers constructed hierarchies of civilization on the frontiers of Europe, just as they did in the exotic New World. Travels within Europe, however, were central in shaping the definitions of the limits of European civilization more precisely than overseas encounters because of the gradualness of the sense of leaving European standards as one moved further into unknown territory. Brian Dolan, *Exploring European Frontiers: British Travellers in the Age of Enlightenment* (London: Macmillan, 2000), 8–11. On this theme, see also Larry Wolff's *Inventing Eastern Europe: The Map of Civilization on the Mind of the Enlightenment* (Stanford, Calif.: Stanford University Press, 1994), and his *Venice and the Slavs: the Discovery of Dalmatia in the Age of Enlightenment* (Stanford, Calif.: Stanford University Press, 2001). Mark Davies explores similar themes in *A Perambulating Paradox: British Travel Literature and the Image of Sweden, c. 1770–1865* (Lund: University of Lund Press, 2000).

12 Much of this account is derived from the extremely valuable collection of articles and sources, *Skaftáreldar 1783–1784: Ritgerðir og Heimildir*, ed. Gísli Ágúst Gunnlaugsson et al. (Reykjavík: Mál og Menning, 1984).

13 Magnús Stephensen, *Island i det attende Aarhundrede* (Copenhagen: Gyldendalske Boghandels Forlag, 1808); Hannes Finnsson, *Om Folkemængdens Formindskelse ved Uaar i Island* (Copenhagen: S. L. Møller, 1831). An Icelandic version of *Island i det attende Aarhundrede* (*Eftirmæli átjándu aldar*) had been published by Stephensen's own press at Leirá in Iceland two years earlier,

but Stephensen reworked the text for the Danish edition. Finnsson's book also appeared first in Icelandic as *Mannfækkun af hallærum* (1796).

14 For a discussion of these environmental problems, see Thorkild Kjærgaard, *The Danish Revolution, 1500–1800: An Ecohistorial Interpretation*, trans. David Hohnen (Cambridge: Cambridge University Press, 1994).

15 Gísli Gunnarsson looks at the effects and efficiency of the monopoly trade in *Monopoly Trade and Economic Stagnation: Studies in the Foreign Trade of Iceland 1602–1787* (Lund: University of Lund Press, 1983).

16 These opinions on the monopoly trade were quite widespread among both Danish and Icelandic officials, although the concern was more for saving the Danish government money than for the freedom of the Icelanders. Also, many officials expressed the opinion that the Icelanders were not capable of managing their own trade. For the views of one of the most important of the Icelandic free-trade advocates, see Skúli Magnússon, *Beskrivelse af Gullbringu- og Kjósar Sýslur*, Bibliotheca Arnamagnæna 4, ed. Jón Helgason (Copenhagen: Einar Munksgaard, 1944), and *Forsøg til en Kort Beskrivelse af Island*, Bibliotheca Arnamagnæna 5, ed. Jón Helgason (Copenhagen: Einar Munksgaard, 1944). Already in the first decades following the Móðuharðindi, leading Icelanders, including some officials in the Danish bureaucracy, propagated the story that the Danish government perceived the island as uninhabitable and proposed to resettle all Icelanders on the Jutland peninsula, where other environmental crises had taken their toll on the population there. Historians who have examined the 1785 land commission records have shown this tale to be wildly exaggerated, although not completely false. Nevertheless, the story was widely believed at the time and still has some status as popular myth today. See Anna Agnarsdóttir, "Ráðabrugg á dulmáli: Huglciðingar um skjal frá 1785," *Ný Saga: Tímarit Söfufélags* 6 (1993): 28–41.

17 Gísli Gunnarsson, *Monopoly Trade and Economic Stagnation*, 144–47.

18 Kjærgaard, *Danish Revolution, 1500–1800*, 139–44.

19 In *Mountain Gloom and Mountain Glory: The Development of the Aesthetics of the Infinite* (Ithaca, N.Y.: Cornell University Press, 1959; repr., Seattle: University of Washington Press, 1997), Marjorie Hope Nicolson explores the transformation in perceptions of mountains, mainly in British poetry, from the seventeenth to the nineteenth century. Although the time frame is slightly different, some of my themes—such as the development of a scientifically ordered world—resonate with hers. Along similar lines, see also Alain Corbin, *The Lure of the Sea: The Discovery of the Seaside in the Western World 1750–1840*, trans. Jocelyn Phelps (Cambridge: Cambridge University Press, 1994). Sumarliði R. Ísleifsson discusses Icelanders' changing perceptions of their own natural world and the influence of foreign travelers in this change in "Erlend myndlist og breytt viðhorf til íslenskrar náttúru á 19. og 20. öld,"

in *Íslenska Söguþingið 28.-31. maí 1997*, vol. 1, ed. Guðmundur J. Guðmunds-son and Eiríkur K. Björnsson (Reykjavík: University of Iceland Press, 1998), 180–88.

20   Stanley's papers, MS, JRL 722, 95, John Rylands Library, University of Man-chester, quoted in Andrew Wawn, "John Thomas Stanley and Iceland: The Sense and Sensibility of an Eighteenth-Century Explorer," *Scandinavian Studies* 53 (1981): 53 (capitalization and punctuation in Stanley's journals is irregular). See also Andrew Wawn, "The Enlightenment Traveller and the Idea of Iceland: The Stanley Expedition of 1789 Reconsidered," in *Scandinavica* 28, no. 1 (1989): 5–16. The published journals from the Stanley expedition—which do not include Stanley's own—are *The Journals of the Stanley Expedition to the Faroe Islands and Iceland*, ed. John F. West (Tórshavn, Faroe Islands: Føroya Fróðskaparfelag, 1970). The scientific papers are in *Transactions of the Royal Society of Edinburgh* 3 (1794): "An Account of the Hot Springs near Rykum in Iceland," 127–37; and "An Account of the Hot Springs near Haukadal in Iceland," 138–53.

21   Excellent pictorial histories of travelers' visions of Iceland include Frank Ponzi, *Ísland á átjándu öld: Myndir úr leiðöngrum Banks og Stanleys* (Reyk-javík: Almenna bókafélagið, 1980), and *Ísland á nítjándu öld: Leiðangrar og listamenn* (Reykjavík: Almenna bókafélagið, 1986); also Sumarliði R. Ísleifs-son, *Ísland: framandi land* (Reykjavík: Mál og menning, 1996).

22   This point is emphasized by Sigurjón Baldur Hafsteinsson in his "Rite of Pas-sage through the Lens: Photographs of Iceland in British Travel Accounts, 1875–1905," *Gardar* 27 (1996): 5–47: "Travellers seem to have come to Iceland not to experience the indigenous culture of the Icelanders. Rather, it served more as an important background for the interest of travelers in Iceland's dra-matic nature and history" (11).

23   For the details of the costumes, Dayes probably had reference to a dress brought back by Stanley. Icelandic women's attire seems to have been of par-ticular interest to British travelers; specimens are noted several times in the journals and were brought home by Stanley, Mackenzie, and Hooker in 1809, although the last one was lost on a shipboard fire.

24   The debate is outlined in Roy Porter, *The Making of Geology: Earth Science in Britain 1660–1815* (Cambridge: Cambridge University Press, 1977). On Mack-enzie, see Andrew Wawn, "Gunnlaugs Saga Ormstunga and the Theatre Royal Edinburgh 1812: Melodrama, Mineralogy and Sir George Mackenzie," *Scandi-navica* 21, no. 2 (1982): 139–51.

25   Andrew Wawn, ed., *The Icelandic Journal of Henry Holland, 1810* (London: Hakluyt Society, 1987), 254–55.

26   George Steuart Mackenzie and Henry Holland, *Travels in the Island of Iceland 1810* (Edinburgh: Constable, 1811). Reports on similar rock formations in the Faroe Islands were published in *Transactions of the Royal Society of Edinburgh*

7 (1815): G. S. Mackenzie, "An Account of some Geological Facts Observed in the Faroe Islands," 213–27; and Thomas Allen, "An Account of the Mineralogy of the Faroe Islands," 229–67.

27 Charles Lyell, *Principles of Geology, Being an Attempt to Explain the Former Changes of the Earth's Surface, by Reference to Causes Now in Operation*, vol. 2 (London: J. Murray, 1830–33), 424–28.

28 Magnús Stephensen, *Kort Beskrivelse over den nye Vulcans Ildsprudning i Vester-Skaptefields Syssel paa Island i Aaret 1783* (Copenhagen: Nicolaus Möller, 1785); Sveinn Pálsson's manuscript, printed as "Eldritið," in *Ferðabók Sveins Pálssonar*, vol. 2, ed. Jón Eyþórsson (Reykavík: Örn og Örlygur, 1983), 553–99; and Ebenezer Henderson, *Iceland; or the Journal of a Residence in that Island during the Years 1814 and 1815* (Edinburgh: Oliphant, Waugh, and Innes, 1818). Sigurður Þórarinsson traces these connections in his article "Annáll Skaftárelda," in *Skaftáreldar 1783–1784: Ritgerðir og Heimildir*, ed. Gísli Ágúst Gunnlaugsson et al., 11–36.

29 S. M. Holm, *Om Jordbranden paa Island i Aaret 1783* (Copenhagen, 1784); and Jón Steingrímsson, "Eldritið," in *Æfisagan og önnur rit*, ed. Kristján Albertsson (Reykjavík: Helgafell, 1973). An English translation of Jón Steingrímsson's text has been published as *Fires of the Earth: The Laki Eruption 1783–1784*, trans. Keneva Kunz (Reykjavík: University of Iceland Press, 1998).

30 On the European response to the Lisbon earthquake, see Ulrich Löffler, *Lissabons Fall-Europas Schrecken: Die Deutung des Erdbeben von Lissabon im deutschsprachigen Protestismus des 18. Jahrhunderts* (Berlin: Walter de Gruyter, 1999); Charles B. Brooks, *Disaster at Lisbon: The Great Earthquake of 1755* (Long Beach, Calif.: Shangton Longley, 1994), 168–94; and Martin Stuber, "Gottesstrafe oder Forschungsobjekt? Zur Resonanz von Erdbeben, Überschwemmungen, Seuchen und Hungerkrisen im Korrespondentennetz Albrecht von Hallers," in *Am Tag danach: Zur Bewältigung von Naturkatastrophen in der Schweiz 1500–2000*, ed. Christian Pfister (Bern: Haupt, 2002), 39–54. The most famous reaction is Voltaire's poem, "Désatre de Lisbonne"; for a comment on this, see Ira O. Wade, *Voltaire and Candide: A Study in the Fusion of History, Art, and Philosophy* (London: Kennikat Press, 1959), 104–15.

31 On such political and nationalistic readings of landscape, see Stephen Daniels, *Fields of Vision: Landscape Imagery and National Identity in England and the United States* (Princeton, N.J.: Princeton University Press, 1993); Angela L. Miller, *The Empire of the Eye: Landscape Representation and American Cultural Politics, 1825–1875* (Ithaca, N.Y.: Cornell University Press, 1993); and, for the German case, Thomas M. Lekan, *Imagining the Nation in Nature: Landscape Preservation and German Identity, 1885–1945* (Cambridge, Mass.: Harvard University Press, 2004).

32 Richard Ringler discusses the intellectual and social milieu of Icelandic stu-

dents in Copenhagen in his *Bard of Iceland: Jónas Hallgrímsson, Poet and Scientist* (Madison: University of Wisconsin, 2002), 26–29.

33   See, for example, Gísli Gunnarsson, *Monopoly Trade and Economic Stagnation*; and Harald Gustafsson, *Mellan kung och allmoge: ämbetsmän, beslutsprocess och inflytande på 1700-talets Island* (Stockholm: Almqvist and Wiksell, 1985).

34   Þorvaldur Thoroddsen, *De vulkanske Udbrud paa Island i Aaret 1783* (Copenhagen: Hoffensberg and Traps, 1879), 6. Þorvaldur Thoroddsen was not himself particularly nationalistic in his thinking. He was a geographer and a major figure in the study of climate in Iceland. In contrast to another school of climate scholars dominant in the nineteenth century, he held that the climate in Iceland had not fundamentally changed since the settlement period. Human inflexibility and lack of foresight, Icelandic as well as Danish, was the cause of the changing fortunes of Iceland. On Thoroddsen, see A. E. J. Ogilvie and T. Jónsson, "'Little Ice Age' Research: A Perspective from Iceland," in *The Iceberg in the Midst: Northern Research in Pursuit of a "Little Ice Age,"* ed. Astrid E. Ogilvie and Trausti Jónsson, 19–25 (Boston: Kluwer Academic Publishers, 2001). On the writing of Icelandic history, see Ingi Sigurðsson, *Íslenzk Sagnfræði frá miðri 19. öld til miðrar 20. aldar* (Reykjavík: University of Iceland Press, 1986).

35   Lekan, *Imagining the Nation in Nature*, 22.

36   Lord Dufferin, *Letters from the High Latitudes* (London: John Murray, 1854), 97–98.

37   Jón Stefánsson, "Iceland: Its History and Inhabitants," *Journal of the Transactions of the Victoria Institute, or Philosophical Society of Great Britain* 38 (1902): 62–63.

38   For a discussion of the Little Ice Age, see Brian M. Fagan, *The Little Ice Age: How Climate Made History, 1300–1850* (New York: Basic Books, 2000). On climatic changes in Iceland in this period, see Astrid E. J. Ogilvie, "Local Knowledge and Traveller's Tales: A Selection of Climatic Observations in Iceland," in *Iceland: Modern Processes and Past Environments*, ed. C. Caseldine et al. (Amsterdam: Elsevier, 2005), 257–88.

39   Nineteenth-century geologists (and later, historians and sociologists as well) sometimes referred to Iceland as a "laboratory"—a common theme from the literature of scientific exploration throughout the nineteenth century, which called islands and remote areas of all sorts "nature's laboratories." This trope is discussed by Gillian Beer in "Writing Darwin's Islands: England and the Insular Condition," in *Inscribing Science: Scientific Texts and the Materiality of Communication*, ed. Timothy Lenoir (Stanford, Calif.: Stanford University Press, 1998), 119–39; and by Roy MacLeod in "Imperial Reflections in the Southern Seas: The Funafufi Expeditions, 1896–1904," in *Nature in Its*

Greatest Extent: Western Science in the Pacific, ed. Roy MacLeod and Philip F. Rehbock (Honolulu: University of Hawai'i Press, 1988), 159–91. See also Roy MacLeod and Philip F. Rehbock, eds., *Darwin's Laboratory: Evolutionary Theory and Natural History in the Pacific* (Honolulu: University of Hawai'i Press, 1994). The theme of Iceland as a laboratory is also discussed in the context of the deCODE controversy in the epilogue.

40 Another participant in the expedition was the German chemist Robert Wilhelm Bunsen, who analyzed the chemical composition of magma. For a history of volcanic science, see Haraldur Sigurðsson, *Melting the Earth: The History of Ideas on Volcanic Eruptions* (Oxford: Oxford University Press, 1999). Bunsen's paper on the magma composition is "Ueber die Processe der vulkanischen Gesteinsbildungen Islands," *Annalen der Physik und Chemie* 83 (1851): 197–272.

41 *Danmark* (Copenhagen: E. M. Bærentzen and Co., 1856).

42 Sumarliði R. Ísleifsson, *Ísland*, 175. The pictures of Frederick Theodore Kloss, who accompanied the Danish prince Frederik Carl Christian on his visit to Iceland in 1834, have similar qualities to Larson's. See Fr. T. Kloss, *Prospecter af Island malede efter Naturen paa den, i Fölge med Hans Kongelige Höihed, Prinds til Danmark Frederik Carl Christian's i Sommeren 1834 foretagene Reise* (Copenhagen, 1835). On the Danish Golden Age painters, see Kasper Monrad, ed., *Danish Painting: The Golden Age, a Loan Exhibition from the Statens Museum for Kunst, Copenhagen, 5 September–20 November 1984* (London: National Gallery, 1984). The text that accompanies the pictures in *Danmark*, as in the records of the Stanley expedition, is somewhat at variance with these calm images and presents a wilder picture of Icelandic (as well as Faroese and Greenlandic) nature.

43 The year 1783 was hardly the last time that the Icelanders suffered a disastrous volcanic eruption, however. The eruption of Askja in 1875 triggered an agricultural crisis, especially in the East Fjords, and was in part responsible for nineteenth-century Icelandic immigration to Canada, where the newcomers founded a settlement in Manitoba called New Iceland.

44 Gunnar Karlsson, "Icelandic Nationalism and the Inspiration of History," in *The Roots of Nationalism: Studies in Northern Europe*, ed. Rosalind Mitchison (Edinburgh: John Donald Publishers, 1980), 83.

45 Orla Lehmann, review of B. Einarson's *Om de danske Provindsialstænder med specielt Hensyn paa Island, Maanedsskrift for Litteratur* 7 (1832): 524.

46 For a more detailed discussion of the sagas and nationalism, see Jesse L. Byock, "Modern Nationalism and the Icelandic Sagas," in *Northern Antiquity: The Post-medieval Reception of Edda and Saga*, ed. Andrew Wawn (Middlesex, U.K.: Hisarlik Press, 1994), 163–88.

47 For a study of parallel developments in the Faroe Islands, see Tom Nauerby,

No Nation Is an Island: Language, Culture, and National Identity in the Faroe Islands (Århus, Denmark: Århus University Press, 1996). For further discussion of cultural nationalism in Scandinavia, see Jens Rahbeck Rasmussen, "The Danish Monarchy as a Composite State," in *European Identities: Cultural Diversity and Integration in Europe since 1700*, ed. Nils Arne Sørensen (Odense, Denmark: Odense University Press, 1995), 23–36.

48   A history of Icelandic art is provided by Björn Th. Björnsson in *Íslenzk myndlist á 19. og 20. öld. Drög að sögulegt yfirliti* (Reykjavík: Helgafell, 1964). I have not examined Icelandic films here as a source of insight into Icelandic views of the country's nature, but Íris Ellenberger has done so in her *Íslandskvikmyndir 1916–1966: Ímyndir, sjálfsmynd og vald* (Reykjavík: University of Iceland, 2007).

49   On this movement, see Adalsteinn Ingólfsson, "Earth, Air, and Water: Georg Gudni and the Icelandic Landscape Tradition," in *Georg Guðni: the Mountain*, ed. Hannes Sigurðsson (Akureyri, Iceland: Akureyri Art Museum, 2007), 119.

50   Frank Ponzi, *Finnur Jónsson: Íslenskur brautryðjandi* (Reykjavík: Almenna bókafélagið, 1983).

51   Thanks to Edward Huijbens and Hildigunnur Ólafsdóttir for drawing the phenomena of "volcanic tourism" to my attention, in which Icelanders drive out to observe volcanic eruptions from a safe distance as soon as such events are reported in the news. This activity clearly indicates a considerable shift from the way that Icelandic volcanoes were understood in the eighteenth century. Another indication of the modern domestification of Icelandic volcanism might be the brand of candy that is sold under the name Hraun (lava). It is a puffed rice cake covered with chocolate and comes in sizes like Risar Hraun (giant lava) and Hraun bitar (lava bites). The manufacturer is Góa, a well-known Icelandic confectionary company.

52   Sigurður H. Þorsteinsson, ed., *Íslenzk Frímerki* (Reykjavík: Ísafold, 1990), 55, 79; Don Brandt, *Exploring Iceland through Stamps: A Philatelic Odyssey* (Reykjavík: Iceland Review, 1991).

53   William Jackson Hooker, *Journal of a Tour in Iceland in the Summer of 1809*, vol. 1 (London: Longman, 1813), 174. See Sumarliði R. Ísleifsson, "Erlend myndlist," for a discussion of Icelanders' attitudes toward Icelandic nature.

54   W. G. Collingwood and Jón Stefánsson, *A Pilgrimage to the Saga-Steads of Iceland* (Ulverston, U.K.: W. Holmes, 1899), v.

55   Kenneth Olwig's book, *Nature's Ideological Landscape: A Literary and Geographic Perspective on Its Development and Preservation on Denmark's Jutland Heath* (London: George Allen and Unwin, 1985), shows how Danish perceptions of the marshes of Jutland changed between 1750 and the present. Nature in Jutland, as in Iceland, was both romanticized and condemned by opposing interests. The discussion about Jutland's nature and how it should be treated,

however, took place mostly within the Danish state, as the region attracted
fewer foreign visitors than Iceland did.

56 Kjærgaard, *Danish Revolution*, 100–5.

57 Ibid., 135–37.

58 Oddgeir Stephensen and Jón Sigurðsson, eds., *Lovsamling for Island* (a collection of the laws concerning Iceland), vol. 4 (Copenhagen: Universitets-
Boghandler Andr. Fred. Höst., 1853–59), 278–96.

59 As discussed in Kirsten Hastrup, *Nature and Policy in Iceland 1400–1800: An
Anthropological Analysis of History and Mentality* (Oxford: Oxford University
Press, 1990), 65–66.

60 A political reading of the Danish Golden Age painters suggests that this
turn toward the Danish landscape, rather than to the classical subjects, and
the efforts to portray the landscape of the kingdom as serene and controlled,
could be understood in the context of a politically and economically weak and
diminished state in the nineteenth century. The paintings were not specifically
responses to political circumstances, but their popularity can be seen as reso-
nating with themes in political life about strengthening the Danish kingdom
from within in order to compensate for what had been lost outside the boundaries of the state. Some aspects of the Danish Golden Age and its political implications are taken up by Hans Hertel and Bente Scavenius in "Hjemme og ude,
oppe og nede: Guldalderens konstraster," in *Guldalderens Verden: 20 historier
fra nær og fjern*, ed. Bente Scavenius (Copenhagen: Gyldendal, 1996), 9–21.

61 This is a different Jón Stefánsson from the one cited above, who was the
coauthor of the Collingwood book and the promoter of Icelandic-British
connections.

62 For examples of these types of power arrangements, see Ingjerd Hoëm,
"The Scientific Endeavor and the Natives," in *Visions of Empire*, ed. Miller
and Reill, 305–25; Mark David Spence, *Dispossessing the Wilderness: Indian
Removal and the Making of the National Parks* (Oxford: Oxford University
Press, 1999); and James Secord, "Narrative Landscapes: Interpreting the Scot-
tish Highlands" (unpublished MS, cited with permission of the author).

2 | NORDIC BY NATURE

Epigraph: Paul Gaimard and Xavier Marmier, *Voyages de la Commission Scientifique du Nord, en Scandinavie, en Laponie, au Spitzberg et aux Feröe, pendant les années 1838, 1839, et 1840* (Paris: Arthus Bertrand, 1842), 2.

1 Carl Julian Graba, *Tagebuch geführt auf einer Reise nach Färö im Jahre 1828*
(Hamburg: Perthes and Besser, 1830), 18.

2 Brian W. Ogilvie, "Travel and Natural History in the Sixteenth Century," in

Sammeln in der Frühen Neuzeit, Preprint no. 50, edited by Brian W. Ogilvie, Anke te Heesen, and Martin Gierl, 27 (Berlin: Max-Planck-Institut für Wissenschaftsgeschichte, 1996). See also Ogilvie's *The Science of Describing: Natural History in Renaissance Europe* (Chicago: University of Chicago Press, 2006).

3   These are described and analyzed in Alix Cooper, *Inventing the Indigenous: Local Knowledge and Natural History in Early Modern Europe* (Cambridge: Cambridge University Press, 2007). See also Cooper's "'The Possibilities of the Land': The Inventory of 'Natural Riches' in the Early Modern German Territories," in *Oeconomies in the Age of Newton,* ed. Margaret Schabas and Neil de Marchi (Durham, N.C.: Duke University Press, 2003), 129–53, and "The Indigenous versus the Exotic: Debating Natural Origins in Early Modern Europe," *Landscape Research* 28, no. 1 (2003): 51–60.

4   James L. Larson, *Interpreting Nature: The Science of the Living Form from Linnaeus to Kant* (Baltimore, Md.: Johns Hopkins University Press, 1994), 99–131.

5   However, the Danish Royal Scientific Society's efforts to publish a description of King Christian VI's journey through Norway in 1733 ultimately failed due to the costs. A history of the society in English is provided by Olaf Pedersen in *Lovers of Learning: A History of the Royal Danish Academy of Science and Letters 1742–1992* (Copenhagen: Det Kongelige Danske Videnskabernes Selskab, 1992). The society was also interested in participating in Carsten Niebuhr's 1761–67 expedition to the Near and Far East, but because the society was dependent on the Danish Cancelli (Danske Kancelli), and Niebuhr's expedition was organized by the German Cancelli (Tyske Kancelli), these plans did not come to fruition. It had, however, connections to other European scientific societies and was involved in the Pan-European project to observe the transit of Venus in 1761 and 1769.

6   Eggert Ólafsson and Bjarni Pálsson, *Vice-lavmand Eggert Olafsens og Landphysici Biarne Povelsens Reise igiennem Island, foranstaltet af Videnskaberne Sælskab i Kiøbenhavn* (Sorøe, Denmark: Jonas Lindgren, 1772). The German translation appeared in 1774, the French in 1802, and the English in 1805 (*Travels in Iceland: Performed 1752–1757 by Order of His Danish Majesty* [London: Barnard and Sultzer, 1805]).

7   So much so that one anonymous British commentator derided it as "accurate and circumstantial, yet it is unfortunately clogged with repetitions, and the facts are recounted in so tedious and uninteresting a manner, that it requires a most phlegmatic temper, and a large fund of patience, to go through the whole of this work, for it is filled with a long and dull recital of events, methodized in the most formal manner possible." Uno von Troil, introduction to *Letters on Iceland* (London: W. Richardson, 1780), ix, which is a translation of his *Brev rörande en Resa til Island* from his 1772 expedition with Banks.

8   The eighteenth century was not, however, the first time that Icelanders wrote natural histories. In the seventeenth century, natural history was a popular genre and prominent Icelanders, including Vísi-Gísli (Gísli Magnússon), Þorlákur Skúlason, Brynjólfur Sveinsson, and Jón Guðmundsson, also described their own country, believing that as natives they were in the best position to write factual accounts; see Gísli Magnússon, "Consignatio Instituti seu Rationes: Greinargarð um fyriрætlun," in *Gísli Magnússon (Vísi-Gísli): Ævisaga, ritgerðir, bréf*, ed. Jakob Benediktsson (Reykjavík, 1939), 48–85. Vísi-Gísli was among the first Icelanders to be interested in technological and economic reform in Iceland. Þorlákur Skúlason's and Brynjólfur Sveinsson's texts are published as *Two Treatises on Iceland from the 17th Century*, ed. Jakob Benediktsson, Bibliotheca Arnamagnæna 3 (Copenhagen: Einar Munksgaard, 1943). See also Halldór Hermannsson, *Jón Guðmundsson and His Natural History of Iceland* (Ithaca, N.Y.: Cornell University Press, 1924). Unlike many of these other authors, Jón was an unschooled man, and his book is an interesting mixture of some superstitious stories and pertinent observations, which can be taken as an example of the wide variety of material included in natural histories in the early period of the genre.

9   In addition to Magnús Stephensen's book discussed in the preceding chapter, *Island i det attende Aarhundrede*, many other treatises of this type were produced, most only available in Icelandic and Danish archives; examples include Hans Christian Bech, "Om Handel paa Island skrevet Anno 1781," MS, JS 37, fol. 1, Landsbókasafn Íslands, and Niels Horrebow, *Relation og Betænkning om Islands Oeconomie og nærværende Tilstand og hvorledes Landet kan komme i Stand*, 1742, 4to, Thott, Det Kongelige Bibliotek. Some published examples are Skúli Magnússon's essays on conditions in Iceland and agricultural reform, which were submitted for competitions of Det Danske Landhusholdingsselskab (the Danish Society for Farming Households): *Beskrivelse af Gullbringu- og Kjósar Sýslur* and *Forsøg til en Kort Beskrivelse af Island*. For a study of the Icelandic administrative bureaucracy, social networks, and their political influence see Einar Hreinsson, "En stat, en förvaltning, två nätverk: Den danske förvaltningen på Island 1770–1870," in *Att Synliggöra det Osynliga: Sex uppsatser om socialt handlande och sociala nätverk*, ed. Tomas Nilson (Gothenberg, Sweden: Institute for History, 2000), 114–39, and *Nätverk och nepotism: den regionala förvaltningen på Island 1770–1870* (Gothenberg, Sweden: University of Gothenberg, 2003).

10 Bech, "Om Handel paa Island," Landsbókasafn Íslands. Mathias Jochumssen [Vagel], a Norwegian trader in the early eighteenth century, attributed Icelandic poverty to many of the same causes as Bech did; see his *Anmerkninger ofver Jsland og dessen Indbyggere: Innberetning etter reiser på Island 1729–1731*, ed. Oddvar Vasstveit (Oslo: University of Oslo Press, 1977). Hrefna Róberts-

dóttir, in her *Wool and Society: Manufacturing Policy, Economic Thought and Local Production in 18th-Century Iceland* (Gothenberg, Sweden: Makadam, 2008), has made a thorough study of the way in which both Icelandic and Danish officials thought about the state and economy in the Danish kingdom. She finds that officials thought of the Danish kingdom as containing a series of overlapping regions, with a strong dividing line between Norway and Denmark. Northern Norway was seen as separate from the rest of Norway, and Iceland and the Faroes were grouped together with it. Greenland was sometimes seen as one of the North Atlantic provinces "but seems also to have been viewed as quite far away, though maybe not as remote as the colonies in the West Indies, Africa, and India" (89–90).

11   Isl. Journ. A. Nr. 1528, Rtk., 32.20, Þjóðskjalasafn Íslands. On the Nye Indretninger, see also Hrefna Róbertsdóttir, "Áætlun um allsherjarviðreisn Íslands 1751–1752," in *Landnám Ingólfs: Nýtt safn til sögu þess* (Reykjavík: Félagið Ingólfur, 1996), 29–88, and *Landsins forbetran: Innréttingar og verkþekking í ullarvefsmiðjum átjándu aldar* (Reykjavík: University of Iceland Press, 2001). Skúli Magnússon and Nye Indretninger have been the subjects of considerable research by Icelandic historians; see Jón Jónsson, *Skúli Magnússon landfógeti 1711–1911* (Reykjavík: Sigurður Kristjánsson, 1911); Lýður Björnsson, "Ágrip af sögu Innréttinganna," in *Reykjavík í 1100 ár*, ed. Helgi Þorláksson (Reykjavík: Sögufélagið, 1974), 117–45, and *Íslands hlutafélag: Rekstrarsaga Innréttinganna* (Reykjavík: Hið íslenzka bókmenntafélag, 1998); also, in English, Gísli Ágúst Gunnlaugsson, "The Granting of Privileges to Industry in Eighteenth Century Iceland," *Scandinavian Journal of History* 7, no. 3 (1982): 195–204.

12   For example, many of the authors of these natural histories and improvement treatises were members of the Lærdómslistafélagið, an association founded in 1779 by Icelanders living in Copenhagen that published many Enlightenment-inspired tracts about Iceland. On some of the personal connections among these figures, see Ingi Sigurðsson's *Hugmyndaheimur Magnúsar Stephensens* (Reykjavík: University of Iceland Press, 1996), and his edited volume, *Upplýsingin á Íslandi: Tíu ritgerðir* (Reykjavík: University of Iceland Press, 1990). Other personal relationships among this Enlightenment elite are discussed in Lýður Björnsson, *Íslands hlutafélag*; Jón Jónsson, *Skúli Magnússon landfógeti*; and Einar Hreinsson, "En stat, en förvaltning, två nätverk," and *Nätverk och nepotism*.

13   The literature on the role of states in shaping natural environments is vast, but some important contributions are James C. Scott, *Seeing Like a State: How Certain Schemes to Improve the Human Condition Have Failed* (New Haven, Conn.: Yale University Press, 1998); James Fairhead and Melissa Leach, *Misreading the African Landscape: Society and Ecology in a Forest-Savanna Mosiac* (Cambridge: Cambridge University Press, 1996); and Richard Dray-

ton, *Nature's Government: Science, Imperial Britain, and the "Improvement" of the World* (New Haven, Conn.: Yale University Press, 2000).

14   Lisbet Koerner, "Purposes of Linnaean Travel: A Preliminary Research Report," in *Visions of Empire: Voyages, Botany, and the Representation of Nature*, ed. David Phillip Miller and Peter Hanns Reill (Cambridge: Cambridge University Press, 1996), 125. Koerner's *Linnaeus: Nature and Nation* (Cambridge, Mass.: Harvard University Press, 1999), goes into more detail about Linnaeus's acclimatization experiments and the importance of the frontier region of Lapland in constructing his visions of the possibilities of Scandinavian nature. On the connections between economic thought and scientific descriptions of territory as a general practice beyond Linnaeus, see Mattias Legnér, *Fäderneslandets rätta beskrivning: Mötet mellan antikvarisk forskning och ekonomisk nyttokult i 1700-talets Sverige* (Helsinki: Svenska litteratursällskapet i Finland, 2004). On the role of mercantilism within Denmark, see Kristof Glamann and Erik Oxenbøll, *Studier i dansk merkantilisme: Omkring tekster af Otto Thott* (Copenhagen: University of Copenhagen Akademisk Forlag, 1983).

15   Martha Baldwin draws attention to a similar discourse in seventeenth-century Denmark in the pharmaceutical and medical professions that, in conjunction with royal patronage, promoted native medicines over imported ones. See her "Danish Medicines for Danes and the Defense of Indigenous Medicines," in *Reading the Book of Nature: The Other Side of the Scientific Revolution*, ed. Allen G. Debus and Michael T. Walton (Kirksville, Mo.: Sixteenth Century Journal Publishers, 1998), 163–80.

16   Michael A. Osborne, *Nature, the Exotic, and the Science of French Colonialism* (Bloomington: University of Indiana, 1994), esp. 62–97 and 145–71. See also Eugene Cittadino, *Nature as the Laboratory: Darwinian Plant Ecology in the German Empire* (Cambridge: Cambridge University Press, 1990), which focuses on the intellectual rather than economic aspects of this practice. On the history of the acclimatization in colonial contexts, see Michael A. Osborne, "Acclimatizing the World: A History of the Paradigmatic Colonial Science," *Osiris* 15 (2000): 135–51.

17   On this theme, see David Arnold, *Colonizing the Body: State Medicine and Epidemic Disease in Nineteenth-Century India* (Berkeley: University of California Press, 1993), and Arnold's edited volume, *Warm Climates and Western Medicine: The Emergence of Tropical Medicine, 1500–1900* (Amsterdam: Rodopi, 1996).

18   See Louis Bobé, "Hans Egede, Grønlands Missionær og Kolonisator," *Meddelelser om Grønland* 129, no. 1 (Copenhagen, 1944): 1–344, esp. 168–72. For a general history of the Danish settlements in Greenland, see Mads Lide-

gaard, *Grønlands historie* (Copenhagen: A. Busck, 1991); Finn Gad, *Grønland* (Copenhagen: Politikens Danmarkshistorie, 1984); Henning Bro, *Grønland: Kilder til en dansk kolonihistorie* (Copenhagen: Det Grønlandske Selskab, 1993); and, in English, Finn Gad, *A History of Greenland*, trans. Ernst Dupont (London: C. Hurst, 1970). See also Clarence J. Glacken, *Traces on the Rhodian Shore: Nature and Culture in Western Thought from Ancient Times to the End of the Eighteenth Century* (Berkeley: University of California Press, 1967), about eighteenth-century theories relating to people and climate.

19 For the details of the eighteenth-century environmental history of Jutland, see the discussion in Thorkild Kjærgaard, *The Danish Revolution, 1500–1800: An Ecohistorial Interpretation*, trans. David Hohnen (Cambridge: Cambridge University Press, 1994).

20 Anna Agnarsdóttir, "Ráðabrugg á dulmáli: Hugleiðingar um skjal frá 1785," *Ný Saga: Tímarit Sögufélags* 6 (1993): 28–41.

21 "Iutska folked," Stift. III 95, Þjóðskjalasafn Íslands. This document is also reproduced in Lýður Björnsson, *Íslands hlutafélag*, 55–57.

22 The introduction of reindeer into new territories to replace other herding animals has in fact been a frequent practice in Alaska, Greenland, and South Georgia Island, among other places, although the Icelandic experiment was among the earliest—if not the very first—such attempt, occurring nearly 150 years before similar projects. For some general comparative history of reindeer introduction, see N. Leader-Williams, *Reindeer on South Georgia* (Cambridge: Cambridge University Press, 1988), esp. 3–52.

23 Oddgeir Stephensen and Jón Sigurðsson, eds., *Lovsamling for Island*, vol. 3 (Copenhagen: Universitets-Boghandler Andr. Fred. Höst., 1853–59), 63.

24 The most complete history of reindeer in Iceland is Ólafur Þorvaldsson, *Hreindýr á Íslandi 1771–1960* (Reykjavík: Bókaútgáfa Menningarsjóðs, 1960). Other useful sources include Skarphéðinn G. Þórisson, *Hreindýrarannsóknir 1979–1981* (Reykjavík: Orkustofnan, 1983), 13–21; Helgi Valtýsson, *Á hreindýraslóðum: Öræfatöfrar Íslands* (Akureyri: Bókaútgáfan Norðri, 1945), 111–228; and Guðmundur Þorláksson, "Af Rendyrets Saga i Island," *Grønland* (1956): 173–78. The reindeer project is also mentioned by Magnús Stephensen in his *Island i det attende Aarhundrede*, 75–76.

25 Oddgeir Stephensen and Jón Sigurðsson, *Lovsamling for Island*, vol. 4, 588–89.

26 Ibid., vol. 5, 683.

27 Ibid., 393–94.

28 Ibid.

29 The phenomenon of "ungulate irruption" occurring with introduced reindeer and other herbivores is well-known worldwide and is described in Leader-Williams, *Reindeer on South Georgia*. Several cases of the environmental

effects of these irruptions—which occur when ungulates (herbivores with large, horny hooves) increase exponentially in response to an excess of food, overshooting the capacity of the plant communities to sustain them—are described in Elinor G. K. Melville, *A Plague of Sheep: Environmental Consequences of the Conquest of Mexico* (Cambridge: Cambridge University Press, 1994).

30 Oddgeir Stephensen and Jón Sigurðsson, *Lovsamling for Island*, vol. 5, 683–84.

31 Ibid., vol. 6, 177–78, and 349–50.

32 Cited in Guðmundur Þorláksson, "Af Rendyrets Saga i Island," 176.

33 Ibid., 178.

34 The hydroelectric dam currently being built at Kárahnjúkar in east Iceland, which has been the subject of considerable environmental concern, threatens the grazing pastures of the reindeer living there. Some species of birds, fish, insects, and mosses are also endangered by the project. For a discussion of the politics and environmental impact of the dam, see Mark Lynas, "Damned Nation," *The Ecologist*, December 2003/January 2004; and Susan De Muth, "Power Driven," *Guardian*, November 29, 2003.

35 Kristján Sveinsson's account of the import of musk-oxen from Greenland to Iceland in 1929 and 1930 shows some interesting parallels with the story of the reindeer. The idea did not originate in Iceland but with a group in Denmark that was concerned about the preservation of northern nature, since the musk-oxen were threatened in Greenland by overhunting. The Icelandic parliament agreed to bring the animals to Iceland, which would serve as a nature preserve for them, but they died of illness. The project was undertaken against the advice of zoologists consulted by the Danish group and seems to have been supported by no scientific evidence stronger than the desire to believe that animals originating in Greenland naturally would flourish in Iceland. See Kristján Sveinsson, "Íslensk sauðnautasaga, 1905–1931," *Ný Saga: Tímarit Sögufélags* 10 (1998): 85–102.

36 Niels Horrebow, *Tilforladelige Efterretninger om Island* (Copenhagen, 1752); Eggert Ólafsson and Bjarni Pálsson, *Reise igiennem Island*; Erik Pontoppidan, *Det förste Forsög paa Norges naturlige historie* (Copenhagen: Berlingske Arvingers Bogtrykkerie, 1752–53); Olaus Olavius, *Oeconomisk Reyse igiennem de nordvestlige, nordlige, og nordostlige Kanter af Island* (Copenhagen, 1780). On the activities of scientific societies, see James E. McClellan III, *Science Reorganized: Scientific Societies in the Eighteenth Century* (New York: Columbia University Press, 1985). Jacques Revel argues that, in the case of the French state, collecting statistics and drawing maps were similar techniques to writing natural histories in defining a territory; see his "Knowledge of the Territory," *Science in Context* 4, no. 1 (1991): 131–61.

37   These are discussed by Sumarliði R. Ísleifsson in his *Ísland: framandi land* (Reykjavík: Mál og menning, 1996), 11–71. He argues that there was a change in the mid-eighteenth century in the picture of Iceland in travel books along similar lines as I see here.

38   Arngrimus Jonas (as he was called in English), *Brevis commentarius de Islandia*, in *The Principal Navigations, Voyages, Traffiques and Discoveries of the English Nation*, ed. Richard Hakluyt, vols. 4 and 8 (Glasgow: Hakluyt Society, 1903).

39   Horrebow, *Tilforladelige Efterretninger om Island*. This quotation is from the English translation, *The Natural History of Iceland*, ed. A. Linde et al. (London, 1758), vii. The reception of this book in Britain, like that of Eggert Ólafsson and Bjarni Pálsson's *Reise igiennem Island* (see note 7 in this chapter), was very critical. Horrebow's systematic approach of devoting one chapter to each form of animal life in Iceland was ridiculed, and it was his chapter on snakes (reading in full, "No snakes of any kind are to be met with throughout the whole island") that Samuel Johnson famously claimed to be able to recite by heart. The book also appeared in German (1753), Dutch (1756), and French (1764) translations but was not translated into Icelandic until 1966.

40   Johann Anderson's *Nachrichten von Island, Grönland, und der Strasse Davis* (Hamburg, 1746) was translated into Danish in 1748, with some of the sections most critical of the Danish monopoly of trade in the North Atlantic omitted. Dutch (1750), French (1754), and Italian (1754) editions of the book also appeared.

41   Horrebow, *Natural History*, 19–20.

42   There appears to have been some royal dissatisfaction with his services, but the exact nature of this is unclear.

43   The Danish Royal Scientific Society, unlike its British counterpart, was closely tied to royal favor in the eighteenth century: it had no general allowance until 1774 but was forced to apply to the Danish Crown for grants for individual projects. Christian VI's royal letter to Johan Ludvig Holstein and Hans Gram, the founders of the society, in 1743 instructed them to "first and foremost . . . pay attention to anything that is in any way connected with the histories of Our realms and countries." Quoted in Pedersen, *Lovers of Learning*, 41. Horrebow's trip, unlike Eggert and Bjarni's, was not directed through the society but was funded by the king, although Horrebow's reports were read at the society's meetings in 1750. Pedersen, *Lovers of Learning*, 70.

44   Eggert Ólafsson and Bjarni Pálsson, *Reise igiennem Island*, book 2, section 788, 95–96. In her "From Hell to Homeland: Eggert Ólafsson's *Reise igiennem Island* and the Construction of Icelandic Identity," in *Images of the North: Histories-Identities-Ideas*, ed. Sverrir Jakobsson (Amsterdam: Rodopi, 2009), 131–38, Karin Schaer points out that the book does not compare Iceland to other

countries as often as other eighteenth-century natural histories did; rather, one part of Iceland is compared with another. She claims that this "develops an image of Icelandic nature as something deeply different to that of other European countries, yet adjures defense of such differences" (134). While it is true that the book portrays Icelandic nature as different from Danish nature, it also stresses that these differences should not be understood as supernatural phenomena but as explicable by the regular processes of nature.

45 Olavius, *Oeconomisk Reyse*, 1. Olavius, who traveled in Iceland during the summers of 1775–77, was assigned the task of writing about the northern and eastern regions of Iceland, since these areas of the island had not been investigated by the land commission in 1770–71 (Landnefndarinn fyrri). This land commission was a significant undertaking on the part of the Danish state. It consisted of three officials and a secretary (two Danes and two Icelanders), received letters from almost 1 percent of the Icelandic population, and presented a final bill of over 7,924 riksdaler (a cow cost about 7 riksdaler in Iceland at this time). The four men traveled throughout the southern and western areas of Iceland, while Olavius was appointed to write about the northern and eastern regions of the country. This work was published as *Oeconomisk Reyse igiennem de nordvestlige, nordlige, og nordostlige Kanter af Island*. On the 1770 land commission, see Harald Gustafsson, *Mellan kung och allmoge: ämbetsmän, beslutsprocess och inflytande på 1700-talets Island* (Stockholm: Almqvist and Wiksell), 1985.

46 Olavius, *Oeconomisk Reyse*, 5.

47 Horrebow, *Relation og Betænkning om Islands Oeconomie*, Det Kongelige Bibliotek.

48 Although this was not necessarily the case; Friedrich August Ludwig Thienemann, who went to Iceland in 1820–21, believed that Icelandic nature was unique and different from the rest of the northern countries and that the Icelandic mouse was a different species than its European cousin. At the same time, he also had a high opinion of the Icelandic people. Indeed, the argument could be equally well made (and was made, especially in the nineteenth century, as other cultural connections between Europe and Iceland developed) in the opposite direction—that people living in a unique nature would naturally be a superior people. Friedrich August Ludwig Thienemann, *Reise im Norden Europa's, vorzüglich in Island, in den Jahren 1820 bis 1821* (Leipzig: Carl Heinrich Reclam, 1827). According to Thienemann, by 1820 large herds of reindeer were fending for themselves in the uninhabited desert interior of Iceland.

49 Gunnar Karlsson, *Iceland's 1100 Years: The History of a Marginal Society* (Reykjavík: Mál og menning, 2000), 175; Harald Gustafsson, *Political Interaction in the Old Regime: Central Power and Local Society in the Eighteenth-Century Nordic States*, trans. Alan Crozier (Lund: Studentlitteratur, 1994), 43.

Epigraph: Francis Spufford, *I May Be Some Time: Ice and the English Imagination* (New York: Picador, 1996), 190.

1   Thomas Tarnovius, *Ferøers Beskrifvelser. Færoensia: Textus & Investigationes*, vol. 2, ed. Håkon Hamre (Copenhagen: Einar Munksgaard, 1950), 54. At about the same time Jón Eggertsson complained of the same problem in Iceland; see Jón Eggertsson, "Adskilligt om Islands Beschafenhed og Vilkor," MS, 1738, fol. 4, Thott, Det Kongelige Bibliotek.

2   Jørgen Landt, *Forsøg til en Beskrivelse over Færøerne* (Copenhagen: Breum, 1800), 302–3.

3   David E. Nye, *America as Second Creation: Technology and Narratives of New Beginnings* (Cambridge, Mass.: MIT Press, 2003). For another example of how foreign travelers understood exotic places through their material culture, see Susan B. Hanley, *Everyday Things in Premodern Japan: The Hidden Legacy of Material Culture* (Berkeley: University of California, 1997), esp. 51–76.

4   Auguste Comte, Thomas Carlyle, and Henry Thomas Buckle were among those who wrote human histories that linked industrial and social progress. See Auguste Comte, "A Brief Appraisal of Modern History," in *The Crisis of Industrial Civilization: The Early Essays of Auguste Comte*, ed. Ronald Fletcher (London: Heinemann, 1974), 79–111; Thomas Carlyle, *Critical and Miscellaneous Essays* (London: Chapman and Hall, 1896); and Henry Thomas Buckle, *History of Civilization in England* (Oxford: Oxford University Press, 1925–31). Herbert L. Sussman, *The Victorians and the Machine: The Literary Response to Technology* (Cambridge, Mass: Harvard University Press, 1968), discusses how Victorian writers such as Dickens, H. G. Wells, and Kipling considered the social aspects of technology. In *Victorian Anthropology*, George W. Stocking Jr. analyzes Victorian narratives of progress in human history more generally, in terms of anthropological differences between the races (New York: Macmillan, 1987).

5   For an elaboration of this discussion, see Michael Adas, *Machines as the Measures of Men: Science, Technology, and Ideologies of Western Dominance* (Ithaca, N.Y.: Cornell University Press, 1989); Daniel R. Headrick, *The Tools of Empire: Technology and European Imperialism in the Nineteenth Century* (Oxford: Oxford University Press, 1981), and *The Tentacles of Progress: Technology Transfer in the Age of Imperialism, 1850–1940* (Oxford: Oxford University Press, 1988); Peter Hulme, "Polytropic Man: Tropes of Sexuality and Mobility in Early Colonial Discourse," in *Europe and Its Others*, vol. 2, ed. Francis Barker et al. (Colchester: University of Essex, 1985), 17–32, and *Colonial Encounters: Europe and the Native Caribbean, 1492–1797* (London: Methuen, 1986).

6   Uno von Troil, *Brev rörande en Resa til Island* (Uppsala: Magnus Swederus Bokhandel, 1777), 116.

7   Ida Pfeiffer, *Visit to Iceland and the Scandinavian North*, translated from German (London: Ingram, Cooke, and Co., 1852), 175–76.

8   Richard F. Burton, *Ultima Thule; or, A Summer in Iceland*, vol. 1 (London: William P. Nimmo, 1875), 338.

9   Ibid., 155.

10   Konrad von Maurer, *Íslandsferð 1858*, trans. Baldur Hafstað (Reykjavík: Ferðafélag Íslands, 1997), 44–5. Von Maurer was a friend and supporter of the Icelandic independence leader Jón Sigurðsson, discussed in chapter 1. In his travel account, von Maurer laid particular emphasis on the literary creativity of the medieval Icelanders and their nineteenth-century efforts to restore their country to the time of the "Free State." His main writings on Iceland were a history of medieval Iceland, *Island von seiner ersten Entdeckung bis zum Untergange des Freistaats* (Munich: Kaiser, 1874), and a treatise on medieval Icelandic law, *Die Entstehung des Isländischen Staats und seiner Verfassung* (Munich: Kaiser, 1852). Some of the correspondence with Jón, including their discussions on Icelandic history, is published in Jón Jensson and Þorleifur H. Bjarnason, eds., *Bréf Jóns Sigurðssonar* (Reykjavík: Hið íslenska Bókmenntafélags, 1911).

11   Else Roesdahl, *Hvalrostand, elfenben, og nordboerne i Grønland* (Odense, Denmark: Odense University Press, 1995).

12   Brian M. Fagan, *The Little Ice Age: How Climate Made History, 1300–1850* (New York: Basic Books, 2000).

13   In the mid-fourteenth century, an emissary of the Norwegian king, Ívar Bárðarson, reported that the western Norse settlement had been occupied by the Inuit, although the Norse settlers may have lasted another 150 years on the eastern farms. For theories about the demise of the Norse population in Greenland, see James H. Barrett, ed., *Contact, Continuity, and Collapse: The Norse Colonization of the North* Atlantic (Turnhout, Belgium: Brepols, 2003); Kirsten Seaver, *The Frozen Echo: Greenland and the Exploration of North America, ca A.D. 1000–1500* (Stanford, Calif.: Stanford University Press, 1997); and T. H. McGovern, "Management for Extinction in Norse Greenland," in *Historical Ecology: Cultural Knowledge and Changing Landscapes*, ed. C. Crumley (Santa Fe, N.M.: School of American Research Press, 1994), 127–54, and "Climate, Correlation, and Causation in Norse Greenland," *Arctic Anthropology* 28, no. 2 (1991): 77–100. Jared Diamond's recent book, *Collapse: How Societies Choose to Fail or Succeed* (New York: Viking, 2005), contains a summary of some of McGovern's ideas.

14   See Hans Egede, *Relation Angaaende den Grønlandske Mission 1738* and *Det Gamle Grønlands Nye Perlustration eller Naturel-Historie og Beskrivelse over*

det Gamle Grønland 1741 together in the edition edited by Finn Gad (Copenhagen: Rosenkilde and Bagger, 1971). The English edition is *A Description of Greenland, by Hans Egede Who Was a Missionary in That Country for Twenty-five Years* (London: T. and J. Allman, 1818). The *Relation* was continued by Hans Egede's sons, Poul and Niels Egede, published as *Continuation af Hans Egedes Relationer fra Grønland*, and Niels Egede also wrote a one-hundred-page natural history of Greenland, *Beskrivelse over Grønland*; both were published in a modern edition in *Meddelelser om Grønland* 120 (1939). Louis Bobé has written a rather laudatory biography of Egede: *Hans Egede: Colonizer and Missionary of Greenland* (Copenhagen: Rosenkilde and Bagger, 1952), which is a translation and revised edition of Bobé's "Hans Egede, Grønlands Missionær og Kolonisator," *Meddelelser om Grønland* 129, no. 1 (1944): 1–344.

15 Egede, "Fortale til Læseren," unpaginated introduction to *Det Gamle Grønlands Nye Perlustration*.

16 Egede, *Det Gamle Grønlands Nye Perlustration*, 106–8.

17 His grandfather is the Arngrímur Jónsson discussed in chapter 2, who was also the author of *Brevis commentarius de Islandia* in addition to *Groenlandia*.

18 Arngrímur Jónsson Vídalín, *Den Tredie Part af Det saa kaldede Gamle og Nye Grønlands Beskrivelse* (Copenhagen: Det Grønlandske Selskab, 1971).

19 Finn Gad, *A History of Greenland*, vol. 1, trans. Ernst Dupont (London: C. Hurst, 1970), 257.

20 Poetry composed in the Norse style also existed from medieval Greenland: *Atlamál* (Lay of Atli), one of the Eddic poems, and *Norðrsetudrápa*, a poem about a northern hunting ground of the Greenlanders. The thirteenth-century Icelander Snorri Sturluson, whom medieval scholars believe to have been the author of some of the major Icelandic sagas, had also written about a type of poetical meter invented by the Norse Greenland settlers.

21 On seventeenth-century European-Greenlandic contact, see Gad, *History of Greenland*, vol. 1, 217–57.

22 On North Atlantic whaling, see Trausti Einarsson, *Hvalveiðar við Ísland, 1600–1939* (Reykjavík: Menningarsjóð, 1987); J. N. Tønnessen and A. O. Johnsen, *The History of Modern Whaling*, translated and condensed version of *Den Moderne Hvalfangsts Historie: Opprinelse og Utvikling*, by R. I. Christophersen (Berkeley: University of California: 1982); John R. Bockstoce, *Whales, Ice, and Men: The History of Whaling in the Western Arctic* (Seattle: University of Washington, 1986); Bjørn L. Basberg, Jan Erik Ringstad, and Einar Wexelsen, eds., *Whaling and History: Perspectives on the Evolution of the Industry* (Sandefjord, Norway: Sandefjord Whaling Museum, 1993); and Sune Dalgård, *Dansk-norsk Hvalfangst* (Copenhagen: G. E. C. Gad, 1962).

23 These figures are from R. Müller, "Fortegnelse over præster i Grønland fra 1721 til 1910," *Det Grønlandske Aarsskrift* (1912): 62–69; and Heinz Israel, *Kultur-*

wandel grönländischer Eskimo im 18. Jahrhundert: Wandlungen in Gesellschaft und Wirtschaft unter dem Einfluß der Herrnhuter Brüdermission (Berlin: Akademie Verlag, 1969), 202–3. Thanks to Thorkild Kjærgaard for helping me with this reference.

24 See Kathrine Kjærgaard and Thorkild Kjærgaard, *Ny Herrnhut i Nuuk 1733–2003* (Nuuk: University of Greenland, 2003), which estimates that the number of conversions in the Moravian mission was close to twice as many as in the Danish by the middle of the eighteenth century (23).

25 In 1771, a Danish missionary, Henrik Christopher Glahn, anonymously published a book "correcting the errors" of a Moravian missionary, David Crantz, whose 1767 *Historie von Grönland* discussed the natural history of Greenland and customs of the people (Crantz's work is discussed at greater length later in this chapter). Glahn's *Anmærkninger over de tre første bøger af Hr. David Crantzes Historie om Grønland* took Crantz to task over many points of accuracy and was less critical of the native beliefs and practices of the Inuit than Crantz had been. A mid-nineteenth-century Danish official, Hinrich Johannes Rink (also discussed later in this chapter), also criticized the Moravians' attitude toward the Inuit. Glahn's text is available in an edition edited by Mads Lidegaard, *Glahns Anmærkninger: 1700-tallets Grønlændere* (Copenhagen: Det Grønlandske Selskab, 1991).

26 This translation of Olearius is from Gad, *History of Greenland*, vol. 1, 247–48. The original is from Olearius's 1656 *Beschreibung der muscowitischen und persischen Reyse*. Inuit were presented as prisoners of the English captain Martin Frobisher in 1577 and at the Danish court of Christian IV in 1606; on these cases, see Michael Harbsmeier, *Stimmen aus dem äußersten Norden: Wie die Grönländer Europa für sich entdeckten* (Stuttgart: Jan Thorbecke Verlag, 2001), and "Bodies and Voices from Ultima Thule: Inuit Explorations of the Kablunat from Christian IV to Knud Rasmussen," in *Narrating the Arctic: A Cultural History of Nordic Scientific Practices*, ed. Michael Bravo and Sverker Sörlin (Canton, Mass.: Science History Publications, 2002), 33–71.

27 David Crantz, *Historie von Grönland enthaltend die Beschreibung des Landes und der Einwohner und insbesondere die Geschichte der dortigen Mission der Evangelischen Brüder zu Neu-Herrnhut und Lichtenfels* (Leipzig: Heinrich Detlef Ebers, 1765), 200–201. A condensed English edition of this book appeared as *The History of Greenland, Containing a Description of That Country and Its Inhabitants Translated from the High-Dutch* (London: Brethen's Society, 1767). The book was also translated into Dutch (1767) and Swedish (1769) and was widely cited as the authority on the natural history of Greenland in the eighteenth century, only to be replaced by Hinrich Rink's work in 1857 (see later in this chapter). Other eighteenth-century natural histories of Greenland included Egede's; Glahn's *Anmærkninger*; Lars Dalager, *Grøn-*

landske Relationer: Indeholdende Grønlændernes Liv og Levnet, deres Skikke og Vedtægter samt Temperament og Superstitioner tillige Nogle korte Reflectioner over Missionen, ed. Louis Bobé (Copenhagen: G. E. C. Gad, 1915); and Otto Fabricius, *Fuldstændig Beskrivelse over Grønland,* ed. H. Ostermann, *Meddelelser om Grønland* 129, no. 4 (1946). Dalager, like Egede, was involved in projects of technology transfer and material improvement in Greenland, although of a less far-reaching variety.

28 Egede, "Fortale til Læseren," unpaginated introduction to *Det Gamle Grønlands Nye Perlustration.*

29 There are exceptions, however, to this general trend. The Danish captain Gustav Holm claims the main purpose of his 1884–85 expedition to east Greenland was the search for the old eastern settlement. Unlike Egede, however, he did not actually expect to find any Scandinavian descendants there. For the report of the voyage, see Gustav Holm, *The Ammassalik Eskimo: Contributions to the Ethnology of the East Greenland Natives,* ed. William Thalbitzer, *Meddelelser om Grønland* 39, part 1 (Copenhagen: Bianco Luno, 1914), 5.

30 The gender dimension of polar exploration is discussed by Lisa Bloom, *Gender on Ice: American Ideologies of Polar Explorations* (Minneapolis: University of Minnesota Press, 1993). Bloom's reading is critiqued by Michael F. Robinson in *The Coldest Crucible: Arctic Exploration and American Culture* (Chicago: University of Chicago Press, 2006), see p. 177. For a discussion of Franklin, see Spufford's book, *I May Be Some Time.* Nansen's account of his Greenland trip is Fridtjof Nansen, *The First Crossing of Greenland,* trans. Hubert Gepp (London: Longmans, 1893).

31 On KGH's policies, see the documents and discussion in Henning Bro, *Grønland: Kilder til en dansk kolonihistorie* (Copenhagen: Det Grønlandske Selskab, 1993), 57–60, and 91–101.

32 Spufford, *I May Be Some Time,* 124–26. To the great displeasure of Lady Jane Franklin, who had organized an international search for her husband, Rae reported that the Inuit found human bones with human teeth marks—evidence of cannibalism—in the last known site of the Franklin party.

33 E. S. Dodge, *The Polar Rosses: John and James Clark and Their Explorations* (New York: Barnes and Noble, 1973). On polar science, see G. E. Fogg, *A History of Antarctic Science* (Cambridge: Cambridge University Press, 1992); Michael Bravo and Sverker Sörlin, eds., *Narrating the Arctic: A Cultural History of Nordic Scientific Practices* (Canton, Mass.: Science History Publications, 2002); Trevor Levere, *Science and the Canadian Arctic: A Century of Exploration, 1818–1918* (Cambridge: Cambridge University Press, 1983); G. H. Liljequist, *High Latitudes: A History of Swedish Polar Travels and Research* (Stockholm: Streiffert, 1993); and the volume edited by Urban Wråkberg, *The*

Centennial of S. A. Andrée's North Pole Expedition (Stockholm: Royal Swedish Academy of Sciences, 1999).

34 Differing judgments on Scott's alleged character flaws and errors that led to his and his men's death on their return trip from the South Pole can be found in Roland Huntford, *The Last Place on Earth* (New York: Atheneum, 1985); Diana Preston, *A First-Rate Tragedy: Captain Scott's Antarctic Expeditions* (London: Constable, 1997); David Thomson, *Scott, Shackleton, and Amundsen: Ambition and Tragedy in the Antarctic* (New York: Adrenaline, 2002); and in Susan Solomon, *The Coldest March: Scott's Fatal Antarctic Expedition* (New Haven, Conn.: Yale University Press, 2001).

35 Robert G. David, *The Arctic in the British Imagination, 1814–1914* (Manchester, U.K.: Manchester University Press, 2000), 247–48.

36 Spufford, *I May Be Some Time*, 190–91.

37 In his *German Exploration of the Polar World: A History, 1870–1940* (Lincoln: University of Nebraska, 2002), David Thomas Murphy explains the positive accounts of the Inuit in the writings of German explorers such as Heinrich Klutschak and Rudolph Franke in terms of the insignificant economic relationship between Germany and the Arctic. According to Murphy, "Germans had no need to vilify the Eskimo, since they had no claims on Eskimo land and little to interest them economically in the Eskimo" (172). This claim obviously does not apply to the relationship between the Danes and Inuit. Michael Harbsmeier, in his *Stimmen aus dem äußersten Norden* argues that cultural rather than economic factors played a larger role, that it was the long history of contact between Greenland and Europe and the frequent visits of Greenlandic Inuit to the European continent that raised the status of the Inuit in European estimations. See also his article, "Bodies and Voices from Ultima Thule," 33–37 . On the German experience of the poles, see also Cornelia Lüdecke, *Die deutsche Polarforschung seit der Jahrhundertwende und der Einfluß Erich von Drygalskis* (Bremerhaven, Germany: Alfred-Wegener-Institut für Polar-und Meersforschung, 1995).

38 Hinrich Rink, *Danish Greenland: Its People and Products* (1877; rcpr., Montreal: McGill-Queen's University Press, 1974), 112–13. See also Rink's *Eskimoiske eventyr og sagn* (Copenhagen: C. A. Reitzel, 1866). The English edition is *Tales and Traditions of the Eskimo, with a Sketch of Their Habits, Religion, Language and Other Peculiarities*, ed. Robert Brown (Edinburgh: W. Blackwood, 1875).

39 Hinrich Rink, *Om monopolhandelen paa Grønland* (Copenhagen: A. F. Høst, 1852), and *Samling af Betænkninger og Forslag vedkommende den kongelige grønlandske Handel* (Copenhagen: L. Kleins, 1856).

40 William Morris, *Icelandic Journals* (London: Mare's Nest, 1996).

41 Vilhjálmur Stefánsson, *The Friendly Arctic: The Story of Five Years in Polar Regions*, 2nd ed. (New York: Macmillan, 1943), 3. It is likely that he either developed his theory of the historical stages of polar exploration with—or borrowed it from—Knud Rasmussen, who gives a very similar outline in his *Polarforskningens saga*, vol. 7 of *Jordens erobring* (Copenhagen: Chr. Erichsens Forlag, 1930), 391–93.

42 Vilhjálmur was not, however, very consistent in his attitude toward Inuit culture throughout his long career as a polar explorer. In his *My Life with the Eskimo* (New York: Macmillan, 1913), published eight years earlier, he claims that since "Eskimos support themselves by the most primitive implements" in polar regions then "we, armed with modern rifles, would be able to live in that sort of country as long as we pleased and to go about in it as we liked" (2). In a revitalization of the eighteenth-century myth, he proposed that the "Copper Eskimos" (also called the "Blond Eskimos") living on Victoria Island were the descendants of Norse settlers. After a splash of publicity followed by heavy criticism from anthropologists, he retreated from this claim. See William R. Hunt, *Stef: A Biography of Vilhjalmur Stefansson, Canadian Arctic Explorer* (Vancouver: University of British Columbia Press, 1986), 57–63. Vilhjálmur's notebooks are have been published in Gísli Pálsson, ed., *Writing on Ice: The Ethnographic Notebooks of Vilhjalmur Stefansson* (Hanover, N.H.: University Press of New England, 2001). He is also the subject of a recent biography, also by Gísli Pálsson, *Travelling Passions: The Hidden Life of Vilhjalmur Stefansson*, trans. Keneva Kunz (Hanover, N.H.: University Press of New England, 2003).

43 Knud Rasmussen, *Fra Grønland til Stillehavet: Rejser og mennesker fra 5. Thule-ekspedtion* (Copenhagen: Gyldendal, 1925), 4–5.

44 See Bloom,.*Gender on Ice*, for some of the details of the Cook-Peary dispute. The final word on the matter seems to be Robert M. Bryce's voluminous *Cook and Peary: The Polar Controversy, Resolved* (Mechanicsburg, Penn.: Stackpole Books, 1997), which concludes that neither Cook nor Peary reached the pole.

45 Robert Peary, *The North Pole: Its Discovery in 1909 under the Auspices of the Peary Arctic Club* (New York: Stokes, 1910), 5, 47.

46 Ibid., 128.

47 See Skúli Sigurðsson, "The Dome of the World: Iceland, Doomsday Technologies and the Cold War," in *Aspects of Arctic and Sub-Arctic History*, ed. Ingi Sigurðsson and Jón Skaptason (Reykjavík: University of Iceland, 2000), 463–73, and "Electric Memories and Progressive Forgetting," in *The Historiography of Contemporary Science and Technology*, ed. Thomas Söderqvist (Amsterdam: Harwood Academic Publishers, 1997), 129–49.

48 Finn Gad, *Grønland under krigen* (Copenhagen: G. E. C. Gads Forlag, 1946), 6.

49 Árni Sverrisson, "Small Boats and Large Ships: Social Continuity and Technical Change in the Icelandic Fisheries, 1800–1960," *Technology and Culture*

43, no. 2 (2002): 227–53. Guðmundur Jónsson discusses the conservative tendencies of the Icelandic elite toward farming in his "Institutional Change in Icelandic Agriculture, 1780-1940," *Scandinavian Economic History Review* 41, no. 2 (1993): 101–28. The attitude of the officials toward fishing is discussed by Christina Folke Ax in "De uregerlige: Den islandske almue og øvrighedens reformforsøg, 1700–1870" (Ph.D. diss., University of Copenhagen, Department of History, 2003), 115–25. On changes in the Icelandic fisheries, see also Magnús S. Magnússon, *Iceland in Transition: Labour and Social-Economic Change before 1940* (Lund: University of Lund, 1985).

4 | TRANSLATING AND CONVERTING

Epigraphs: C. W. Schultz-Lorentzen, *Det Grønlandske Folk og Folkesind* (Copenhagen: Department for Greenlandic Affairs, 1951), 20; Peter Høeg, *Frøken Smillas fornemmelse for sne* (Copenhagen: Rosinante, 1992), 88–89.

1   Holm's account of this voyage is in *The Ammassalik Eskimo: Contributions to the Ethnology of the East Greenland Natives*, ed. William Thalbitzer. This contains a translation and expansion of Holm's original Danish account, along with other texts from East Greenland expeditions. There is an account written by a participant from Greenland, also edited by William Thalbitzer, titled *Den Grønlandske Kateket Hansêraks Dagbog* (Copenhagen: G. E. C. Gad, 1933).

2   William Thalbitzer, *A Phonetical Study of the Eskimo Language, Based on Observations Made on a Journey in North Greenland 1900-01*, trans. Sophia Bertelsen (Copenhagen: Bianco Luno, 1904), 10–11. Thalbitzer's attitude toward the impact of missionary work in Danish Greenland seems to have been ambivalent, and it probably changed throughout his long career. For example, in this same text he praises the missionaries for having brought "enlightenment" and "civilization" to Greenland, "grafting European enlightenment . . . onto a primitive population" (63–65). On the other hand, writing about the East Greenlanders in his foreword to Holm's *Ammassalik Eskimo*, he notes his good fortune at being able to collect the folklore of the people before they became Christianized: "now [we] . . . can realize the magnitude and wealth of the spiritual life which animated the tribe before it became Christianized. Happily, at the time of my visit . . . the inhabitants of Ammassalik were pagan and unable to read and write" (2).

3   Lamin Sanneh, *Encountering the West: Christianity and the Global Cultural Process: the African Dimension* (Maryknoll, N.Y.: Orbis Books, 1993), 17–19.

4   For some examples, see Sara Pugach, "Lost in Translation: Carl Büttner's Contribution to the Development of African Language Studies in German," and Derek R. Petersen, "Language Work and Colonial Politics in Eastern Africa:

The Making of Standard Swahili and 'School Kikuyu,'" both in David L. Hoyt and Karen Oslund, eds., *The Study of Language and the Politics of Community in Global Context, 1740–1940*, (Lanham, Md.: Rowman and Littlefield, 2006), 151–84, and 185–214.

5   Pugach, "Lost in Translation," 165.

6   Urs Bitterli, *Cultures in Contact: Encounters between European and Non-European Cultures, 1492-1800*, trans. Ritchie Robertson (Stanford, Calif.: Stanford University Press, 1989), 47.

7   Margit Mogensen, "Nordboudstillingen i Paris 1900: iscenesættelse af kolonimagten," in *Danmark og verdensudstillingerne i 19. århundrede: de store udstillinger i politisk, økonomisk, teknologisk, og kulturelt lys*, 1–17 (Copenhagen: University of Copenhagen, 1997), 14.

8   Poul Egede, *Dictionarium Grönlandico-Danico-Latinum* (Copenhagen: G. F. Kisel, 1750). Fifty-four years later, Otto Fabricius brought out a new dictionary, under the title *Den grönlandske ordbog, forbedret og forøget* (Copenhagen: C. F. Schubart, 1804). Fabricius's dictionary omits the Latin translations of words, the preface written in Latin, and the preface written in Greenlandic contained in Egede's dictionary. This suggests, as Fabricius indicates in his (Danish) preface, that his dictionary is mostly intended as a practical "in the field" handbook for the Danish missionaries.

9   Finn Gad, *Grønland* (Copenhagen: Politikens Danmarkshistorie, 1984), 124–26.

10 Languages are in fact not exclusively inflective or agglutinative—many have elements of both characteristics. The scientific classification depends on the main technique used by language speakers to produce changes of meaning.

11 Schultz-Lorentzen, *Det Grønlandske Folk og Folkesind*, 10. He translates the Greenlandic word into Danish as *"vi har egentlig faaet en kraftig ordre til at gaa ud at fiske hajer."*

12 Hans Egede, *Det Gamle Grønlands Nye Perlustration eller Naturel-Historie og Beskrivelse over det Gamle Grønland 1741*, ed. Finn Gad (Copenhagen: Rosenkilde and Bagger, 1971), 23.

13 Samuel Kleinschmidt's biography is given in the comprehensive study by Henrik Wilhjelm, *"Af tilbøielighed er jeg grønlandsk": Om Samuel Kleinschmidts Liv og Værk* (Copenhagen: Det Grønlandske Selskab, 2001).

14 Ibid., 16.

15 Samuel Kleinschmidt, *Grammatik der grönländischen Sprache mit teilweisem Einschluß des Labradordialekts* (Berlin: Walter de Gruyter, 1851), vii.

16 Wilhjelm, *"Af tilbøielighed er jeg grønlandsk,"* 123.

17 For a study of the Moravians as a transnational missionary society, see Gisela Mettele, *Weltbürgertum oder Gottesreich? Die Herrnhuter Brüdergemeine als transnationale Gemeinschaft 1760-1857* (Göttingen, Germany: Vandenhoeck

and Ruprecht, 2005). According to Mettele, a career path like Kleinschmidt's, who remained in Greenland for his entire missionary service, was unusual, although it was becoming less so by the end of the nineteenth century, when the central control of the order was weakening. During the eighteenth century the Moravians almost always moved every ten years. Furthermore, Kleinschmidt's self-identification as a Greenlander was also quite atypical for the Moravians, who were actively opposed to identifying themselves with any one nation but rather saw themselves as members of a transnational brotherhood of pilgrims. In 1859 Kleinschmidt formally separated from the Moravians, and he began to teach at a Danish school in Godthåb. See also Mettele's "Eine 'Imagined Community' jenseits der Nation: Die Herrnhuter Brüdergemeinde als transnationale Gemeinschaft," *Geschichte und Gesellschaft* 32 (2006): 45–68, esp. 51–52. A history of the Moravians in Greenland, written from the Moravian perspective, is provided in Gerhardt J. Vollprecht, "Die Brüdermission in Grönland und Labrador," in *Unitas Fratrum/Moravian Studies*, ed. Mari P. van Buijtenen, Cornelis Dekker, Huib Leeuwenberg (Utrecht, Netherlands: Rijksarchief, 1975), 225–40.

18   Franz Bopp, *Vergleichende Grammatik des Sanskrit, Send, Armenischen, Griechischen, Lateinischen, Litauischen, Altsluvischen, Gothischen und Deutschen*, 2 vols. (Berlin: F. Dümmler, 1868–71).

19   In Kleinschmidt's Danish-Greenlandic dictionary, *Den grønlandske ordbog* (Copenhagen: Louis Kleins, 1871), which he completed based on the text of H. F. Jørgenson, Kleinschmidt claimed that one of the purposes of the dictionary was to correct mistaken pronunciations in the language and eliminate provincial usages (see p. v). On the story of the compilation of the Greenlandic dictionary and the disputes over Greenlandic orthography, see Wilhjelm, *"Af tilbøielighed er jeg grønlandsk,"* 287–325.

20   Thalbitzer, *Phonetical Study of the Eskimo Language*, xv.

21   Louis L. Hammerich, *Vesteskimoernes land* (Copenhagen: Geislers Forlag, 1982). Hammerich evaluated the abilities of various missionaries he met in Alaska quite differently. Some he judged to speak the language well and also to have good understanding of the grammar, but others were "hopeless" in their knowledge of formal language study and moreover so involved in their religious duties that they had no interest in Inuit linguistics (44–48). An account published by one of the missionaries Hammerich consulted is Ferdinand Drebert, *Alaska Missionary* (Bethlehem, Penn.: Moravian Books, 1959). Drebert's observations on the Inuit language spoken in Alaska, mostly about translation problems, are on pages 135–40. Among the linguists of Hammerich's generation, Knut Bergsland, who held a university chair in Oslo, was also often generous in his evaluations of missionary contribution to language study.

22 Hinrich Rink, *Om Eskimoernes Herkomst* (Copenhagen: Thieles bogtrykkeri, 1890), vol. 1, 288.

23 According to Thalbitzer, Henry made this case in an unpublished paper read at the Congress of Americanists in Brussels in 1879. See William Thalbitzer, "The Aleutian Language Compared with the Greenlandic," *International Journal of American Linguistics* 2, no. 3 (1921): 56. Henry published his grammar of the Aleut language in the same year, *Esquisse d'une grammaire raisonnée de la langue aléoute d'aprés la grammaire et le vocabulaire de Ivan Véniaminov* (Paris: Maisonneuve, 1879); see pages 2–3 for a brief discussion of the relationship between the indigenous languages of North America and Siberia.

24 For reasons of consistency and to avoid confusion, I use the normally pejorative word "Eskimo" in the context of describing the work of this school of linguists.

25 William Thalbitzer, "Et Manuskript af Rasmus Rask om Aleuternes Sprog, sammenlignet med Grønlændernes," *Oversigt over det Kgl. Danske Videnskabernes Selskabs Forhandlinger* (Copenhagen, 1916), 211–49 (an edition of Rask's unpublished manuscript, "Om det grönlandske sprog"). Rask suggested here that the Greenlandic language was closely connected with the language of northwest North America. See also Thalbitzer, "Aleutian Language Compared with the Greenlandic."

26 Knut Bergsland, *A Grammatical Outline of the Eskimo Language of West Greenland* (Oslo: Skrivemaskinstua, 1955), and *Aleut Dialects of Atka and Attu* (Philadelphia: American Philosophical Society, 1959).

27 David Crantz, *Historie von Grönland enthaltend die Beschreibung des Landes und der Einwohner und insbesondere die Geschichte der dortigen Mission der Evangelischen Brüder zu Neu-Herrnhut und Lichtenfels* (Leipzig: Heinrich Detlef Ebers, 1765), 27–31.

28 C. C. Uhlenbeck, *Oude aziatische contacten van het Eskimo* (Amsterdam: N. V. Noord-Hollandsche uitgevers maatschappij, 1941).

29 C. C. Uhlenbeck, *Eskimo en Oer-Indogermaansch* (Amsterdam: Noord-Hollandsche uitgevers maatschappij, 1935), 188

30 William Thalbitzer, *Uhlenbeck's Eskimo-Indo European Hypothesis: A Critical Revision* (Copenhagen: Travaux du Cercle Linguistique de Copenhague, 1945), 96.

31 Uhlenbeck, *Eskimo en Oer-Indogermaansch*, 180.

32 Fridtjof Nansen, *Eskimoliv* (Oslo: H. Aschehoug, 1891), 248–53.

33 Thalbitzer, *Die kultischen Gottheiten der Eskimo*, trans. Walter Zombat Zombatfalva (Leipzig: B. G. Teuber, 1928), 417–19.

34 A classic work on this theme of European intellectual history is Frank Edward Manuel, *The Eighteenth Century Confronts the Gods* (Cambridge, Mass.: Harvard University Press, 1959).

35   Louis L. Hammerich, *The Eskimo Language* (Oslo: University of Olso Press, 1970), 33–37. See also Hammerich's article, "Can Eskimo Be Related to Indo-European?" *International Journal of American Linguistics* 17 (1951): 217–23.

36   According to the explanation in Hammerich, *Eskimo Language*, the names of the numbers in Greenlandic are derived from the parts of the body, and people only have twenty fingers and toes all together (29).

37   Probably the most famous example of the relationship between the environment and language in the Inuit case is the alleged number of words that "Eskimos" have for snow. The story that the Inuit have "hundreds" of words for snow grew out of articles by the anthropologist Franz Boas and his student Benjamin Lee Whorf, who asserted that there were four separate words for snow. As Laura Martin and Geoffrey Pullum have discussed, this number was then multiplied by successive popular articles on the subject. The effect of this was, ironically, to give the Inuit language an exotic character in the popular imagination, linking their language with stories of unfamiliar customs such as wife sharing and eating raw meat, which was the view that Boas and Whorf were originally arguing against. See Laura Martin, "'Eskimo Words for Snow': A Case Study in the Genesis and Decay of an Anthropological Example," *American Anthropologist* 88 (1986): 418–23; and Geoffrey Pullum, *The Great Eskimo Vocabulary Hoax and Other Irrelevant Essays on the Study of Language* (Chicago: University of Chicago Press, 1991).

38   Hammerich, *Eskimo Language*, 29.

39   That year, the *International Journal of American Linguistics* 17 (1951) devoted the issue to celebrating Kleinschmidt's work, focusing on the relationships of the Eskimo languages to other languages. It contained articles by Louis L. Hammerich, "The Cases of Eskimo," 18–22; Otto Rosling, "Samuel Petrus Kleinschmidt," 63–65; Morris Swadesh, "Unaalio and Proto-Eskimo," 66–70; Knut Bergsland, "Aleut Demonstratives and the Aleut-Eskimo Relationship," 167–79; Gordon Marsh and Morris Swadesh, "Eskimo Aleut Correspondences," 209–16; and by Hammerich again, "Can Eskimo Be Related to Indo-European?" 217–23.

40   Hammerich, "Can Eskimo Be Related to Indo-European?" 217.

41   The two leading proponents of the theory after Uhlenbeck—Thalbitzer and Hammerich—did not survive to promote their views. Thalbitzer died in 1958 and Hammerich in 1975, five years after he last published on the subject of Indo-European and Eskimo-Aleut connections. The idea of relationships between Indo-European and Eskimo-Aleut still exists in a form within the Nostratic hypothesis, which asserts that the proto-languages of Indo-European, Eskimo-Aleut, Afro-Asiatic, Dravidian, Altaic, Uralic, and possibly Japanese and Korean all descended from a language called Nostratic, spoken fifteen thousand years ago by hunter-gatherers in Europe, Africa, Asia, and

the Middle East. This hypothesis is only supported by a few scholars today, however.

5 | READING BACKWARD

Epigraph: Jóhann Sigurjónsson, *Fjalla-Eyvindur*, in *Modern Icelandic Plays*, trans. Henninge Krohn Schanche (New York: American Scandinavian Foundation, 1916), 13–14.

1 Nuuk in Greenland is larger, with about 15,000 inhabitants compared to Tórshavn's about 13,000, although Greenland as a whole is less densely populated than the Faroes.

2 Bayard Taylor, *Egypt and Iceland in the Year 1874* (New York: G. P. Putnam's Sons, 1886), 235–36. Taylor was a friend of Willard Fiske, the librarian and Icelandic collector at Cornell University, and was himself a translator of Goethe. Many Icelanders of this period did in fact travel; eighteenth- and nineteenth-century Icelandic officials were educated in Copenhagen and had often traveled in Europe. On the social background of this group, see Einar Hreinsson, *Nätverk och nepotism: den regionala förvaltningen på Island 1770–1870* (Gothenberg, Sweden: University of Gothenberg, 2003).

3 Samuel Kneeland, *An American in Iceland: An Account of Its Scenery, People, and History* (Boston: Lockwood, Brooks, and Company, 1876), reports that "the study of the classics is very general, and the traveler is, as we were, often surprised to find persons in humble life able to converse in Latin" (245). This observation is probably somewhat exaggerated; it would be remarkable indeed to find Icelandic farmers at the end of the nineteenth century able to hold conservations in Latin, although they might well have known some Latin words. The only person Kneeland actually reports holding a Latin conservation with is a priest. Nevertheless, the idea that Icelanders commonly and routinely spoke Latin was a widespread one at this time. In his novel *Brekkukotsannáll* (*The Fish Can Sing*) Halldór Laxness makes fun of the Icelandic tendency to regard Latin as the sine qua non of a good education.

4 The extent to which the thirteenth-century texts were based on older oral sources became a point of debate among literary scholars and had implications for Icelandic cultural identity. In the first decades of the twentieth century, one group of scholars (the "book prose" school) argued that the texts were based on oral narratives but were substantially reshaped by thirteenth-century authors, while another group (the "free prose" school) held that they were a straightforward writing down of oral stories from the settlement period. Members of the book prose school, which included prominent Icelandic intellectuals such as Sigurður Nordal, thought that it would raise estima-

tions of Icelandic culture, both within in Iceland and in other nations, if the sagas could be shown to be the creation of singularly gifted Icelandic authors in the thirteenth century. Since this discussion took place during a time when the saga manuscripts were still kept in Denmark, there were nationalist dimensions as well to the book prose–free prose discussions. For a further discussion, see Jesse L. Byock, "Modern Nationalism and the Icelandic Sagas," in *Northern Antiquity: The Post-medieval Reception of Edda and Saga*, ed. Andrew Wawn (Middlesex, U.K.: Hisarlik Press, 1994), 163–88.

5   For some commentary on this dual picture of the Scandinavians in Great Britain, see Susie I. Tucker, "Scandinavica for the Eighteenth-Century Common Reader," in *The Saga Book of the Viking Society*, 26 (1962–65): 233–47; also John L. Greenway, *The Golden Horns: Mythic Imagination and the Nordic Past* (Athens: University of Georgia Press, 1977), esp. 73–98; and Edward J. Cowan, "Icelandic Studies in Eighteenth and Nineteenth Century Scotland," *Studia Islandica* 31 (1972): 109–51.

6   Ole Worm, *Reuer seu Danica literature antiqvissima vulgo Gothica dicta* (Copenhagen: Typis Martzan, 1651).

7   An introduction to the early saga scholarship and these themes is provided in Ellen Jørgensen, *Historieforskning og historieskrivning i Danmark indtil Aar 1800* (Copenhagen: Gyldendal, 1964); also Greenway, *Golden Horns*; and Cowan, "Icelandic Studies in Eighteenth and Nineteenth Century Scotland." See also the edited volume by Svenolof Karlsson, *Frihetens källa: Nordens betydelse för Europa* (Stockholm: The Nordic Council, 1992); and the one by Else Roesdahl and Preben Meulengracht Sørensen, *The Waking of Angantyr: The Scandinavian Past in European Culture; Den nordiske fortid i europæisk kultur* (Århus: Århus University Press, 1996). On the importance of Icelandic culture and the sagas in nineteenth-century Britain, see Andrew Wawn, *The Vikings and the Victorians: Inventing the Old North in Nineteenth-Century Britain* (Cambridge: D. S. Brewer, 2000); and Sigrún Pálsdóttir, "Icelandic Culture in Victorian Thought: British Interpretations (c. 1850–1900) of the History, Politics and Society of Iceland" (Ph.D. diss., University of Oxford, Faculty of Modern History, 2000).

8   Neither Loti nor Verne ever traveled to Iceland, but Verne took much of his information about Iceland from the eight volumes by Paul Gaimard and Xavier Marmier, *Voyage en Islande et au Groenland, execute pendant les années 1835 et 1836* (Paris: Arthus Bertrand, 1838–52), and *Voyages de la Commission Scientifique du Nord, en Scandinavie, en Laponie, au Spitzberg et aux Feröe, pendant les années 1838, 1839, et 1840* (Paris: Arthus Bertrand, 1842). In this respect, Verne's realism contrasts sharply with Loti's romantic vision of Iceland. On the French voyages and their idea of Iceland, see Einar Hreinsson, "Frakkar á Fróni: Samskipti Frakka og Íslendinga, 1600-1800," *Sagnir* 15

(1984): 4–11; and Kirsten-Elizabeth Høgsbro, "Fransk visit i dansk idyl: Xavier Marmiers besøg i København i 1837," in *Guldalderens Verden: 20 Historier fra nær og fjern*, ed. Bente Scavenius (Copenhagen: Gyldendal, 1996), 92–99.

9   Pierre Loti, *Iceland Fisherman*, trans. W. P. Baines (London: J. M. Dent and Sons, 1935), 51.

10   Von Maurer's travel diary was published in an Icelandic translation as *Íslandsferð 1858*, trans. Baldur Hafstað (Reykjavík: Ferðafélag Íslands, 1997). His main work on Iceland included a history of medieval Iceland, *Island von seiner ersten Entdeckung bis zum Untergange des Freistaats* (Munich: Kaiser, 1874); a treatise on medieval Icelandic law, *Die Entstehung des Isländischen Staats und seiner Verfassung* (Munich: Kaiser, 1852); and a translation of Icelandic folktales into German, *Isländische Volkssagen der Gegenwart vorwiegend nach mündlicher Überlieferung, gesammelt und verdeutscht* (Leipzig: J. C. Hinrichs, 1860). On Morris, see William Morris, *Icelandic Journals* (Fontwell, Sussex: Centaur Press, 1969). Morris also studied Icelandic with Eiríkur Magnússon at Oxford, translated sagas, and wrote poetry with Old Norse themes. Auden and MacNeice's book is *Letters from Iceland* (London: Faber and Faber, 1937).

11   Árni Magnússon, an Icelander who was archivist of the Danish king's private archive and later a professor at the University of Copenhagen, was mainly responsible for bringing the saga manuscripts from Iceland to Denmark. He collected saga manuscripts while working for the Danish Crown on the Icelandic census in 1702–12. He bequeathed his collection to the University of Copenhagen, which originally housed the manuscripts in the Royal Library (Det Kongelige Bibliotek). An unknown number were lost in the great Copenhagen fire of 1728. After Icelandic independence from Denmark in 1944, Iceland successfully pressed the Danish government for return of the manuscripts. In 1965, the Danish parliament agreed, and the first shipments of sagas came back to Iceland in 1971.

12   Lars S. Vikør, "Northern Europe: Languages as Prime Markers of Ethnic and National Identity," in *Language and Nationalism in Europe*, ed. Stephen Barbour and Cathie Carmichael (Oxford: Oxford University Press, 2000), 125.

13   Derek R. Peterson, "Language Work and Colonial Politics in Eastern Africa," 185–214.

14   The nineteenth-century politics of Schleswig and Holstein are notoriously complex, but the disputes between Denmark and the German Federation essentially centered on whether the two duchies were unified or separate and how they should be defined under the Danish constitution. Denmark had claimed Holstein in 1806, arguing that it was historically unified with Schleswig. Then the Danish king Frederik VI allowed it to join the German Federation, while remaining duke of the territory himself. Denmark lost both

Schleswig and Holstein to Prussia and Austria in the wars of 1864 but received a part of northern Schleswig back after World War I. For further details of the cultural politics of Denmark and Germany, see Ole Feldbæk, ed. *Danmarks-identitetshistorie*, vol. 2, *Et yndigt land*, and vol. 3, *Folkets Danmark* (Copenhagen: C. A. Reitzel, 1992).

15 The studies of Norwegian language politics include Einar Haugen, *Language Conflict and Language Planning: The Case of Modern Norwegian* (Cambridge, Mass.: Harvard University Press, 1966); Gregg Bucken-Knapp, *Elites, Language, and the Politics of Identity: The Norwegian Case in Comparative Perspective* (Albany: SUNY Press, 2003); and Andrew Robert Linn, *Constructing the Grammars of a Language: Ivar Aasen and Nineteenth Century Norwegian Linguistics* (Münster, Germany: Nodus Publikationen, 1997). Some of the primary documents in these debates have been collected in Eskil Hanssen, ed., *Om norsk språkhistorie* (Oslo: University of Oslo Press, 1970). On Norwegian national identity, see also Øystein Sørensen, ed., *Jakten på det Norske: Perspecktiver på utviklingen av en norsk nasjonal identitet på 1800-tallet* (Oslo: Gyldendal, 1998).

16 Haugen, *Language Conflict and Language Planning*, 54–61.

17 The *-else* suffix is functionally similar to the German *-ung*, as in *Bedeutung*. M. O'C. Walshe, *Introduction to the Scandinavian Languages* (London: Andre Deutsche, 1965).

18 Tom Nauerby, *No Nation Is an Island: Language, Culture, and National Identity in the Faroe Islands* (Århus, Denmark: Århus University Press, 1996), 40–41.

19 Ibid.

20 Some of the fundamental tenets of linguistics emerged from this work, such as the idea that languages change according to regular and universal laws. Following this principle, Grimm described the series of sound changes that differentiated the group of Germanic languages from the larger family of Indo-European languages in 1822. Grimm's Law, as it is known today, was actually first formulated by Rasmus Rask in his Danish grammar of Old Norse, *Undersögelse om det gamle Nordiske eller Islandske Sprogs Oprindelse* (Copenhagen: Gyldendalske Forlag, 1818). The law states that the Germanic languages shifted the *p, t, k* of Indo-European to *f, þ*, and *X* (spelled often as *ch*). Certain exceptions to this rule were later explained in 1857 by the Danish linguist Karl Verner through an analysis of the accent of Indo-European. The innovative feature of this work was the emphasis on individual sounds and letters rather than on entire words.

21 One history of language study is R. H. Robins, *A Short History of Linguistics* (London: Longman, 1990). I have also used Orrin W. Robinson, *Old English and Its Closest Relatives: A Survey of the Earliest Germanic Languages* (Stan-

ford, Calif.: Stanford University Press, 1992); John T. Waterman, *A History of the German Language* (Seattle: University of Washington Press, 1966); and Philip Baldi, *An Introduction to the Indo-European Languages* (Carbondale: Southern Illinois University Press, 1983).

22 Rask, *Undersögelse om det gamle Nordiske eller Islandske Sprogs Oprindelse.*

23 Rasmus Kristian Rask, *A Grammar of the Icelandic or Old Norse Tongue*, trans. George Webbe Dasent (London: William Pickering, 1843; repr., Amsterdam: John Benjamin, 1976), 229.

24 J. C. Svabo, *Inberetninger fra en Reise i Færøe 1781 og 1782*, ed. N. Djurhuus (Copenhagen: Selskabet til Udgivelse af Færøske Kildskrifter og Studier, 1959), 265–66.

25 Hans Christian Lyngbye, *Færøiske qvæder om Sigurd Fofnersbane og hans æt* (Randers, Denmark: S. Sigmenhoff, 1822).

26 V. U. Hammershaimb, "Færøiske Sproglære," *Annaler for nordisk Oldkyndighed og Historie* (1854): 233–316, and three articles in *Annaler for nordisk Oldkyndighed og Historie* (1846): "Færøiske Trylleformular," "Færøiske Sagn, meddelte af V. U. Hammershaimb," and "Bemærkninger med Hensyn til den færøiske Udtale," 347–65.

27 Nauerby, *No Nation Is an Island*, 42–43.

28 Details about Faroese political history are provided in Jonathan Wylie, *The Faroe Islands: Interpretations of History* (Lexington: University of Kentucky Press, 1987); Jonathan Wylie and David Margolin, *The Ring of Dancers: Images of Faroese Culture* (Philadelphia: University of Pennsylvania, 1981); John F. West, *Faroe: The Emergence of a Nation* (New York: Paul S. Eriksson, 1972); and Vagn Wåhlin, "Faroese History and Identity: National Historical Writing," *North Atlantic Studies* 1, no. 1 (1989): 21–32.

29 Nauerby, *No Nation Is an Island*, 47.

30 Svend Grundtvig, *Dansken paa Færøerne: Sidestykke til Tysken i Slesvig* (Copenhagen: C. A. Reitzel, 1845; repr., ed. Hans Bekker-Nielsen, Odense, Denmark: Odense University Press, 1978), 15. The pamphlet was originally published anonymously under the pseudonym "A Faroese," although Grundtvig was in fact Danish. He was the son of N. F. S. Grundtvig, the founder of the Danish folk high school system. The Faroese high schools were founded in 1899 and were the first schools to teach in Faroese.

31 Ibid., 27.

32 Ibid., 36–37.

33 Hammershaimb, essays in *Annaler for nordisk Oldkyndighed og Historie* (1846).

34 The existence of a saga manuscript about the early history of the islands after settlement (*Færeyinga Saga*, translated as *The Saga of the Faroe Islanders*) also lent credibility to this claim.

35 Hammershaimb's "Færøiske Sproglære" essay in *Annaler for nordisk Oldkyndighed og Historie* (1854): 233–316.

36 Cited in Nauerby, *No Nation Is an Island*, 77–80.

37 Jakob Jakobsen, *Det norrøne sprog på Shetland* (Copenhagen: I. Cohens, 1897). Jakobsen also published a Norn-English dictionary, *Etymologisk ordbog over det norrøne sprog på Shetland* (Copenhagen: Prior, 1921, with an English edition in 1928–32), and a collection of Faroese folktales, *Færøske folkesagn og æventyr* (Copenhagen: S. L. Møller, 1898–1901).

38 Christian Pløyen, *Erindringer fra en Reise til Shetlandsøerne, Örkenøerne og Skotland i Sommeren* 1839 (Copenhagen: C. W. Reizel, 1840).

39 The sentence is taken from Nauerby, *No Nation Is an Island*, 92–93.

40 Grundtvig, *Dansken paa Færøerne*, 73–76.

41 Nauerby, *No Nation Is an Island*, 88.

42 Jakobsen, "Nogle ord om færøsk, samt et forslag til en ny færøsk retskrivning," in *Greinir og Ritgerðir*, ed. Chr. Matras (Tórshavn, Faroe Islands: H. H. Jacobsen, 1957), 23–43. Many of these claims and counterclaims were originally exchanged in the new Faroese newspaper, *Dimmalætting* (Dawning), established in 1878.

43 Wylie, *Faroe Islands*, 137.

44 Nauerby, *No Nation Is an Island*, 87–88.

45 For a discussion of the exchange between nineteenth-century linguistics and evolutionary biology, see Stephen G. Alter, *Darwinism and the Linguistic Image: Language, Race, and Natural Theology in the Nineteenth Century* (Baltimore: Johns Hopkins University Press, 1999). According to Hans Aarsleff, in the first half of the nineteenth century "comparative anatomy became the model science, and its principles were quickly adopted in language study and anthropology." Hans Aarsleff, *From Locke to Saussure: Essays on the Study of Language and Intellectual History* (Minneapolis: University of Minnesota Press, 1982), 33.

46 Arngrímur Jónsson, *Crymogæa*, translated and introduced by Jakob Benediktsson (Reykjavík: Sögufélagið, 1985), 103. For a historical treatment of the idea of purism in Icelandic, see Kjartan G. Ottósson, *Íslensk málhreinsun: Sögulegt yfirlit* (Reykjavík, Íslensk málnefnd, 1990). In his doctoral dissertation, "Det reine språket: Om purisme i dansk, svensk, færøysk og norsk" (University of Bergen, Institute for Nordic Studies, 2001), Endre Brumstad looks at purism in Norwegian, Swedish, Danish, and Faroese and argues that purism in Scandinavia was modeled on purist developments in the very languages—French, German, and English—against which the Scandinavians tried to defend their own.

47 An example of this effort, as discussed in chapter 3, is Egede's *Det Gamle*

Grønlands Nye Perlustration. See also Finn Gad, *Grønland* (Copenhagen: Politikens Danmarkshistorie, 1984), 148–50, for an overview.

48 Gísli Pálsson claims that "Icelandic society may be exceptional in its reliance on linguistic concepts for cultural reproduction," a statement that would hold up equally well in the Faroes. Gísli Pálsson, *The Textual Life of Savants: Ethnography, Iceland, and the Linguistic Turn* (Chur, Switzerland: Harwood Academic Publishers, 1995), 135.

49 The error is made by overgeneralizing the form from the correct usage, as in *"mér þóknast að gera það"* ("I like to do it," i.e., "it suits me to do it").

50 Nauerby, *No Nation Is an Island,* 93–94.

51 A pronunciation guide for Faroese can be found in W. B. Lockwood, *An Introduction to Modern Faroese* (Copenhagen: Munksgaard, 1964). Einar Haugen makes this observation about the comprehensibility of Faroese Danish in his introduction to Wylie and Margolin, *Ring of Dancers.*

52 For examples of the rhetorical use of the Icelandic example in these discussions, see Michael Bjerre, "Færøerne vil have frihed som Island"; and Henning Mols Jensen, "Politisk ja til Færø-aftale," *Berlingske Tidende,* August 20, 1998, 6. Independence parties in Greenland have often made similar comparisons to the Icelandic model.

53 The anthropologist Kirsten Hastrup discusses some of the social consequences of the narrative of Icelandic timelessness in her "Uchronia and the two histories of Iceland, 1400–1800," in *Other Histories,* ed. Kirsten Hastrup (New York: Routledge, 1992), 102–20.

EPILOGUE

Epigraph: Quoted in Anne Brydon, "The Eye of the Guest: Icelandic Nationalist Discourse and the Whaling Issue" (Ph.D. diss., McGill University, Department of Anthropology, 1991), 144.

1 For a satiric comment on the widespread use of such Icelandic symbolism, see Harald Gustafsson, "Magiska jöklar och primuskök: funderingar kring schablonbildar av Island i allmänhet och Halldór Laxness i synnerhet," *Gardar* 23 (1992): 38–42. See also Magnús Einarsson, "The Wandering Semioticians: Tourism and the Image of Modern Iceland," in *Images of Contemporary Iceland: Everday Lives and Global Contexts,* ed. Gísli Pálsson and E. Paul Durrenberger (Iowa City: University of Iowa Press, 1996), 215–35, on the tourist experience of modern Iceland.

2 Keiko was only actually filmed in the first of these movies, the 1993 film, *Free Willy.* Animatronic models were used in the two sequels, *Free Willy 2: The*

Adventure Home and *Free Willy 3: The Rescue*. See Kenneth Brower, *Freeing Keiko: The Journey of a Killer Whale from Free Willy to the Wild* (New York: Gotham, 2005).

3 Michael Fortun juxtaposes the figures of Keiko and Kári in his *Promising Genomics: Iceland and deCODE Genetics in a World of Speculation* (Berkeley: University of California, 2008), esp. 65–81. The book is an anthropological investigation of the deCODE episode, both inside Iceland and internationally. Fortun's main use of the Keiko and Kári pairing is to analyze the quality and quantity of media attention devoted to both. My intention is to compare the logic behind these contemporary debates to the historical images of Iceland.

4 E. Paul Durrenberger, "Epidemiology of Iceland on the Brain," in *Icelandic Essays: Explorations in the Anthropology of Modern Life*, ed. E. Paul Durrenberger (Iowa City: University of Iowa Press, 1992), 3.

5 As is often the case when history merges with anthropology or ethnology, the personal identity and background of researchers have sometimes become themselves the object of inquiry in the deCODE matter. Therefore—in the interest of full disclosure—I provide here a little personal background. I first became acquainted with the deCODE matter through the historian of science Skúli Sigurðsson. At that time, in the summer of 1998, I was a graduate student and Skúli had provided informal mentorship and introductions in Iceland for me for some years (he was not, however, on my dissertation committee or a formal reader for my thesis). In the following years, Skúli emerged as vocal and outspoken critic of deCODE, both within Iceland and internationally. Until late 2002, after my graduation, I did not pursue the deCODE episode as a research topic, although I continued to follow the developments in the newspapers and in conversations with other scholars, including Skúli. As someone who was not and would never be affected personally by the HSD law, I did not feel compelled to take an ethical position on the matter. My argument in this chapter has nothing to do with the ethics of genetic research, therefore I have not researched this aspect of the deCODE discussion. I do not claim to be morally neutral and to have no opinions whatsoever about the HSD law (or about Icelandic whaling, for that matter), which I think would be a difficult and perhaps implausible position to maintain. I have long felt, however, that others are better informed about the ethics (and the science) of the matter than I am. I am, of course, extremely grateful to Skúli for his help in researching the issue—as well as in many other respects.

6 An English translation of this law is available at the Mannvernd Web site, www.mannvernd.is. The group Mannvernd, which organized itself in opposi-

tion to deCODE's proposal, has collected articles about the company at this
site. DeCODE's Web site is www.decode.is.

7　The text of this declaration can be found at the World Medical Association
　Web site, www.wma.net/e.

8　As quoted in *Iceland Investment News* 1 (1998), www.invest.is. Guðni Th.
　Jóhannesson's account of the deCODE episode, *Kári í jötunmóð: Saga Kára
　Stefánssonar og íslenkrar erfðagreiningar* (Reykjavík: Nýja Bókafélagið, 1999),
　discusses the concept of the Icelandic people as a "limited natural resource,"
　as Kári described them in 1996 (96–100).

9　The question of the genetic homogeneity of the Icelandic population later
　became an issue of scientific debate; see Einar Árnason, "Genetic Heterogene-
　ity of the Icelanders," *Annuals of Human Genetics* 67 (2003): 5–16.

10　For examples of this language, see Dirk Schümer, "Die lukrativen Gene der
　Wikinger: Island wird zum Labor der Biotechnologie," *Frankfurt Allgemeine
　Zeitung*, September 16, 2000, 1; W. Wayt Gibbs, "Natural-Born Guinea Pigs,"
　Scientific American 278 (February 1998), 34; Christoph Keller, "Die Isländer,
　unsere Labormäuse," *Das Magazin*, October 3, 1998, 13–24; and Stephen D.
　Moore, "Roche Research Chief Bets Firm's Future on Genetic Research . . .
　Iceland as a Giant Gene Lab," *Wall Street Journal*, July 18, 1998. Other images
　common to journalists' accounts of deCODE include "sagas/Vikings," "fish-
　ing/gene pool," "buying and selling genes."

11　Richard Lewontin, "People Are Not Commodities," *New York Times*, January
　23, 1999, A19. For more examples of this argument, see Jamaica Potts, "At Least
　Give the Native Glass Beads: An Examination of the Bargain Made between
　Iceland and deCODE Genetics with Implications for Global Bioprospect-
　ing," *Virginia Journal of Law and Technology* 8 (2002): 1–40; Jean Yves Nau,
　"L'exploitation d'un patrimonie genetique unique," *Le Monde*, December 18,
　1998, 22; and Lopeti Senituli and Margaret Boyes, "Whose DNA? Tonga and
　Iceland: Biotech, Ownership, and Consent," paper presented at the Austral-
　asian Bioethics Association Annual Conference," Adelaide, Australia, Febru-
　ary 14–16, 2002.

12　Gísli Pálsson and Paul Rabinow, "Iceland: the Case of the National Human
　Genome Project," *Anthropology Today* 15, no. 5 (October 1999): 14–18.

13　Guðjón Guðmundsson, "Dáður vestra en umdeildur hér," *Morgunblaðið*
　(hereafter abbreviated *MbI.*), September 5, 1998. See also Susan Orlean's
　article, "Where's Willy?" *The New Yorker*, September 23, 2002. Anne Bry-
　don's excellent article, "The Predicament of Nature: Keiko the Whale and the
　Cultural Politics of Whaling in Iceland," *Anthropological Quarterly* 79, no.
　2 (Spring 2006): 225–60, explores the issues that Keiko's return created for
　Iceland from an anthropological perspective.

14　For an account of this case, see Susan G. Davies, *Spectacular Nature: Corpo-*

rate Culture and the Sea World Experience (Berkeley: University of California Press, 1997).

15 See Helgi Geirsson, "Étum Keikó og byrjum hvalveiðar strax," *MbI.*, September 25, 2001, 42. In the same issue, see also Ólafur Hannibalsson, "Hryðju-verkamenn á Íslandi," 32.

16 For an example of this, see Michael Spector, "Iceland Decoded," *The New Yorker*, January 18, 1999, 40–51.

17 In *Kári í jötunmoð*, Guðni Jóhannesson credits these projects for providing inspiration for Kári's research (65–67).

18 On this history, see Gísli Pálsson, *Anthropology and the New Genetics* (Cambridge: Cambridge University Press, 2007), 68–78, and 97–101. For the early twentieth-century history of genetic research in Iceland, especially the introduction of Mendel's work, see Steindór J. Erlingsson, *Genin okkar: líftæknin og íslenskt samfélag* (Reykjavík: Oddi, 2002), 34–37. This book analyzes the deCODE episode from a science studies perspective.

19 Further details on the IWC policy can be found at the IWC Web site, www.iwcoffice.org, and in Robert L. Friedheim, "Introduction: The IWC as a Contested Regime," *Toward a Sustainable Whaling Regime*, ed. Robert L. Friedheim (Seattle: University of Washington, 2001), 3–48.

20 For a history of North Atlantic whaling, see J. N. Tønnessen and A. O. Johnsen, *The History of Modern Whaling*, translated and condensed version of *Den Moderne Hvalfangsts Historie: Opprinelse og Utvikling*, by R. I. Christophersen (Berkeley: University of California Press, 1982), 25–32; and Trausti Einarsson, *Hvalveiðar við Ísland, 1600–1939* (Reykjavík: Menningarsjóð, 1987). For discussion of the Icelandic case, see also Anne Brydon's dissertation, "Eye of the Guest," her "Icelandic Nationalism and the Whaling Issue," *North Atlantic Studies* 2, no 2.:185–91, and "Whale-Siting: Spatiality in Icelandic Nationalism," in *Images of Contemporary Iceland*, ed. Gísli Pálsson and Durrenberger, 25–45.

21 This argument is elaborated in Finn Lynge, *Arctic Wars, Animal Rights, Endangered Peoples*, trans. Marianne Stenbæk (Hanover, N.H.: University Press of New England, 1992.), a translation of *Kampen om de vilde dyr*. See also George Wenzel, *Animal Rights, Human Rights: Ecology, Economy, and Ideology in the Canadian Arctic* (Toronto: University of Toronto Press, 1991).

22 Some of the most central articulators of this claim in the United States have been Scott McVay, Robbins Barstow, and Roger Payne. See Scott McVay, "The Last of the Great Whales," *Scientific American* 215, no. 2 (August 1966), 13–21; and Robbins Barstow, *Meet the Great Ones: An Introduction to Whales and Other Cetaceans* (Wethersfield, Conn.: Cetacean Society International, 1987). The quotes here are from Barstow's *Whales Alive: Report of Global Confer-*

ence on the Non-consumptive Utilisation of Cetacean Resources (Wethersfield, Conn.: Cetacean Society International, 1983), 19.

23 "Hvalur í hættu," *MbI.*, July, 16, 1980, 1. An article on a threatened boycott of fish from the whale-catching nations of Japan, Norway, Peru, and Russia organized by the Animal Welfare Institute did not even mention the possibility that Iceland might also be affected by such a ban. "Hvetja menn til að kaupa ekki fisk frá hvalveiðiþjóðunum," *MbI.*, July 22, 1983, 16.

24 "Friður með hvölum," *MbI.*, July 15, 1980, 30.

25 For an example of this discussion in Iceland see Ingvar Agnarsson, "Eitt af fyrstu skrefunum til bættrar lífsstefnu," *MbI.*, July 5, 1983, 45.

26 Eggert H. Kjartansson, "Ferðin með Green Peace," *MbI.*, August 14, 1980, 16–17, and "Rainbow Warrior ennþá í El Ferrol," *MbI.*, June 21, 1980, 1.

27 "Vísindalegur hvalveiðar," *MbI.*, July 21, 1985, 26.

28 On this, see Mats Ris, "Conflicting Cultural Values: Whale Tourism in Northern Norway," *Arctic* 46, no. 2 (1993): 156–63; Arne Kalland, "Management by Totemization: Whale Symbolism and the Anti-Whaling Campaign," *Arctic* 46, no. 2 (June 1993): 124–33; and Stein R. Mathisen, "'Real Barbarians Eat Whales: Norwegian Identity and the Whaling Issue," in *Making Europe in Nordic Contexts*, ed. Pertti J. Anttonen (Turku, Finland: University of Turku, 1996), 105–36. See also Eyðun Andreassen, "Ordinary Europeans from Northern Norway to the Mediterranean: On Gender and Identity in the Faroe Islands," also in *Making Europe in Nordic Contexts*, 77–104. For an elaboration of this viewpoint, see the 1991 publication by the Faroese Ministry of Fisheries, *Whales and Whaling in the Faroe Islands*.

29 For an account of the Sea Shepherd Conservation Society's mission and activities, see the writings of its founder, Paul Watson, a former member of Greenpeace: *Ocean Warrior: My Battle to End the Illegal Slaughter on the High Seas* (Toronto: Key Porter Books, 1994). The Sea Shepherd Web site gives further information about the organization's current nature protection programs, www.seashepherd.org. For North Atlantic writing on the Sea Shepherd Society, see "Það gerist aldrei hér . . ." *MbI.*, July 12, 1986, 11; Ólafur Hannibalsson, "Hryðjuverkamenn á Íslandi," *MbI.*, September 25, 2001, 32, compares Sea Shepherd's activities to the September 11, 2001, attacks on the United States. From the Norwegian newspaper *Aftenposten*, on Sea Shepherd activities in Norway, see "Miljøterror straffes ikke," November 20, 1996; "Paul Watson løslates i neste uke," June 10, 1997, "Watson fornøyd etter forliset," November 12, 1997; and "Hevder han senket Bastesens båt," November 18, 1997, all available in the newspaper's online archive, www.aftenposten.no.

30 "Norge får hvalstøtte, gir elefantstøtte," *Aftenposten*, May 15, 1997; see also

Eyþór Arnalds, "Ljóti andarunginn," *MbI.*, June 27, 1998. This position was met with heavy criticism of Norway in the international press.

31   More information about the programs and goals of these organizations can be found at these various Web sites: www.nammco.no; www.highnorth.no; www.worldcouncilofwhalers.com; www.inuitcircumpolar.com (for the Inuit Circumpolar Council).

32   For a statement of PETA's philosophy, see its official Web site, www.peta.org. For another version of this philosophy, see Peter Singer, *Animal Liberation*, 2nd ed. (New York: Ecco, 1990).

33   Although others do not; see, for example, David G. Victor, "Whale Sausage: Why the Whaling Regime Does Not Need to Be Fixed," in *Toward a Sustainable Whaling Regime*, ed. Friedman, 292–310. See also Peter J. Stoett, *The International Politics of Whaling* (Vancouver: University of British Columbia Press, 1997).

34   The court decision is available in translation at the Mannvernd Web site, www.mannvernd.is.

35   Gísli Pálsson, *Anthropology and the New Genetics*, 143.

36   On the development of the whale-watching industry as part of Icelandic tourism, see Angela Walk, "Þróun hvalaskoðunar á Íslandi" (bachelor's thesis, University of Iceland, 2005); and Niels Einarsson, "From Good to Eat to Good to Watch: Whale Watching, Adaptation, and Change in Icelandic Fishing Communities," *Polar Research* 28, no. 1 (2009): 129–38.

BIBLIOGRAPHY

In accordance with Icelandic conventions, Icelandic authors are listed under their first names. Names beginning with Þ appear at the end of this list.

ARCHIVAL SOURCES

ICELANDIC

Landsbókasafn Íslands (National Library of Iceland)

Hans Christian Bech, "Om Handel paa Island skrevet Anno 1781" [Trade in Iceland, written in 1781], MS, JS 37, fol. 1.

Henry Holland, letter to his father, Peter Holland, August 2, 1811, Lbs. 4925 4to, 21.

Þjóðskjalasafn Íslands (National Archives of Iceland)

Skjalasafn rentukammers (Rtk.)
Isl. Journ. A. Nr. 1528, Rtk. 32.20.

Skjalasafn Stiftamtmanns (Stift.)
"Iutska folked" [The People from Jutland], Stift. III 95.

DANISH

Det Kongelige Bibliotek (The Royal Library, Copenhagen)

Otto Thott Collection (Thott)

Niels Horrebow, *Relation og Betænkning om Islands Oeconomie og nærværende Tilstand og hvorledes Landet kan komme i Stand* [Report and Thoughts about Iceland's Economy and Current Condition, and How the Country Could Improve its Situation], 1742, 4to.

Jón Eggertsson, "Adskilligt om Islands Beschafenhed og Vilkor" [Various Ideas about the Icelandic Economy and Conditions], MS, 1738, fol. 4.

PUBLISHED AND SECONDARY SOURCES

Aarsleff, Hans. *From Locke to Saussure: Essays on the Study of Language and Intellectual History.* Minneapolis: University of Minnesota Press, 1982.

Adalsteinn Ingólfsson. "Earth, Air, and Water: Georg Gudni and the Icelandic Landscape Tradition." In *Georg Guðni: The Mountain*, edited by Hannes Sigurðsson, 109–32. Akureyri, Iceland: Akureyri Art Museum, 2007.

Adas, Michael. *Machines as the Measure of Men: Science, Technology, and Ideologies of Western Dominance.* Ithaca, N.Y.: Cornell University Press, 1989.

Alter, Stephen G. *Darwinism and the Linguistic Image: Language, Race, and Natural Theology in the Nineteenth Century.* Baltimore, Md.: Johns Hopkins University Press, 1999.

Anderson, Benedict. *Imagined Communities.* London: Verso, 1991.

Anderson, Johann. *Nachrichten von Island, Grönland, und der Strasse Davis* [Stories from Iceland, Greenland, and the Davis Strait]. Hamburg, 1746.

Anna Agnarsdóttir. "Great Britain and Iceland 1800–1820." Ph.D. diss., London School of Economics, Department of International History, 1989.

———. "Ráðabrugg á dulmáli: Hugleiðingar um skjal frá 1785" [A Secret Scheme: Some Reflections on a Document from 1785]. *Ný Saga: Tímarit Sögufélags* 6 (1993): 28–41.

———. "Sir Joseph Banks and the Exploration of Iceland." In *Sir Joseph Banks: A*

Global Perspective, edited by R. E. R. Banks, B. Elliott, J. G. Hawkes, D. King-Hele, and G. L. L. Lucas, 31–48. Richmond, U.K.: Royal Botanic Gardens, 1994.

Anttonen, Pertt J., ed. *Making Europe in Nordic Contexts*. Turku, Finland: University of Turku, 1996.

Arneborg, Jette. "Det europæiske landnám: Nordboerne i Grønland, 985–1450 e.v.t." [The European Settlement: Scandinavians in Greenland, 985–1450]. In *Grønlands forhistorie*, edited by Hans Christian Gulløv, 264–65. Copenhagen: Gyldendal, 2004.

Arngrímur Jónsson. *Crymogæa*. Translated and introduced by Jakob Benediktsson. Reykjavík: Sögufélagið, 1985.

Arngrímur Jónsson Vídalín. *Den Tredie Part af Det saa kaldede Gamle og Nye Grønlands Beskrivelse* [The Third Part of the So-Called Description of Old and New Greenland]. Copenhagen: Det Grønlandske Selskab, 1971.

Arngrimus Jonas [Arngrímur Jónsson]. *Brevis commentarius de Islandia* [Short Commentary on Iceland]. In *The Principal Navigations, Voyages, Traffiques and Discoveries of the English Nation*, edited by Richard Hakluyt, vols. 4 and 8. Glasgow: Hakluyt Society, 1903.

Árni Sverrisson. "Small Boats and Large Ships: Social Continuity and Technical Change in the Icelandic Fisheries, 1800–1960." *Technology and Culture* 43, no. 2 (2002): 227–53.

Arnold, David. *Colonizing the Body: State Medicine and Epidemic Disease in Nineteenth-Century India*. Berkeley: University of California Press, 1993.

———, ed. *Warm Climates and Western Medicine: The Emergence of Tropical Medicine, 1500–1900*. Amsterdam: Rodopi, 1996.

Auden, W. H., with Louis MacNeice. *Letters from Iceland*. London: Faber and Faber, 1937.

Ax, Christina Folke. "At gøre en forskel: opfattelse og anvendelse af danske og islandske genstande og sprog i Reykjavik i sidste halvdel af 1700-tallet" [Constructing Difference: Conceptions and Use of Danish and Icelandic Household Objects and Language in Reykjavík in the Last Half of the Eighteenth Century]. *1066: Tidsskrift for historie* 31, no. 4 (2002): 3–13.

———. "De uregerlige: Den islandske almue og øvrighedens reformforsøg, 1700–1870" [The Unruly: Popular Response to Elite Reform Initiatives in Iceland, 1700–1870]. Ph.D. diss., University of Copenhagen, Department of History, 2003.

Bagge, Sverre, and Knut Mykland. *Norge i dansketiden* [Norway under Danish Rule]. Copenhagen: Politikens Danmarkshistorie, 1987.

Baldi, Philip. *An Introduction to the Indo-European Languages*. Carbondale: Southern Illinois University Press, 1983.

Baldwin, Martha. "Danish Medicines for Danes and the Defense of Indigenous Medicines." In *Reading the Book of Nature: The Other Side of the Scientific*

Revolution, edited by Allen G. Debus and Michael T. Walton, 163–80. Kirksville, Mo.: Sixteenth Century Journal Publishers, 1998.

Barrett, James H., ed. *Contact, Continuity, and Collapse: The Norse Colonization of the North Atlantic*. Turnhout, Belgium: Brepols, 2003.

Barstow, Robbins. *Meet the Great Ones: An Introduction to Whales and Other Cetaceans*. Wethersfield, Conn.: Cetacean Society International, 1987.

———. *Whales Alive: Report of Global Conference on the Non-consumptive Utilisation of Cetacean Resources*. Wethersfield, Conn.: Cetacean Society International, 1983.

Barth, Fredrik, ed. *Ethnic Groups and Boundaries: The Social Organization of Culture Difference*. Bergen, Norway: University of Bergen Press, 1969.

Basberg, Bjørn L., Jan Erik Ringstad, and Einar Wexelsen, eds. *Whaling and History: Perspectives on the Evolution of the Industry*. Sandefjord, Norway: Sandefjord Whaling Museum, 1993.

Beer, Gillian. "Writing Darwin's Islands: England and the Insular Condition." In *Inscribing Science: Scientific Texts and the Materiality of Communication*, edited by Timothy Lenoir, 119–39. Stanford, Calif.: Stanford University Press, 1998.

Bencard, Mogens. "Two 17th-Century Eskimos at Rosenborg Palace." *Meddelelser om Grønland: Man and Society* 12 (1989): 47–55.

Bergsland, Knut. "Aleut Demonstratives and the Aleut-Eskimo Relationship." *International Journal of American Linguistics* 17 (1951): 167–79.

———. *Aleut Dialects of Atka and Attu*. Philadelphia: American Philosophical Society, 1959.

———. *A Grammatical Outline of the Eskimo Language of West Greenland*. Oslo: Skrivemaskinstua, 1955.

Bitterli, Urs. *Cultures in Contact: Encounters between European and Non-European Cultures, 1492–1800*. Translated by Ritchie Robertson. Stanford, Calif.: Stanford University Press, 1989.

Bjerre, Michael. "Færøerne vil have frihed som Island" [The Faroes Want to Be Free Like Iceland]. *Berlingske Tidende*, August 20, 1998, 6.

Björn Th. Björnsson. *Íslenzk myndlist á 19. og 20. öld. Drög að sögulegt yfirliti* [Nineteenth- and Twentieth-Century Icelandic Painting: A Historical Overview]. Reykjavík: Helgafell, 1964.

Björn Þorsteinsson. "Henry VIII and Iceland." *Saga Book of the Viking Society* 15 (1957–61): 65–101.

———. *Island*. Copenhagen: Politikens Danmarkshistorie, 1985.

Bloom, Lisa. *Gender on Ice: American Ideologies of Polar Explorations*. Minneapolis: University of Minnesota Press, 1993.

Bobé, Louis. *Hans Egede: Colonizer and Missionary of Greenland*. Copenhagen: Rosenkilde and Bagger, 1952.

————. "Hans Egede, Grønlands Missionær og Kolonisator." *Meddelelser om Grønland* 129, no. 1 (1944): 1–344.

Bockstoce, John. *Whales, Ice, and Men: The History of Whaling in the Western Arctic.* Seattle: University of Washington Press, 1986.

Bopp, Franz. *Vergleichende Grammatik des Sanskrit, Send, Armenischen, Griechischen, Lateinischen, Litauischen, Altslavischen, Gothischen und Deutschen* [A Comparative Grammar of the Sanskrit, Zend, Armenian, Greek, Latin, Lithuanian, Old Slavic, Gothic, and German Languages]. 2 vols. Berlin: F. Dümmler, 1868–71.

Brandt, Don. *Exploring Iceland through Stamps: A Philatelic Odyssey.* Reykjavík: Iceland Review, 1991.

Bravo, Michael, and Sverker Sörlin, eds. *Narrating the Arctic: A Cultural History of Nordic Scientific Practices.* Canton, Mass.: Science History Publications, 2002.

Bro, Henning. *Grønland: Kilder til en dansk kolonihistorie* [Greenland: Sources for Danish Colonial History]. Copenhagen: Det Grønlandske Selskab, 1993.

Brockway, Lucile H. *Science and Colonial Expansion: The Role of the British Royal Botanic Gardens.* New York: Harcourt, Brace, Jovanovich, 1979.

Brooks, Charles B. *Disaster at Lisbon: The Great Earthquake of 1755.* Long Beach, Calif.: Shangton Longley, 1994.

Brower, Kenneth. *Freeing Keiko: The Journey of a Killer Whale from Free Willy to the Wild.* New York: Gotham, 2005.

Brown, DeNeen L. "Trail of Frozen Tears: The Cold War Is Over, but to the Native Greenlanders Displaced by It, There's Still No Peace." *Washington Post,* October 22, 2002, C1.

Brumstad, Endre. "Det reine språket: Om purisme i dansk, svensk, færøysk og norsk" [The Pure Tongue: Purism in Danish, Swedish, Faroese, and Norwegian]. Ph.D. diss., University of Bergen, Institute for Nordic Studies, 2001.

Bruun, Daniel. *Færøerne, Island og Grønland paa verdensudstillingen i Paris 1900* [The Faroes, Iceland, Greenland at the World's Fair Exhibit in Paris 1900]. Copenhagen: Nielsen and Lydiche, 1901.

Bryce, Robert M. *Cook and Peary: The Polar Controversy, Resolved.* Mechanicsburg, Penn.: Stackpole Books, 1997.

Brydon, Anne. "The Eye of the Guest: Icelandic Nationalist Discourse and the Whaling Issue." Ph.D. diss., McGill University, Department of Anthropology, 1991.

————. "Icelandic Nationalism and the Whaling Issue." *North Atlantic Studies* 21, no. 2 (1990): 185–91.

————. "Whale-Siting: Spatiality in Icelandic Nationalism." In *Images of Contemporary Iceland: Everday Lives and Global Contexts,* edited by Gísli Pálsson and E. Paul Durrenberger, 25–45. Iowa City: University of Iowa Press, 1996.

———. "The Predicament of Nature: Keiko the Whale and the Cultural Politics of Whaling in Iceland." *Anthropological Quarterly* 9, no. 2 (Spring 2006): 225–60.

Bucken-Knapp, Gregg. *Elites, Language, and the Politics of Identity: The Norwegian Case in Comparative Perspective.* Albany: SUNY Press, 2003.

Buckle, Henry. *History of Civilization in England.* 3 vols. Oxford: Oxford University Press, 1925–31.

Bunsen, Robert Wilhelm. "Ueber die Processe der vulkanischen Gesteinsbildungen Islands" [About the Processes of Volcanic Rock Formation in Iceland]. *Annalen der Physik und Chemie* 83 (1851): 197–272.

Burton, Richard F. *Ultima Thule; or, A Summer in Iceland.* 2 vols. London: William P. Nimmo, 1875.

Byock, Jesse L. "Modern Nationalism and the Icelandic Sagas." In *Northern Antiquity: The Post-medieval Reception of Edda and Saga,* edited by Andrew Wawn, 163–88. Middlesex, U.K.: Hisarlik Press, 1994.

Cañizares-Esguerra, Jorge. *How to Write the History of the New World: History, Epistemologies, and Identities in the Eighteenth-Century Atlantic World.* Stanford, Calif.: Stanford University Press, 2001.

Canney, Nicholas. *Kingdom and Colony: Ireland in the Atlantic World, 1560–1800.* Baltimore, Md.: Johns Hopkins University Press, 1988.

Carlyle, Thomas. *Critical and Miscellaneous Essays.* London: Chapman and Hall, 1896.

Carter, Harold B. *Sir Joseph Banks, 1743–1820.* London: Natural History Museum, 1988.

Chambers, Neil, ed. *Scientific Correspondence of Sir Joseph Banks, 1765–1820.* London: Pickering and Chatto, 2007.

Cittadino, Eugene. *Nature as the Laboratory: Darwinian Plant Ecology in the German Empire.* Cambridge: Cambridge University Press, 1990.

Cohen, Michael P. "Comment: Resistance to Wilderness." *Environmental History* 1, no. 1 (1996): 33–42.

Collingwood, W. G., and Jón Stefánsson. *A Pilgrimage to the Saga-Steads of Iceland.* Ulverston, U.K.: W. Holmes, 1899.

Comte, Auguste. "A Brief Appraisal of Modern History." In *The Crisis of Industrial Civilization: The Early Essays of Auguste Comte,* edited by Ronald Fletcher, 79–111. London: Heinemann, 1974.

Cooper, Alix. "The Indigenous versus the Exotic: Debating Natural Origins in Early Modern Europe." *Landscape Research* 28, no. 1 (2003): 51–60.

———. *Inventing the Indigenous: Local Knowledge and Natural History in Early Modern Europe.* Cambridge: Cambridge University Press, 2007.

———. "'The Possibilities of the Land': The Inventory of 'Natural Riches' in the Early Modern German Territories." In *Oeconomies in the Age of Newton,* edited by Margaret Schabas and Neil de Marchi, 129–53. Durham, N.C.: Duke University Press, 2003.

Corbin, Alain. *The Lure of the Sea: The Discovery of the Seaside in the Western World, 1750–1840*. Translated by Jocelyn Phelps. Cambridge: Cambridge University Press, 1994.

Cowan, Edward J. "Icelandic Studies in Eighteenth and Nineteenth Century Scotland." *Studia Islandica* 31 (1972): 109–51.

Crantz, David. *Historie von Grönland enthaltend die Beschreibung des Landes und der Einwohner und insbesondere die Geschichte der dortigen Mission der Evangelischen Brüder zu Neu-Herrnhut und Lichtenfels*. Leipzig: Heinrich Detlef Ebers, 1765.

———. *The History of Greenland, Containing a Description of That Country and Its Inhabitants Translated from the High-Dutch*. London: Brethen's Society, 1767.

Cronon, William. *Changes in the Land: Indians, Colonists, and the Ecology of New England*. New York: Hill and Wang, 1983.

———. "The Trouble with Wilderness: A Response." *Environmental History* 1, no. 1 (1996): 47–55.

———. "The Trouble with Wilderness: or, Getting Back to the Wrong Nature." *Environmental History* 1, no. 1 (1996): 7–28.

Dalager, Lars. *Grønlandske Relationer: Indeholdende Grønlændernes Liv og Levnet, deres Skikke og Vedtægter samt Temperament og Superstitioner tillige Nogle korte Reflectioner over Missionen* [A Discussion of Greenland: Lifestyle, Customs, Conventions, Temperament and Beliefs of the Greenlanders, along with a Short Discussion of the Missions There], edited by Louis Bobé. Copenhagen: G. E. C. Gad, 1915.

Dalgård, Sune. *Dansk-norsk Hvalfangst* [Whaling in the Danish-Norwegian Kingdom]. Copenhagen: G. E. C. Gad, 1962.

Daniels, Stephen. *Fields of Vision: Landscape Imagery and National Identity in England and the United States*. Princeton, N.J.: Princeton University Press, 1993.

Danmark. Copenhagen: E. M. Bærentzen and Co., 1856.

Daston, Lorraine, and Katharine Park. *Wonders and the Order of Nature, 1150–1750*. New York: Zone Books, 1998.

David, Robert G. *The Arctic in the British Imagination, 1814–1914*. Manchester, U.K.: Manchester University Press, 2000.

Davies, Mark. *A Perambulating Paradox: British Travel Literature and the Images of Sweden, c. 1770–1865*. Lund: University of Lund Press, 2000.

Davies, Susan G. *Spectacular Nature: Corporate Culture and the Sea World Experience*. Berkeley: University of California Press, 1997.

DeCODE. http://www.decode.is.

"Decolonising the Arctic: Nearly Independent Day." *The Economist*, June 21, 2009.

Delanty, Gerard. *Inventing Europe: Idea, Identity, Reality.* New York: St. Martin's Press, 1995.

De Muth, Susan. "Power Driven." *Guardian*, November 29, 2003.

Diamond, Jared M. *Collapse: How Societies Choose to Fail or Succeed.* New York: Viking, 2005.

Dodge, E. S. *The Polar Rosses: John and James Clark and Their Explorations.* New York: Barnes and Noble, 1973.

Dolan, Brian. *Exploring European Frontiers: British Travellers in the Age of Enlightenment.* London: Macmillan, 2000.

Drayton, Richard. *Nature's Government: Science, Imperial Britain, and the "Improvement" of the World.* New Haven, Conn.: Yale University Press, 2000.

Drebert, Ferdinand. *Alaska Missionary.* Bethlehem, Penn.: Moravian Books, 1959.

Dufferin, Lord. *Letters from the High Latitudes.* London: John Murray, 1854.

Dunlap, Thomas R. "Comment: But What Did You Go Out in the Wilderness to See?" *Environmental History* 1, no. 1 (1996): 43–46.

Durrenberger, E. Paul. "Epidemiology of Iceland on the Brain." In *Icelandic Essays: Explorations in the Anthropology of Modern Life*, edited by E. Paul Durrenberger, 1–18. Iowa City: University of Iowa Press, 1992.

Egede, Hans. *A Description of Greenland, by Hans Egede Who Was a Missionary in That Country for Twenty-five Years.* London: T. and J. Allman, 1818.

———. *Det Gamle Grønlands Nye Perlustration eller Naturel-Historie og Beskrivelse over det Gamle Grønland 1741* [The Reemergence of Old Greenland, or a Natural History and Description of Old Greenland] and *Relation Angaaende den Grønlandske Mission 1738* [Report on the Mission in Greenland]. Edited by Finn Gad. Copenhagen: Rosenkilde and Bagger, 1971.

Egede, Niels. *Beskrivelse over Grønland* [Description of Greenland]. *Meddelelser om Grønland* 120 (1939): 223–69.

Egede, Poul. *Dictionarium Grönlandico-Danico-Latinum* [Greenlandic-Danish-Latin Dictionary]. Copenhagen: G. F. Kisel, 1750.

Egede, Poul, and Niels Egede. *Continuation af Hans Egedes Relationer fra Grønland* [A Continuation of Hans Egede's Description of Greenland]. *Meddelelser om Grønland* 120 (1939): 1–219.

Eggert H. Kjartansson. "Ferðin með Green Peace" [Traveling with Green Peace]. *Morgunblaðið*, August 14, 1980, 16–17.

———. "Rainbow Warrior ennþá í El Ferrol" [Rainbow Warrior Still in El Ferrol]. *Morgunblaðið*, June 21, 1980, 1.

Eggert Ólafsson and Bjarni Pálsson. *Travels in Iceland: Performed 1752–1757 by Order of His Danish Majesty.* London: Barnard and Sultzer, 1805.

———. *Vice-lavmand Eggert Olafsens og Land-physici Biarne Povelsens Reise igiennem Island, foranstaltet af Videnskaberne Sælskab i Kiøbenhavn.* Sorøe, Denmark: Jonas Lindgren, 1772.

Einar Árnason. "Genetic Heterogeneity of the Icelanders." *Annuals of Human Genetics* 67 (2003): 5–16.

Einar Hreinsson. "En stat, en förvaltning, två nätverk: Den danske förvaltningen på Island 1770–1870." In *Att Synliggöra det Osynliga: Sex uppsatser om socialt handlande och sociala nätverk* [One State, One Administration, Two Networks: The Danish Administration in Iceland, 1770–1870], edited by Tomas Nilson, 114–39. Gothenberg, Sweden: Institute for History, 2000.

———. "Frakkar á Fróni: Samskipti Frakka og Íslendinga, 1600–1800" [The French in Iceland: Relations between the French and the Icelanders, 1600–1800]. *Sagnir* 15 (1984): 4–11.

———. *Nätverk och nepotism: den regionala förvaltningen på Island 1770–1870* [Networks and Nepotism: Regional Administration in Iceland, 1770–1870]. Gothenberg, Sweden: University of Gothenberg, 2003.

Ekström, Anders. *Den utställda världen: Stockholmutställningen 1897 och 1800-talets världsutställningar* [The World on Display: The 1897 Stockholm Exhibition and the Nineteenth-Century World Fairs]. Stockholm: University of Stockholm, 1994.

Esobar, Arturo. *Encountering Development: The Making and Unmaking of the Third World.* Princeton, N.J.: Princeton University Press, 1995.

Eyðun Andreassen. "Ordinary Europeans from Northern Norway to the Mediterranean: On Gender and Identity in the Faroe Islands." In *Making Europe in Nordic Contexts*, edited by Pertti J. Anttonen, 77–104. Turku, Finland: University of Turku, 1996.

Eyþór Arnalds. "Ljóti andarunginn" [An Ugly Duckling]. *Morgunblaðið,* June 27, 1998.

Fabricius, Otto. *Den grønlandske ordbog, forbedret og forøget* [An Improved and Expanded Greenlandic Dictionary]. Copenhagen: C. F. Schubart, 1804.

———. *Fuldstændig Beskrivelse over Grønland* [A Complete Description of Greenland], edited by H. Ostermann. *Meddelelser om Grønland* 129, no. 4 (1946): 1–110.

Fagan, Brian M. *The Little Ice Age: How Climate Made History, 1300–1850.* New York: Basic Books, 2000.

Fairhead, James, and Melissa Leach. *Misreading the African Landscape: Society and Ecology in a Forest-Savanna Mosaic.* Cambridge: Cambridge University Press, 1996.

Faroese Ministry of Fisheries. *Whales and Whaling in the Faroe Islands.* Tórshavn, Faroe Islands: Faroese Ministry of Fisheries, 1991.

Fea, James. *The Present State of the Orkney Islands Considered, and an Account of a New Method of Fishing on the Coasts of Shetland, Published in 1775.* Edinburgh: W. Brown, 1884.

Feldbæk, Ole, ed. *Danmarks identitetshistorie* [A History of Danish Identity]. 4 vols. Copenhagen: C. A. Reitzel, 1992.

Findlen, Paula. *Possessing Nature: Museums, Collecting, and Scientific Culture in Early Modern Italy*. Berkeley: University of California Press, 1994.

Fogg, G. E. *A History of Antarctic Science*. Cambridge: Cambridge University Press, 1992.

Fortun, Michael. *Promising Genomics: Iceland and deCODE Genetics in a World of Speculation*. Berkeley: University of California Press, 2008.

Franklin, Benjamin. "Meteorological Imaginations and Conjectures." *Memoirs of the Literary and Philosophical Society of Manchester* 2 (1784): 357–61.

Friedheim, Robert L., ed. *Toward a Sustainable Whaling Regime*. Seattle: University of Washington Press, 2001.

"Friður með hvölum" [Peace with the Whales]. *Morgunblaðið*, July 15, 1980, 30.

Gad, Finn. *Grønland*. Copenhagen: Politikens Danmarkshistorie, 1984.

——. *Grønland under krigen* [Greenland during World War II]. Copenhagen: Gads Forlag, 1946.

——. *A History of Greenland*. 2 vols. Translated by Ernst Dupont. London: C. Hurst, 1970.

Gaimard, Paul, and Xavier Marmier. *Voyage en Islande et au Groenland, executé pendant les années 1835 et 1836* [Voyage to Iceland and Greenland Undertaken in 1835 and 1836]. Paris: Arthus Bertrand, 1838–52.

——. *Voyages de la Commission Scientifique du Nord, en Scandinavie, en Laponie, au Spitzberg et aux Feröe, pendant les années 1838, 1839, et 1840* [Journeys of the Nordic Scientific Commission in Scandinavia, Lapland, Spitsbergen, and the Faroe Islands, undertaken in 1838, 1839, and 1840]. Paris: Arthus Bertrand, 1842.

Gascoigne, John. *Joseph Banks and the English Enlightenment: Useful Knowledge and Polite Culture*. Cambridge: Cambridge University Press, 1994.

Gibbs, Wayt W. "Natural-Born Guinea Pigs." *Scientific American* 278 (February 1998): 34.

Gísli Ágúst Gunnlaugsson. "The Granting of Privileges to Industry in Eighteenth Century Iceland." *Scandinavian Journal of History* 7, no. 3 (1982): 195–204.

Gísli Ágúst Gunnlaugsson, Gylfi Már Guðbergsson, Sigurður Þórarinsson, Sveinbjörn Rafnsson, and Þorleifur Einarsson, eds. *Skaftáreldar, 1783–1784: Ritgerðir og heimildir* [The Fires of the Skaftá River, 1783–1784: Essays and Sources]. Reykjavík: Mál og Menning, 1984.

Gísli Gunnarsson. *Monopoly Trade and Economic Stagnation: Studies in the Foreign Trade of Iceland 1602–1787*. Lund: University of Lund Press, 1983.

Gísli Magnússon. "Consignatio Instituti seu Rationes: Greinargarð um fyrirætlun" [An Account of Economic Plans for Iceland]. In *Gísli Magnússon (Vísi-*

Gísli): Ævisaga, ritgerðir, bréf, edited by Jakob Benediktsson, 48–85. Reykjavík: Isafoldarprentsmiðja, 1939.

Gísli Pálsson. *Anthropology and the New Genetics.* Cambridge: Cambridge University Press, 2007.

———. *The Textual Life of Savants: Ethnography, Iceland, and the Linguistic Turn.* Chur, Switzerland: Harwood Academic Publishers, 1995.

———. *Travelling Passions: The Hidden Life of Vilhjalmur Stefansson.* Translated by Keneva Kunz. Hanover, N.H.: University Press of New England, 2003.

———, ed. *Writing on Ice: The Ethnographic Notebooks of Vilhjalmur Stefansson.* Hanover, N.H.: University Press of New England, 2001.

Gísli Pálsson and E. Paul Durrenberger, eds. *Images of Contemporary Iceland: Everyday Lives and Global Contexts.* Iowa City: University of Iowa Press, 1996.

Gísli Pálsson and Paul Rabinow. "Iceland: The Case of the National Human Genome Project." *Anthropology Today* 15, no. 5 (October 1999): 14–18.

Glacken, Clarence J. *Traces on the Rhodian Shore: Nature and Culture in Western Thought from Ancient Times to the End of the Eighteenth Century.* Berkeley: University of California, 1967.

Glamann, Kristof, and Erik Oxenbøll. *Studier i dansk merkantilisme: Omkring tekster af Otto Thott* [Studies in Danish Mercantilism: The Writings of Otto Thott]. Copenhagen: University of Copenhagen Akademisk Forlag, 1983.

Graba, Carl Julian. *Tagebuch geführt auf einer Reise nach Färö im Jahre 1828* [Journal of a Trip to the Faroe Islands in 1828]. Hamburg: Perthes and Besser, 1830.

Greenblatt, Stephen. *Marvelous Possessions: The Wonder of the New World.* Chicago: University of Chicago Press, 1991.

Greenway, John L. *The Golden Horns: Mythic Imagination and the Nordic Past.* Athens: University of Georgia Press, 1977.

Grundtvig, Svend. *Dansken paa Færøerne: Sidestykke til Tysken i Slesvig* [Danish in the Faroes: A Comparison with German in Schleswig]. Copenhagen: C. A. Reitzel, 1845; reprint, edited by Hans Bekker-Nielsen, Odense, Denmark: Odense University Press, 1978.

Guðjón Guðmundsson. "Dáður vestra en umdeildur hér" [Western Achievement, but Controversial Here]. *Morgunblaðið,* September 5, 1998.

Guðmundur Jónsson. "Institutional Change in Icelandic Agriculture, 1780–1940." *Scandinavian Economic History Review* 41, no. 2 (1993): 101–28.

Guðmundur Þorláksson. "Af Rendyrets Saga i Island" [Reindeer in Iceland]. *Grønland* (1956): 173–78.

Guðni Th. Jóhannesson. *Kári í jötunmóð: Saga Kára Stefánssonar og íslenkrar erfðagreiningar* [Kári the Giant: the Story of Kári Stefánsson and deCODE Genetics]. Reykjavík: Nýja Bókafélagið, 1999.

Gunnar Karlsson. "Icelandic Nationalism and the Inspiration of History." In *The*

Roots of Nationalism: Studies in Northern Europe, edited by Rosalind Mitchison, 77–89. Edinburgh: John Donald Publishers, 1980.

———. *Iceland's 1100 Years: The History of a Marginal Society*. Reykjavík: Mál og menning, 2000.

Gustafsson, Harald. "Magiska jöklar och primuskök: funderingar kring schablonbildar av Island i allmänhet och Halldór Laxness i synnerhet" [Magical Glaciers and the Primus Stove: Thoughts on Clichés about Iceland in General, and about Halldór Laxness in Particular]. *Gardar* 23 (1992): 38–42.

———. *Mellan kung och allmoge: ämbetsmän, beslutsprocess och inflytande på 1700-talets Island* [Between the King and the People: Royal Officials, Decision-making, and Influence in Eighteenth-Century Iceland]. Stockholm: Almqvist and Wiksell, 1985.

———. *Political Interaction in the Old Regime: Central Power and Local Society in the Eighteenth-Century Nordic States*. Translated by Alan Crozier. Lund: Studentlitteratur, 1994.

Halldór Hermannsson. *Jón Guðmundsson and His Natural History of Iceland*. Ithaca, N.Y.: Cornell University Press, 1924.

———. *Sir Joseph Banks and Iceland*. Ithaca, N.Y.: Cornell University Press, 1928.

Hammerich, Louis L. "Can Eskimo Be Related to Indo-European?" *International Journal of American Linguistics* 17 (1951): 217–23.

———. "The Cases of Eskimo." *International Journal of American Linguistics* 17 (1951):18–22.

———. *The Eskimo Language*. Oslo: University of Oslo Press, 1970.

———. *Vesteskimoernes land* [The Country of the Western Eskimos]. Copenhagen: Geislers Forlag, 1982.

Hammershaimb, V. U. "Færøiske Sproglære [Faroese Grammar]." *Annaler for nordisk Oldkyndighed og Historie* (1854): 233–316.

———. "Færøiske Trylleformular" [Faroese Magic Rhymes], "Færøiske Sagn, meddelte af V. U. Hammershaimb" [Faroese Sayings], and "Bemærkninger med Hensyn til den færøiske Udtale" [Remarks on Faroese Pronounciation]. *Annaler for nordisk Oldkyndighed og Historie* (1846): 347–65.

Hanley, Susan B. *Everyday Things in Premodern Japan: The Hidden Legacy of Material Culture*. Berkeley: University of California Press, 1997.

Hannes Finnsson. *Om Folkemængdens Formindskelse ved Uaar i Island* [Population Declines in the Famine Years in Iceland]. Copenhagen: S. L. Møller, 1831.

Hanssen, Eskil, ed. *Om norsk språkhistorie* [The History of the Norwegian Language] Oslo: University of Oslo Press, 1970.

Haraldur Sigurðsson. *Melting the Earth: The History of Ideas on Volcanic Eruptions*. Oxford: Oxford University Press, 1999.

Harbsmeier, Michael. "Bodies and Voices from Ultima Thule: Inuit Explorations of the Kablunat from Christian IV to Knud Rasmussen." In *Narrating the Arc-*

tic: A Cultural History of Nordic Scientific Practices, edited by Michael Bravo and Sverker Sörlin, 33–71. Canton, Mass.: Science History Publications, 2002.

———. "Schauspiel Europa: Die außereuropäische Entdeckung Europas im 19. Jahrhundert am Beispiel afrikanischer Texte" [Europe on Stage: The Non-Western Discovery of Europe in the Nineteenth Century in African Texts]. *Historische Anthropologie* 3 (1994): 331–50.

———. *Stimmen aus dem äußersten Norden: Wie die Grönländer Europa für sich entdeckten* [Voices from the Far North: How the Greenlanders Discovered Europe]. Stuttgart: Jan Thorbecke Verlag, 2001.

Hartog, Francois. *The Mirror of Herodotus: The Representation of the Other in the Writing of History*. Translated by Janet Lloyd. Berkeley: University of California Press, 1988.

Hastrup, Kirsten. *Nature and Policy in Iceland, 1400–1800: An Anthropological Analysis of History and Mentality*. Oxford: Oxford University Press, 1990.

———. "Uchronia and the Two Histories of Iceland, 1400–1800." In *Other Histories*, edited by Kirsten Hastrup, 102–20. New York: Routledge, 1992.

Haugen, Einar. *Language Conflict and Language Planning: The Case of Modern Norwegian*. Cambridge, Mass.: Harvard University Press, 1966.

Hays, Samuel P. "Comment: The Trouble with Bill Cronon's Wilderness." *Environmental History* 1, no. 1 (1996): 29–32.

Headrick, Daniel R. *The Tentacles of Progress: Technology Transfer in the Age of Imperialism, 1850–1940*. Oxford: Oxford University Press, 1988.

———. *The Tools of Empire: Technology and European Imperialism in the Nineteenth Century*. Oxford: Oxford University Press, 1981.

Hechter, Michael. *Internal Colonialism: The Celtic Fringe in British National Development, 1536–1966*. Berkeley: University of California Press, 1975.

Helgi Geirsson. "Étum Keikó og byrjum hvalveiðar strax" [Let's Eat Keiko and Begin Whaling-Hunting Right Away]. *Morgunblaðið*, September 25, 2001, 42.

Helgi Valtýsson. *Á hreindýraslóðum: Öræfatöfrar Íslands* [On the Trail of the Reindeer in Iceland]. Akureyri, Iceland: Bókaútgáfan Norðri, 1945.

Henderson, Ebenezer. *Iceland; or the Journal of a Residence in that Island during the Years 1814 and 1815*. Edinburgh: Oliphant, Waugh, and Innes, 1818.

Henry, Victor. *Esquisse d'une grammaire raisonnée de la langue aléoute d'après la grammaire et le vocabulaire de Ivan Véniaminov* [Essay on the Grammar of the Aleut Language, Following Ivan Véniaminov's Grammar and Vocabulary of Aleut]. Paris: Maisonneuve, 1879.

Hertel, Hans, and Bente Scavenius. "Hjemme og ude, oppe og nede: Guldalderens konstraster [At Home and Away, Up and Down: The Contrasts of the Golden Age]." In *Guldalderens Verden: 20 historier fra nær og fjern*, edited by Bente Scavenius, 9–21. Copenhagen: Gyldendal, 1996.

"Hevder han senket Bastesens båt" [Claims to Have Sunk Bastesen's Boat]. *Aften-posten*, November 18, 1997.

High North Alliance. http://www.highnorth.no.

Hind, Robert J. "The Internal Colonial Concept." *Comparative Studies in Society and History* 26, no. 3 (July 1984): 543–68.

Høeg, Peter. *Frøken Smillas fornemmelse for sne* [Smilla's Sense of Snow]. Copenhagen: Rosinante, 1992.

Hoëm, Ingjerd. "The Scientific Endeavor and the Natives." In *Visions of Empire: Voyages, Botany, and the Representation of Nature*, edted by David Phillip Miller and Peter Hanns Reill, 305–25. Cambridge: Cambridge University Press, 1996.

Høgsbro, Kirsten-Elizabeth. "Fransk visit i dansk idyl: Xavier Marmiers besøg i København i 1837 [A French Visit to a Danish Paradise: Xavier Marmier's Visit to Copenhagen in 1837]." In *Guldalderens Verden: 20 Historier fra nær og fjern*, edited by Bente Scavenius, 92–99. Copenhagen: Gyldendal, 1996.

Holm, Gustav. *The Ammassalik Eskimo: Contributions to the Ethnology of the East Greenland Natives*, edited by William Thalbitzer. *Meddelelser om Grønland* 39 (part 1). Copenhagen: Bianco Luno, 1914.

Holm, S. M. *Om Jordbranden paa Island i Aaret 1783* [The 1783 Eruption in Iceland]. Copenhagen, 1784.

Hooker, William Jackson. *Journal of a Tour in Iceland in the Summer of 1809.* 2 vols. London: Longman, 1813.

Horrebow, Niels. *The Natural History of Iceland*. Edited by A. Linde, D. Wilson, T. Durham, G. Keith, P. Davey, et al. London, 1758.

———. *Tilforladelige Efterretninger om Island*. Copenhagen: S. L. Møller, 1752.

Hoyt, David L., and Karen Oslund, eds. *The Study of Language and the Politics of Community in Global Context, 1740-1940*. Lanham, Md.: Rowman and Little-field, 2006.

Hrefna Róbertsdóttir. "Áætlun um allsherjarviðreisn Íslands 1751–1752" [The Plan to Reshape Iceland, 1751–1752]. *Landnám Ingólfs: Nýtt safn til sögu þess* 5 (1996): 29–88.

———. *"Landsins forbetran": Innréttingar og verkþekking í ullarvefsmiðjum átjándu aldar* [The Drive for Economic Improvement: "The New Industries" and the Weaving Factories in the Eighteenth-Century Iceland]. Reykjavík: University of Iceland Press, 2001.

———. *Wool and Society: Manufacturing Policy, Economic Thought and Local Production in 18th-Century Iceland*. Gothenberg, Sweden: Makadam, 2008.

Hulme, Peter. *Colonial Encounters: Europe and the Native Caribbean, 1492-1797*. London: Methuen, 1986.

———. "Polytropic Man: Tropes of Sexuality and Mobility in Early Colonial

Discourse." In *Europe and Its Others*, edited by Francis Barker, Peter Hulme, Margaret Iversen, and Diana Loxley, vol. 2, 17–32. Colchester, U.K.: University of Essex Press, 1985.

Hunt, William R. *Stef: A Biography of Vilhjalmur Stefansson, Canadian Arctic Explorer.* Vancouver: University of British Columbia Press, 1986.

Huntford, Roland. *The Last Place on Earth.* New York: Atheneum, 1985.

"Hvalur í hættu." [Whales in Danger]. *Morgunblaðið*, July 16, 1980, 1.

"Hvetja menn til að kaupa ekki fisk frá hvalveiðiþjóðunum" [Urging a Boycott on Fish from Whale-Hunting nations]. *Morgunblaðið*, July 22, 1983, 16.

Iceland Investment News 1 (1998). http://www.invest.is.

Ingi Sigurðsson. *Hugmyndaheimur Magnúsar Stephensens* [The Mental World of Magnús Stephensen]. Reykjavík: University of Iceland Press, 1996.

———. *Íslenzk Sagnfræði frá miðri 19. öld til miðrar 20. aldar* [The Study of History in Iceland from the Mid-19th to the Mid-20th Century]. Reykjavík: University of Iceland Press, 1986.

———, ed. *Upplýsingin á Íslandi: Tíu ritgerðir* [The Enlightenment in Iceland: Ten Essays]. Reykjavík: University of Iceland Press, 1990.

———. "Viðhorf Íslendinga til Skotlands og Skota á 19. og 20. öld" [Icelandic Views of Scotland and the Scots in the 19th and 20th Centuries]. *Saga* 18 (1980): 115–78.

Ingvar Agnarsson. "Eitt af fyrstu skrefunum til bættrar lífsstefnu" [One of the First Steps to a Better Way of Life]. *Morgunblaðið*, July 5, 1983, 45.

International Journal of American Linguistics 17 (1951).

International Whaling Commission. http://www.iwcoffice.org

Inuit Circumpolar Council. http://www.inuitcircumpolar.com.

Íris Ellenberger. *Íslandskvikmyndir 1916–1966: Ímyndir, sjálfsmynd og vald* [A History of Icelandic Films, 1916–1966: Images, Self-Images, and Power]. Reykjavík: University of Iceland Press, 2007.

Israel, Heinz. *Kulturwandel grönländischer Eskimo im 18. Jahrhundert: Wandlungen in Gesellschaft und Wirtschaft unter dem Einfluß der Herrnhuter Brüdermission* [Changes in the Culture of the Greenlanders in the Eighteenth Century under the Influence of the Moravian Mission]. Berlin: Akademie Verlag, 1969.

Jakobsen, Jakob. "Nogle ord om færøsk, samt et forslag til en ny færøsk retskrivning" [Some Thoughts on Faroese, with a Proposal for a New System for Spelling Faroese]. In *Greinir og Ritgerðir*, edited by Chr. Matras, 23–43. Tórshavn, Faroe Islands: H. H. Jacobsen, 1957.

———. *Det norrøne sprog på Shetland* [The Norn Language in Shetland]. Copenhagen: I. Cohens, 1897.

———. *Etymologisk ordbog over det norrøne sprog på Shetland* [Ethnological Dictionary of the Norn Language of Shetland]. Copenhagen: Prior, 1921.

————. *Færøske folkesagn og æventyr* [Faroese Stories and Tales]. Copenhagen: S. L. Møller, 1898–1901.

Jensen, Henning Mols. "Politisk ja til Færø-aftale" [Faroese Agreement Approved]. *Berlingske Tidende*, August 20, 1998, 6.

Jochumssen, [Vagel] Mathias. *Anmerkninger ofver Jsland og dessen Indbyggere: Innberetning etter reiser på Island 1729–1731* [Reflections on Iceland and Its Inhabitants, Based on Travels in Iceland, 1729–1731], edited by Oddvar Vasstveit. Oslo: University of Oslo Press, 1977.

Jóhann Sigurjónsson. *Fjalla-Eyvindur* [Eyvindur of the Hills]. In *Modern Icelandic Plays*, translated by Henninge Krohn Schanche. New York: American Scandinavian Foundation, 1916.

Jón Jensson and Þorleifur H. Bjarnason, eds. *Bréf Jóns Sigurðssonar* [Letters of Jón Sigurðsson]. Reykjavík: Hið íslenska Bókmenntafélags, 1911.

Jón Jónsson. *Skúli Magnússon landfógeti, 1711–1911* [Sheriff Skúli Magnússon: Reflections Two Hundred Years Later]. Reykjavík: Sigurður Kristjánsson, 1911.

Jón Stefánsson. "Iceland: Its History and Inhabitants." *Journal of the Transactions of the Victoria Institute, or Philosophical Society of Great Britain* 38 (1902): 53–63.

Jón Steingrímsson. "Eldritið." In *Æfisagan og önnur rit*, edited by Kristján Albertsson. Reykjavík: Helgafell, 1973.

————. *Fires of the Earth: The Laki Eruption 1783–1784*. Translated by Keneva Kunz. Reykjavík: University of Iceland Press, 1998.

Jones, W. Glyn. *Denmark: A Modern History*. London: Croom Helm, 1986.

Jørgensen, Ellen. *Historieforskning og historieskrivning i Danmark indtil Aar 1800* [Historical Research and Writing in Denmark before 1800]. Copenhagen: Gyldendal, 1964.

Kalland, Arne. "Management by Totemization: Whale Symbolism and the Anti-Whaling Campaign." *Arctic* 46, no. 2 (June 1993): 124–33.

Karlsson, Svenolof. *Frihetens källa: Nordens betydelse för Europa* [The Well of Freedom: The Meaning of the Nordic Countries for Europe]. Stockholm: The Nordic Council, 1992.

Keller, Christoph. "Die Isländer, unsere Labormäuse" [The Icelanders, Our Laboratory Mice?]. *Das Magazin*, October 3, 1998, 13–24.

Kjærgaard, Kathrine, and Thorkild Kjærgaard. *Ny Herrnhut i Nuuk, 1733–2003* [New Herrenhut in Nuuk, 1733–2003]. Nuuk: University of Greenland, 2003.

Kjærgaard, Thorkild. *The Danish Revolution, 1500–1800: An Ecohistorial Interpretation*. Translated by David Hohnen. Cambridge: Cambridge University Press, 1994.

————. "'Én enda ofantlige ödegard': Den europæiske ødegårdskrise og nordboernes forsvinden fra Grønland" [The Crisis of European Abandoned Farms and the Disappearance of the Scandinavians from Greenland]. Special issue, edited by Andras Mortensen, Alf R. Nielssen, and Jón Th. Thor, *Innussuk* 2 (2006): 121–28.

Kjartan G. Ottósson. *Íslensk málhreinsun: Sögulegt yfirlit* [Purism in Icelandic: A Historical Perspective]. Reykjavík: Íslensk málnefnd, 1990.

Kleinschmidt, Samuel. *Grammatik der grönländischen Sprache mit teilweisem Einschluß des Labradordialekts* [Grammar of the Greenlandic Language, Including Some Reference to the Dialect of Labrador]. Berlin: Walter de Gruyter, 1851.

———. *Den grønlandske ordbog* [The Dictionary of Greenlandic]. Copenhagen: Louis Kleins, 1871.

Kloss, Fr. T. *Prospecter af Island malede efter Naturen paa den, i Fölge med Hans Kongelige Höihed, Prinds til Danmark Frederik Carl Christian's i Sommeren 1834 foretagene Reise* [Icelandic Scenes from the Danish Prince Frederick Carl Christian's Trip in 1834]. Copenhagen, 1835.

Kneeland, Samuel. *An American in Iceland: An Account of Its Scenery, People, and History*. Boston: Lockwood, Brooks, and Company, 1876.

Koerner, Lisbet. "Purposes of Linnaean Travel: A Preliminary Research Report." In *Visions of Empire: Voyages, Botany, and the Representation of Nature*, edited by David Phillip Miller and Peter Hanns Reill, 117–152. Cambridge: Cambridge University Press, 1996.

———. *Linnaeus: Nature and Nation*. Cambridge, Mass.: Harvard University, 1999.

Kristján Sveinsson. "Íslensk sauðnautasaga, 1905–1931" [The History of the Musk-Ox in Iceland, 1905–1931]. *Ný Saga: Tímarit Sögufélags* 10 (1998): 85–102.

———. "Viðhorf Íslendinga til Grænlands og Grænlendinga á 18., 19. og 20. öld" [Icelandic Views of Greenland and Greenlanders from the 18th to the 20th Centuries]. *Saga* 32 (1994): 159–210.

Landt, Jørgen. *Forsøg til en Beskrivelse over Færøerne* [Description of the Faroes]. Copenhagen: Breum, 1800.

Larson, James L. *Interpreting Nature: The Science of the Living Form from Linnaeus to Kant*. Baltimore, Md.: Johns Hopkins University Press, 1994.

Leader-Williams, N. *Reindeer on South Georgia*. Cambridge: Cambridge University Press, 1988.

Legnér, Mattias. *Fäderneslandets rätta beskrivning: Mötet mellan antikvarisk forskning och ekonomisk nyttokult i 1700-talets Sverige* [The Just Description of the Fatherland: The Encounter between Antiquarian Study and the Cult of Economic Utility in Eighteenth-Century Sweden]. Helsinki: Svenska litteratursällskapet i Finland, 2004.

Lehmann, Orla. Review of B. Einarson's *Om de danske Provindsialstænder*

med specielt Hensyn paa Island [The Danish Provinces, Especially Iceland].
Maanedsskrift for Litteratur 7 (1832): 523–37.

Lekan, Thomas M. *Imagining the Nation in Nature: Landscape Preservation and German Identity, 1885–1945.* Cambridge, Mass.: Harvard University Press, 2004.

Levere, Trevor. *Science and the Canadian Arctic: A Century of Exploration, 1818–1918* Cambridge: Cambridge University Press, 1983.

Lewontin, Richard. "People Are Not Commodities." *New York Times*, January 23, 1999, A19.

Lidegaard, Mads, ed. *Glahns Anmærkninger: 1700-tallets Grønlændere* [Eighteenth-Century Greenlanders: Henrik Glahn's *Reflections*]. Copenhagen: Det Grønlandske Selskab, 1991.

———. *Grønlands Historie* [History of Greenland]. Copenhagen: A. Busck, 1991.

Liljequist, G. H. *High Latitudes: A History of Swedish Polar Travels and Research.* Stockholm: Streiffert, 1993.

Linn, Andrew Robert. *Constructing the Grammars of a Language: Ivar Aasen and Nineteenth Century Norwegian Linguistics.* Münster, Germany: Nodus Publikationen, 1997.

Lockwood, W. B. *An Introduction to Modern Faroese.* Copenhagen: Munksgaard, 1964.

Löffler, Ulrich. *Lissabons Fall-Europas Schrecken: Die Deutung des Erdbeben von Lissabon im deutschsprachigen Protestismus des 18. Jahrhunderts* [Lisbon's Catastrophe-Europe's Fear: Interpretations of the Lisbon Earthquake among German Protestants in the 18th Century]. Berlin: Walter de Gruyter, 1999.

Loti, Pierre. *Iceland Fisherman.* Translated by W. P. Baines. London: J. M. Dent and Sons, 1935.

Lüdecke, Cornelia. *Die deutsche Polarforschung seit der Jahrhundertwende und der Einfluß Erich von Drygalskis* [German Polar Exploration in the Twentieth Century and Erich von Drygalskis's Influence]. Bremerhaven, Germany: Alfred-Wegener-Institut für Polar-und Meersforschung, 1995.

Lýður Björnsson. "Ágrip af sögu Innréttinganna" [Overview of the History of the 'New Industries' in Iceland]. In *Reykjavík í 1100 ár*, edited by Helgi Þorláksson, 117–45. Reykjavík: Sögufélagið, 1974.

———. *Íslands hlutafélag: Rekstrarsaga Innréttinganna* [The Icelandic Corporation: The Management of the "New Industries"]. Reykjavík: Hið íslenzka bókmenntafélag, 1998.

Lyell, Charles. *Principles of Geology, Being an Attempt to Explain the Former Changes of the Earth's Surface, by Reference to Causes Now in Operation.* 3 vols. London: J. Murray, 1830–33.

Lynas, Mark. "Damned Nation." *The Ecologist*, December 2003/January 2004.

Lyngbye, Hans Christian. *Færøiske qvæder om Sigurd Fofnersbane og hans æt*

[Faroese Ballads about Sigurd the Dragon-Slayer and His Linage]. Randers, Denmark: S. Sigmenhoff, 1822.

Lynge, Finn. *Arctic Wars, Animal Rights, Endangered Peoples*, translated by Marianne Stenbæk. Hanover, N.H.: University Press of New England, 1992.

Mackay, David. "Agents of Empire: the Banksian Collectors and Evaluation of New Lands," In *Visions of Empire: Voyages, Botany, and the Representation of Nature*, edted by David Phillip Miller and Peter Hanns Reill, 38–57. Cambridge: Cambridge University Press, 1996.

Mackenzie, George Steuart, and Henry Holland. *Travels in the Island of Iceland 1810*. Edinburgh: Constable, 1811.

MacLeod, Roy. "Imperial Reflections in the Southern Seas: The Funafufi Expeditions, 1896–1904." In *Nature in Its Greatest Extent: Western Science in the Pacific*, edited by Roy MacLeod and Philip F. Rehbock, 159–91. Honolulu: University of Hawai'i Press, 1988.

MacLeod, Roy, and Philip F. Rehbock, eds. *Darwin's Laboratory: Evolutionary Theory and Natural History in the Pacific*. Honolulu: University of Hawai'i Press, 1994.

Magnús Einarsson. "The Wandering Semioticians: Tourism and the Image of Modern Iceland." In *Images of Contemporary Iceland: Everday Lives and Global Contexts*, edited by Gísli Pálsson and E. Paul Durrenberger, 215–35. Iowa City: University of Iowa Press, 1996.

Magnús S. Magnússon. *Iceland in Transition: Labour and Social-Economic Change before 1940*. Lund: University of Lund, 1985.

Magnús Stephensen. *Island i det attende Aarhundrede* [Iceland in the Eighteenth Century]. Copenhagen: Gyldendalske Boghandels Forlag, 1808.

———. *Kort Beskrivelse over den nye Vulcans Ildsprudning i Vester-Skaptefields Syssel paa Island i Aaret 1783* [Brief Account of the New Volcanoes in Skaptfell, Iceland in 1783]. Copenhagen: Nicolaus Möller, 1785.

Mannvernd. www.mannvernd.is.

Manuel, Edward Frank. *The Eighteenth Century Confronts the Gods*. Cambridge, Mass.: Harvard University Press, 1959.

Marsh, Gordon, and Morris Swadesh, "Eskimo Aleut Correspondences." *International Journal of American Linguistics* 17 (1951): 209–16.

Martin, Laura. "'Eskimo Words for Snow': A Case Study in the Genesis and Decay of an Anthropological Example," *American Anthropologist* 88 (1986): 418–23.

Mason, Peter. *Deconstructing America: Representations of the Other*. London: Routledge, 1990.

Mathisen, Stein R. "'Real Barbarians Eat Whales: Norwegian Identity and the Whaling Issue." In *Making Europe in Nordic Contexts*, edited by Pertti J. Anttonen, 105–36. Turku, Finland: University of Turku, 1996.

McClellan, James E., III. *Science Reorganized: Scientific Societies in the Eighteenth Century.* New York: Columbia University Press, 1985.

McDonnell, Evelyn. *Army of She: Icelandic, Iconoclastic, Irrepressible Björk.* New York: Random House, 2001.

McGovern, T. H. "Climate, Correlation, and Causation in Norse Greenland." *Arctic Anthropology* 28, no. 2 (1991): 77–100.

———. "Management for Extinction in Norse Greenland." In *Historical Ecology: Cultural Knowledge and Changing Landscapes*, edited by C. Crumley, 127–54. Santa Fe, N.M.: School of American Research Press, 1994.

McKay, Derek. "Great Britain and Iceland in 1809." *The Mariner's Mirror* 59, no. 1 (February 1973): 85–93.

McVay, Scott. "The Last of the Great Whales." *Scientific American* 215, no. 2 (August 1966): 13–21.

Melville, Elinor G. K. *A Plague of Sheep: Environmental Consequences of the Conquest of Mexico.* Cambridge: Cambridge University Press, 1994.

Mettele, Gisela. "Eine 'Imagined Community' jenseits der Nation: Die Herrnhuter Brüdergemeinde als transnationale Gemeinschaft" [An "Imagined Community" Beyond the Nation: The Moravians as a Transnational Community]. *Geschichte und Gesellschaft* 32 (2006): 45–68.

———. *Weltbürgertum oder Gottesreich? Die Herrnhuter Brüdergemeine als globale Gemeinschaft 1727–1857* [The Kingdom of Heaven or on Earth? The Moravians as a Global Community, 1727–1857]. Göttingen, Germany: Vandenhoeck and Ruprecht, 2009.

"Miljøterror straffes ikke" [Environmental Terrorism Goes Unpunished]. *Aftenposten*, November 20, 1996.

Miller, Angela. *The Empire of the Eye: Landscape Representation and American Cultural Politics, 1825–1875.* Ithaca, N.Y.: Cornell University Press, 1993.

Miller, David Philip. "Joseph Banks, Empire, and 'Centers of Calculation' in late Hanoverian London." In *Visions of Empire: Voyages, Botany, and the Representation of Nature*, edited by David Phillip Miller and Peter Hanns Reill, 21–37. Cambridge: Cambridge University Press, 1996.

Miller, David Philip, and Peter Hanns Reill, eds. *Visions of Empire: Voyages, Botany, and the Representation of Nature.* Cambridge: Cambridge University Press, 1996.

Miller, William Ian. *Bloodtaking and Peacemaking: Feud, Law, and Society in Saga Iceland.* Chicago: University of Chicago Press, 1990.

Mitchell, Timothy. *Colonising Egypt.* Cambridge: Cambridge University Press, 1988.

Moe, Nelson. *The View from Vesuvius: Italian Culture and the Southern Question.* Berkeley: University of California Press, 2002.

Mogensen, Margit. *Eventyrets tid: Danmarks deltagelse i Verdensudstillingerne 1851–1900* [The Age of Fairy-Tales: Danish Participation in the World's Fairs, 1851–1900]. Copenhagen: Landbohistorisk Selskab, 1993.

———. "Nordboudstillingen i Paris 1900: iscenesættelse af kolonimagten" [The "Northern-Dwellers" Exhibition in Paris, 1900: A Staging of Colonial Power]. In *Danmark og verdensudstillingerne i 19. århundrede: de store udstillinger i politisk, økonomisk, teknologisk, og kulturelt lys*, 1–17. Copenhagen: University of Copenhagen, 1997.

Monrad, Kasper, ed. *Danish Painting: The Golden Age, a Loan Exhibition from the Statens Museum for Kunst, Copenhagen, 5 September–20 November 1984*. London: National Gallery, 1984.

Moore, Stephen D. "Roche Research Chief Bets Firm's Future on Genetic Research . . . Iceland as a Giant Gene Lab." *Wall Street Journal*, July 18, 1998.

Morris, William. *Icelandic Journals*. Fontwell, Sussex: Centaur Press, 1969.

———. *Icelandic Journals*. London: Mare's Nest, 1996.

Müller, R. "Fortegnelse over præster i Grønland fra 1721 til 1910" [A Listing of Pastors in Greenland from 1721 to 1910]. *Det Grønlandske Aarsskrift* (1912): 62–69.

Murphy, David Thomas. *German Exploration of the Polar World: A History, 1870–1940*. Lincoln: University of Nebraska Press, 2002.

Nansen, Fridtjof. *Eskimoliv* [The Life of the Eskimos]. Oslo: H. Aschehoug, 1891.

———. *The First Crossing of Greenland*, translated by Hubert Gepp. London: Longmans, 1893.

Nash, Roderick. *Wilderness and the American Mind*. New Haven, Conn.: Yale University Press, 1973.

Nau, Jean Yves. "L'exploitation d'un patrimonie genetique unique" [Exploitation of a Unique Genetic Heritage]. *Le Monde*, December 18, 1998, 22.

Nauerby, Tom. *No Nation Is an Island: Language, Culture, and National Identity in the Faroe Islands*. Århus, Denmark: Århus University Press, 1996.

New Source Material on Sir Joseph Banks and Iceland. Occasional Papers, Manuscript Series 5. San Francisco: California State Library, Sutro Branch, 1941.

Nicolson, Marjorie Hope. *Mountain Gloom and Mountain Glory: The Development of the Aesthetics of the Infinite*. Ithaca, N.Y.: Cornell University Press, 1959; reprint, Seattle: University of Washington Press, 1997.

Niels Einarsson. "From Good to Eat to Good to Watch: Whale Watching, Adaptation, and Change in Icelandic Fishing Communities." *Polar Research* 28, no. 1 (2009): 129–38.

Nolte, Hans-Heinrich, ed. *Internal Peripheries in European History*. Göttingen, Germany: Muster-Schmidt, 1991.

"Norge får hvalstøtte, gir elefantstøtte" [Norway Gets African Support on Whaling, and Supports Africans on the Elephants]. *Aftenposten*, May 15, 1997.

North Atlantic Marine Mammal Organization. http://www.nammco.no.

Nutall, Mark. *Protecting the Arctic: Indigenous Peoples and Cultural Survival.* Amsterdam: Harwood, 1998.

Nye, David E. *America as Second Creation: Technology and Narratives of New Beginnings.* Cambridge, Mass.: MIT Press, 2003.

Oddgeir Stephensen and Jón Sigurðsson, eds. *Lovsamling for Island* [A Collection of Laws Concerning Iceland]. 21 vols. Copenhagen: Universitets-Boghandler Andr. Fred. Höst., 1853–59.

Officer, Charles, and Jake Page. *A Fabulous Kingdom: The Exploration of the Arctic.* Oxford: Oxford University Press, 2001.

Ogilvie, Astrid E. J. "Local Knowledge and Traveller's Tales: A Selection of Climatic Observations in Iceland." In *Iceland: Modern Processes and Past Environments,* edited by C. Caseldine, A. Russell, J. Harðardóttir, and Ó. Knedsen, 257–88. Amsterdam: Elsevier, 2005.

Ogilvie, Astrid E. J., and T. Jónsson. "'Little Ice Age' Research: A Perspective from Iceland." In *The Iceberg in the Midst: Northern Research in Pursuit of a "Little Ice Age,"* edited by Astrid E. Ogilvie and Trausti Jónsson, 19–25. Boston: Kluwer Academic Publishers, 2001.

Ogilvie, Brian W. *The Science of Describing: Natural History in Renaissance Europe.* Chicago: University of Chicago Press, 2006.

———. "Travel and Natural History in the Sixteenth Century." In *Sammeln in der Frühen Neuzeit,* Preprint no. 50, edited by Brian W. Ogilvie, Anke te Heesen, and Martin Gierl, 3–28. Berlin: Max-Planck-Institut für Wissenschaftsgeschichte, 1996.

Ólafur Hannibalsson. "Hryðjuverkamenn á Íslandi [Terrorists in Iceland]. *Morgunblaðið,* September 25, 2001, 32.

Ólafur Þorvaldsson. *Hreindýr á Íslandi, 1771–1960* [Reindeer in Iceland, 1771–1960]. Reykjavík: Bókaútgáfa Menningarsjóðs, 1960.

Olaus Olavius. *Oeconomisk Reyse igiennem de nordvestlige, nordlige, og nordostlige Kanter af Island I–II* [Journey through the North, Northwest, and Northeast Regions of Iceland]. Copenhagen, 1780.

Olwig, Kenneth. *Nature's Ideological Landscape: A Literary and Geographic Perspective on Its Development and Preservation on Denmark's Jutland Heath.* London: George Allen and Unwin, 1985.

Orlean, Susan. "Where's Willy?" *The New Yorker,* September 23, 2002.

Osborne, Michael A. "Acclimatizing the World: A History of the Paradigmatic Colonial Science." *Osiris* 15 (2000): 135–51.

———. *Nature, the Exotic, and the Science of French Colonialism.* Bloomington: University of Indiana Press, 1994.

Osterhammel, Jürgen. *Colonialism: A Theoretical Overview.* Translated by Shelley L. Frisch. Princeton, N.J.: Marcus Wiener, 1997.

————. *Kolonialismus: Geschichte-Formen-Folgen.* Munich: C. H. Beck, 1995.

Oxfeldt, Elisabeth. *Nordic Orientalism: Paris and the Cosmopolitan Imagination.* Copenhagen: Museum Tusculanum Press, 2005.

"Paul Watson løslates i neste uke" [Paul Watson to Be Freed Next Week]. *Aftenposten*, June 10, 1997.

Pearson, Michael N. "Littoral Society: The Concept and the Problems." *Journal of World History* 17, no. 4 (2006): 353–73.

Peary, Robert. *The North Pole: Its Discovery in 1909 under the Auspices of the Peary Arctic Club.* New York: Stokes, 1910.

Pedersen, Olaf. *Lovers of Learning: A History of the Royal Danish Academy of Science and Letters 1742–1992.* Copenhagen: Det Kongelige Danske Videnskabernes Selskab, 1992.

People for the Ethical Treatment of Animals. http://www.peta.org.

Petersen, Derek R. "Language Work and Colonial Politics in Eastern Africa: The Making of Standard Swahili and 'School Kikuyu.'" In *The Study of Language and the Politics of Community in Global Context, 1740–1940*, edited by David L. Hoyt and Karen Oslund, 185–214. Lanham, Md.: Rowman and Littlefield, 2006.

Pfeiffer, Ida. *Visit to Iceland and the Scandinavian North.* Translated from German. London: Ingram, Cooke, and Co., 1852.

Pløyen, Christian. *Erindringer fra en Reise til Shetlandsøerne, Örkenøerne og Skotland i Sommeren 1839* [Account of a Trip to the Shetlands, Orkneys, and Scotland in the Summer of 1839]. Copenhagen: C. W. Reizel, 1840.

Pontoppidan, Erik. *Det förste Forsög paa Norges naturlige Historie* [The Natural History of Norway: An Introduction]. Copenhagen: Berlingske Arvingers Bogtrykkerie, 1752–53.

Ponzi, Frank. *Finnur Jónsson: Íslenskur brautryðjandi* [Finnur Jónsson: Icelandic Trailblazer]. Reykjavík: Almenna bókafélagið, 1983.

————. *Ísland á átjándu öld: Myndir úr leiðöngrum Banks og Stanleys* [Iceland in the Eighteenth Century: Pictures from the Banks and Stanley Expeditions]. Reykjavík: Almenna bókafélagið, 1980.

————. *Ísland á nítjándu öld: Leiðangrar og listamenn* [Iceland in the Nineteenth Century: Explorers and Artists]. Reykjavík: Almenna bókafélagið, 1986.

Porter, Roy. *The Making of Geology: Earth Science in Britain 1660–1815.* Cambridge: Cambridge University Press, 1977.

Potts, Jamaica. "At Least Give the Native Glass Beads: An Examination of the Bargain Made between Iceland and deCODE Genetics with Implications for Global Bioprospecting." *Virginia Journal of Law and Technology* 8 (2002): 1–40.

Pratt, Mary Louise. *Imperial Eyes: Travel Writing and Transculturation.* London: Routledge, 1992.

Preston, Diana. *A First-Rate Tragedy: Captain Scott's Antarctic Expeditions.* London: Constable, 1997.

Pugach, Sara. "Lost in Translation: Carl Büttner's Contribution to the Development of African Language Studies in German." In *The Study of Language and the Politics of Community in Global Context, 1740–1940,* edited by David L. Hoyt and Karen Oslund, 151–84. Lanham, Md.: Rowman and Littlefield, 2006.

Pullum, Geoffrey. *The Great Eskimo Vocabulary Hoax and Other Irrelevant Essays on the Study of Language.* Chicago: University of Chicago Press, 1991.

Rask, Rasmus Kristian. *A Grammar of the Icelandic or Old Norse Tongue.* Translated by George Webbe Dasent. London: William Pickering, 1843; reprint, Amsterdam: John Benjamin, 1976.

———. *Undersögelse om det gamle Nordiske eller Islandske Sprogs Oprindelse* [Investigation of the Origins of Old Norse or Icelandic]. Copenhagen: Gyldendalske Forlag, 1818.

Rasmussen, Jens Rahbeck. "The Danish Monarchy as a Composite State." In *European Identities: Cultural Diversity and Integration in Europe since 1700,* edited by Nils Arne Sørensen, 23–36. Odense, Denmark: Odense University Press, 1995.

Rasmussen, Knud. *Fra Grønland til Stillehavet: Rejser og mennesker fra 5. Thule-ekspedtion* [From Greenland to the Pacific: Travels and People of the Fifth Thule Expedition]. Copenhagen: Gyldendal, 1925.

———. *Polarforskningens saga* [A History of Polar Research]. Vol. 7 of *Jordens erobring* [The Conquest of the World]. Copenhagen: Chr. Erichsens Forlag, 1930.

Rauschenberg, Roy. "The Journals of Joseph Banks's Voyage." *Proceedings of the American Philosophical Society* 113 (1973): 184–216.

Revel, Jacques. "Knowledge of the Territory." *Science in Context* 4, no. 1 (1991): 131–61.

Ringler, Richard. *Bard of Iceland: Jónas Hallgrímsson, Poet and Scientist.* Madison: University of Wisconsin Press, 2002.

Rink, Hinrich. *Danish Greenland: Its People and Products.* 1877; reprint, Montreal: McGill-Queen's University Press, 1974.

———. *Eskimoiske eventyr og sagn.* Copenhagen: C. A. Reitzel, 1866.

———. *Om Eskimoernes Herkomst* [Eskimo Origins]. 2 vols. Copenhagen: Thieles bogtrykkeri, 1890.

———. *Om monopolhandelen paa Grønland* [The Monopoly Trade in Greenland]. Copenhagen: A. F. Høst, 1852.

———. *Tales and Traditions of the Eskimo, with a Sketch of Their Habits, Religion, Language and Other Peculiarities.* Edited by Robert Brown. Edinburgh: W. Blackwood, 1875.

———. *Samling af Betænkninger og Forslag vedkommende den kongelige* grønlandske Handel [Collected Thoughts and Suggestions about the Danish Monopoly Trade in Greenland]. Copenhagen: L. Kleins, 1856.

Ris, Mats. "Conflicting Cultural Values: Whale Tourism in Northern Norway." *Arctic* 46, no. 2 (1993): 156–63.

Robins, R. H. *A Short History of Linguistics*. London: Longman, 1990.

Robinson, Michael F. *The Coldest Crucible: Arctic Exploration and American Culture*. Chicago: University of Chicago Press, 2006.

Robinson, Orrin W. *Old English and Its Closest Relatives: A Survey of the Earliest Germanic Languages*. Stanford, Calif.: Stanford University Press, 1992.

Roesdahl, Else. *Hvalrostand, elfenben, og nordboerne i Grønland* [Walrus Tusks, Ivory, and the Scandinavians in Greenland]. Odense, Denmark: Odense University Press, 1995.

Roesdahl, Else, and Preben Meulengracht Sørensen. *The Waking of Angantyr: The Scandinavian Past in European Culture; Den nordiske fortid i europæisk kultur*. Århus, Denmark: Århus University Press, 1996.

Rosling, Otto. "Samuel Petrus Kleinschmidt." *International Journal of American Linguistics* 17 (1951): 63–65.

Ross, Alex. "Björk's Saga." *The New Yorker*, August 23, 2004, 48–59.

Saga Centre. http://www.njala.is/en.

Said, Edward W. *Culture and Imperialism*. New York: Knopf, 1993.

———. *Orientalism*. New York: Vintage Books, 1979.

Sanneh, Lamin. *Encountering the West: Christianity and the Global Cultural Process: The African Dimension*. Maryknoll, N.Y.: Orbis Books, 1993.

Scavenius, Bente, ed. *Guldalderens Verden: 20 historier fra nær og fjern* [The World of the Danish Golden Age: Twenty Essays from Denmark and Beyond]. Copenhagen: Gyldendal, 1996.

Schaer, Karin. "From Hell to Homeland: Eggert Ólafsson's *Reise igiennem Island* and the Construction of Icelandic Identity." In *Images of the North: Histories-Identities-Ideas*, edited by Sverrir Jakobsson, 131–38. Amsterdam: Rodopi, 2009.

Schama, Simon. *Landscape and Memory*. New York: Knopf, 1995.

Schneider, Jane, ed. *Italy's "Southern Question": Orientalism in One Country*. New York: Berg, 1998.

Schümer, Dirk. "Die lukrativen Gene der Wikinger: Island wird zum Labor der Biotechnologie" [Lucrative Genes of the Vikings: Iceland Becomes a Biotech Laboratory]. *Frankfurter Allgemeine Zeitung*, September 16, 2000, 1.

Schultz-Lorentzen, C. W. *Det Grønlandske Folk og Folkesind* [The Greenlanders and their Customs]. Copenhagen: Department for Greenlandic Affairs, 1951.

Scott, James C. *Seeing Like a State: How Certain Schemes to Improve the Human Condition Have Failed*. New Haven, Conn.: Yale University Press, 1998.

Sea Shepherd. http://www.seashepherd.org.

Seaver, Kirsten. *The Frozen Echo: Greenland and the Exploration of North America, ca A.D. 1000–1500*. Stanford, Calif.: Stanford University Press, 1997.

Secord, James. "Narrative Landscapes: Interpreting the Scottish Highlands." MS.

Senituli, Lopeti, and Margaret Boyes. "Whose DNA? Tonga and Iceland: Biotech, Ownership, and Consent." Paper presented at the Australasian Bioethics Association Annual Conference," Adelaide, Australia, February 14–16, 2002.

Shaw, Frances J. *The Northern and Western Isles of Scotland: Their Economy and Society in the Seventeenth Century*. Edinburgh: J. Donald, 1980.

Shelley, Mary Wollstonecraft. *Frankenstein, or The Modern Prometheus*. Edited by James Rieger. Chicago: University of Chicago Press, 1982.

Sigrún Pálsdóttir. "Icelandic Culture in Victorian Thought: British Interpretations c. 1850–1900 of the History, Politics and Society of Iceland." Ph.D. diss., University of Oxford, Faculty of Modern History, 2000.

Sigurður H. Þorsteinsson, ed. *Íslenzk Frímerki* [Icelandic Stamps]. Reykjavík: Ísafold, 1990.

Sigurjón Baldur Hafsteinsson. "Rite of Passage through the Lens: Photographs of Iceland in British Travel Accounts, 1875–1905." *Gardar* 27 (1996): 5–47.

Singer, Peter. *Animal Liberation*. 2nd ed. New York: Ecco, 1990.

Skarphéðinn G. Þórisson. *Hreindýrarannsóknir 1979–1981* [Study on Reindeer, Research Results, 1979–1981]. Reykjavík: Orkustofnan, 1983.

Skúli Magnússon. *Beskrivelse af Gullbringu- og Kjósar Sýslur* [Description of the Gullbringa and Kjósa Districts]. Bibliotheca Arnamagnæna 4. Edited by Jón Helgason. Copenhagen: Einar Munksgaard, 1944.

———. *Forsøg til en Kort Beskrivelse af Island* [Short Description of Iceland]. Bibliotheca Arnamagnæna 5. Edited by Jón Helgason. Copenhagen: Einar Munksgaard, 1944.

Skúli Sigurðsson. "The Dome of the World: Iceland, Doomsday Technologies and the Cold War." In *Aspects of Arctic and Sub-Arctic History*, edited by Ingi Sigurðsson and Jón Skaptason, 463–73. Reykjavík: University of Iceland, 2000.

———. "Electric Memories and Progressive Forgetting." In *The Historiography of Contemporary Science and Technology*, edited by Thomas Söderqvist, 129–49. Amsterdam: Harwood Academic Publishers, 1997.

Smith, Bernard. *European Vision in the South Pacific*. New Haven, Conn.: Yale University Press, 1985.

———. *Imagining the Pacific in the Wake of the Cook Voyages*. Miegunyah, Australia: Melbourne University Press, 1992.

Smith, Hance D. *The Making of Modern Shetland*. Lerwick: Shetland Times, 1977.

Solomon, Susan. *The Coldest March: Scott's Fatal Antarctic Expedition*. New Haven, Conn.: Yale University Press, 2001.

Sørensen, Øystein, ed. *Jakten på det Norske: Perspecktiver på utviklingen av en norsk nasjonal identitet på 1800-tallet* [Searching for "Norwegianism": Perspectives on the Development of Norwegian National Identity in the Nineteenth Century]. Oslo: Gyldendal, 1998.

Spector, Michael. "Iceland Decoded." *The New Yorker*, January 18, 1999, 40–51.

Spence, Mark David. *Dispossessing the Wilderness: Indian Removal and the Making of the National Parks.* Oxford: Oxford University Press, 1999.

Spufford, Francis. *I May Be Some Time: Ice and the English Imagination.* New York: Picador, 1996.

Stark, Peter. *Driving to Greenland.* Springfield, N.J.: Burford Books, 1994.

Steindór J. Erlingsson. *Genin okkar: líftæknin og íslenskt samfélag* [Our Genes: Bioengineering and Icelandic Society]. Reykjavík: Oddi, 2002.

Stocking, George W., Jr. *Victorian Anthropology.* New York: Macmillan, 1987.

Stoett, Peter J. *The International Politics of Whaling.* Vancouver: University of British Columbia Press, 1997.

Stuber, Martin. "Gottesstrafe oder Forschungsobjekt? Zur Resonanz von Erdbeben, Überschwemmungen, Seuchen und Hungerkrisen im Korrespondentennetz Albrecht von Hallers" [Punishment from God or a Subject of Scientific Research?. The Interpretation of Earthquakes, Floods, Epidemic, and Famine in Albrecht von Haller's Circle]. In *Am Tag danach: Zur Bewältigung von Naturkatastrophen in der Schweiz 1500-2000,* edited by Christian Pfister, 39–54. Bern: Haupt, 2002.

Sumarliði R. Ísleifsson. "Erlend myndlist og breytt viðhorf til íslenskrar náttúru á 19. og 20. öld" [Foreign Art and the Changing Views of Icelandic Nature in the 19th and 20th Centuries]. In *Íslenska Söguþingið 28.-31. maí 1997,* vol. 1, edited by Guðmundur J. Guðmundsson and Eiríkur K. Björnsson, 180–88. Reykjavík: University of Iceland Press, 1998.

———. *Ísland: framandi land* [Iceland through Foreign Eyes]. Reykjavík: Mál og menning, 1996.

Sussman, Herbert L. *The Victorians and the Machine: The Literary Response to Technology.* Cambridge, Mass.: Harvard University Press, 1968.

Svabo, J. C. *Inberetninger fra en Reise i Færøe 1781 og 1782* [Impressions from a Trip to the Faroes in 1781-1782]. Edited by N. Djurhuus. Copenhagen: Selskabet til Udgivelse af Færøske Kildskrifter og Studier, 1959.

Sveinn Pálsson. "Eldritið" [Essay on Volcanism]. In *Ferðabók Sveins Pálssonar,* vol. 2, edited by Jón Eyþórsson, 553–99. Reykavík: Örn og Örlygur, 1983.

Sverrir Jakobsson. "'Black Men and Malignant-Looking': The Place of the Indigenous Peoples of North America in the Icelandic World View." In *Approaches to Vínland: A Conference on the Written and Archaeological Sources for the Norse Settlements in the North Atlantic Region and Exploration of America,* edited by Andrew Wawn and Þórunn Sigurðardóttir, 88–104. Reykjavík: Sigurður Nordal Institute, 2001.

Swadesh, Morris. "Unaalio and Proto-Eskimo." *International Journal of American Linguistics* 17 (1951): 66–70.

Tarnovius, Thomas. *Ferøers Beskrifvelser. Færoensia: Textus et Investigationes* [Description of the Faroes]. Vol. 2. Edited by Håkon Hamre. Copenhagen: Einar Munksgaard, 1950.

Taylor, Bayard. *Egypt and Iceland in the Year 1874*. New York: G. P. Putnam's Sons, 1886.

Thalbitzer, William. "The Aleutian Language Compared with the Greenlandic." *International Journal of American Linguistics* 2, no. 3 (1921): 40–57.

———, ed. *Den Grønlandske Kateket Hansêraks Dagbog* [Journal of the Greenlandic Catechist Hansêrak]. Copenhagen: Gads Forlag, 1933.

———. *Die kultischen Gottheiten der Eskimo* [Eskimo Religious Rituals and Beliefs]. Translated by Walter Zombat Zombatfalva. Leipzig: B. G. Teuber, 1928.

———. "Et Manuskript af Rasmus Rask om Aleuternes Sprog, sammenlignet med Grønlændernes" [Rasmus Rask's Manuscript on Aleut, Compared with Greenlandic], *Oversigt over det Kgl. Danske Videnskabernes Selskabs Forhandlinger*, 211–49. Copenhagen, 1916.

———. *A Phonetical Study of the Eskimo Language, Based on Observations Made on a Journey in North Greenland, 1900-01*. Translated by Sophia Bertelsen. Copenhagen: Bianco Luno, 1904.

———. *Uhlenbeck's Eskimo-Indo European Hypothesis: A Critical Revision.* Copenhagen: Travaux du Cercle Linguistique de Copenhague, 1945.

Thienemann, Friedrich August Ludwig. *Reise im Norden Europa's, vorzüglich in Island, in den Jahren 1820 bis 1821* [A Journey in the North, Especially in Iceland, in 1820–1821]. Leipzig: Carl Heinrich Reclam, 1827.

Thisted, Kirsten. "'Dengang i de ikke rigtigt gamle dage': Grønlandsk fortælletradition som kilde til 1700-tallets kulturmøde" ['In the Time Not So Very Long Ago': Greenlandic Folktales as Sources for Cultural Encounters in the Eighteenth Century]. In *Digternes paryk: studier i 1700-tallet*, edited by Marianne Alenius, Pil Dahlerup, Søren Peter Hansen, Hans Hertel, and Peter Meisling, 73–86. Copenhagen: Museum Tusculanums Forlag, 1997.

Thomson, David. *Scott, Shackleton, and Amundsen: Ambition and Tragedy in the Antarctic*. New York: Adrenaline, 2002.

Tønnessen, J. N., and A. O. Johnsen. *The History of Modern Whaling.* Translated and condensed version of *Den Moderne Hvalfangsts Historie: Opprinelse og Utvikling*, by R. I. Christophersen. Berkeley: University of California Press, 1982.

Transactions of the Royal Society of Edinburgh 3 (1794): 127–53.

Transactions of the Royal Society of Edinburgh 7 (1815): 213–67.

Trausti Einarsson. *Hvalveiðar við Ísland, 1600–1939* [Whaling in Iceland]. Reykjavík: Menningarsjóð, 1987.

Tucker, Susie I. "Scandinavica for the Eighteenth-Century Common Reader." *Saga Book of the Viking Society* 26 (1962–65): 233–47.

Uhlenbeck, C. C. *Eskimo en Oer-Indogermaansch* [Eskimo and the Indo-European Languages]. Amsterdam: Noord-Hollandsche uitgevers maatschappij, 1935.

———. *Oude aziatische contacten van het Eskimo* [Asian Influences in the Eskimo Language]. Amsterdam: N. V. Noord-Hollandsche uitgevers maatschappij, 1941.

Ulfstein, Geir. *The Svalbard Treaty: From Terra Nullius to Norwegian Sovereignty.* Oslo: University of Olso Press, 1995.

Valtur Ingimundarson. *Í eldlínu kalda stríðsins: Samskipti Íslands og Bandaríkjanna, 1945–1960* [On the Firing Line of the Cold War: Icelandic-American Relations, 1945–1960]. Reykjavík: University of Iceland Press, 1996.

Victor, David G. "Whale Sausage: Why the Whaling Regime Does Not Need to Be Fixed." In *Toward a Sustainable Whaling Regime*, edited by Robert L. Friedman, 292–310. Seattle: University of Washington Press, 2001.

Vikør, Lars S. "Northern Europe: Languages as Prime Markers of Ethnic and National Identity." In *Language and Nationalism in Europe*, edited by Stephen Barbour and Cathie Carmichael, 105–29. Oxford: Oxford University Press, 2000.

Vilhjálmur Stefánsson. *The Friendly Arctic: The Story of Five Years in Polar Regions.* 2nd ed. New York: Macmillan, 1943.

———. *My Life with the Eskimo.* New York: Macmillan, 1913.

"Vísindalegur hvalveiðar" [Scientific Whaling]. *Morgunblaðið*, July 21, 1985, 26.

Vollprecht, Gerhardt J. "Die Brüdermission in Grönland und Labrador" [The Moravian Missions in Greenland and Labrador]. In *Unitas Fratrum/Moravian Studies*, edited by Mari P. van Buijtenen, Cornelis Dekker, and Huib Leeuwenberg, 225–40. Utrecht, Netherlands: Rijksarchief, 1975.

von Maurer, Konrad. *Die Entstehung des Isländischen Staats und seiner Verfaßung* [The Origins of the Icelandic State and its Constitution]. Munich: Kaiser, 1852.

———. *Isländische Volkssagen der Gegenwart vorwiegend nach mündlicher Überlieferung, gesammelt und verdeutscht* [Icelandic Folktales from the Past, Collected and Translated]. Leipzig: J. C. Hinrichs, 1860.

———. *Íslandsferð 1858* [A Journey to Iceland in 1858]. Translated by Baldur Hafstað. Reykjavík: Ferðafélag Íslands, 1997.

———. *Island von seiner ersten Entdeckung bis zum Untergange des Freistaats* [Iceland from the First Settlers to the End of the Commonwealth]. Munich: Kaiser, 1874.

von Troil, Uno. *Brev rörande en Resa til Island*. Uppsala: Magnus Swederus Bokhandel, 1777.

———. *Letters on Iceland*. London: W. Richardson, 1780.

Wade, Ira O. *Voltaire and Candide: A Study in the Fusion of History, Art, and Philosophy*. London: Kennikat Press, 1959.

Wåhlin, Vagn. "Faroese History and Identity: National Historical Writing." *North Atlantic Studies* 11 (1989): 21–32.

Walk, Angela. "Þróun hvalaskoðunar á Íslandi" [The Development of the Whale-Watching Industry in Iceland]. Bachelor's thesis, University of Iceland, 2005.

Walshe, M. O'C. *Introduction to the Scandinavian Languages*. London: Andre Deutsche, 1965.

Waterman, John T. *A History of the German Language*. Seattle: University of Washington Press, 1966.

Watson, Paul. *Ocean Warrior: My Battle to End the Illegal Slaughter on the High Seas*. Toronto: Key Porter Books, 1994.

"Watson fornøyd etter forliset" [Watson Shipwrecked but Buoyant]. *Aftenposten*, November 12, 1997.

Wawn, Andrew. "The Enlightenment Traveller and the Idea of Iceland: The Stanley Expedition of 1789 Reconsidered." *Scandinavica* 28, no. 1 (1989): 5–16.

———. "Gunnlaugs Saga Ormstunga and the Theatre Royal Edinburgh 1812: Melodrama, Mineralogy and Sir George Mackenzie." *Scandinavica* 21, no. 2 (1982): 139–51.

———. "John Thomas Stanley and Iceland: The Sense and Sensibility of an Eighteenth-Century Explorer." *Scandinavian Studies* 53 (1981): 52–76.

———. *The Vikings and the Victorians: Inventing the Old North in Nineteenth-Century Britain*. Cambridge: D. S. Brewer, 2000.

Wawn, Andrew, ed. *The Icelandic Journal of Henry Holland, 1810*. London: Hakluyt Society, 1987.

Weber, Eugen. *Peasants into Frenchmen: The Modernization of Rural France, 1870-1914*. Stanford, Calif.: Stanford University Press, 1976.

Weißhaupt, Winfried. *Europa sieht sich mit fremden Blick. Werke nach dem Schema der "Lettres persanes" in der europäischen, insbesondere der deutschen Literatur des 18. Jahrhunderts* [Europe Looking at Itself through the Eyes of the Other: The Genre of "Persian Letters" in German and European Literature of the 18th Century], 2 vols. Frankfurt: Peter Lang, 1979.

Wenzel, George. *Animal Rights, Human Rights: Ecology, Economy, and Ideology in the Canadian Arctic*. Toronto: University of Toronto Press, 1991.

West, John F. *Faroe: The Emergence of a Nation*. New York: Paul S. Eriksson, 1972.

———, ed. *The Journals of the Stanley Expedition to the Faroe Islands and Iceland*. Tórshavn, Faroe Islands: Føroya Fróðskaparfelag, 1970.

Whyte, Nicholas. *Science, Colonialism, and Ireland*. Cork, Ireland: Cork University Press, 1999.

Wilhjelm, Henrik. *"Af tilbøielighed er jeg grønlandsk": Om Samuel Kleinschmidts liv og værk* ["Greenlandic by Inclination": Samuel Kleinschmidt's Life and Work]. Copenhagen: Det Grønlandske Selskab, 2001.

Withers, Charles. "The Historical Creation of the Scottish Highlands." In *The Manufacture of Scottish History*, edited by I. Dounachies and C. Whatley, 143–56. Edinburgh: Polygon, 1992.

Wolf, Eric R. *Europe and the People without History*. Berkeley: University of California Press, 1982.

Wolff, Larry. *Inventing Eastern Europe: The Map of Civilization on the Mind of the Enlightenment*. Stanford, Calif.: Stanford University Press, 1994.

———. *Venice and the Slavs: The Discovery of Dalmatia in the Age of Enlightenment*. Stanford, Calif.: Stanford University Press, 2001.

World Council of Whalers. http://www.worldcouncilofwhalers.com.

World Medical Association. http://www.wma.net/e.

Worm, Ole. *Reuer seu Danica literature antiqvissima vulgo Gothica dicta* [Old Norse Literature]. Copenhagen: Typis Martzan, 1651.

Wråkberg, Urban, ed. *The Centennial of S. A. Andrée's North Pole Expedition*. Stockholm: Royal Swedish Academy of Sciences, 1999.

Wylie, Jonathan. *The Faroe Islands: Interpretations of History*. Lexington: University of Kentucky Press, 1987.

Wylie, Jonathan, and David Margolin. *The Ring of Dancers: Images of Faroese Culture*. Philadelphia: University of Pennsylvania Press, 1981.

"Það gerist aldrei hér . . ." [This never happens here . . .]. *Morgunblaðið*, July 12, 1986, 11.

Þorlákur Skúlason and Brynjólfur Sveinsson. *Two Treatises on Iceland from the 17th Century*. Edited by Jakob Benediktsson. Bibliotheca Arnamagnæna 3. Copenhagen: Einar Munksgaard, 1943.

Þorvaldur Thoroddsen. *De vulkanske Udbrud paa Island i Aaret 1783* [Volcanic Eruptions in Iceland in 1783]. Copenhagen: Hoffensberg and Traps, 1879.

INDEX

WEYERHAEUSER ENVIRONMENTAL CLASSICS

CYCLE OF FIRE BY STEPHEN J. PYNE